Gold Wings, Blue Sea

Gold Wings, Blue Sea

A NAVAL AVIATOR'S STORY

CAPTAIN ROSARIO RAUSA, U.S. NAVAL RESERVE

NAVAL INSTITUTE PRESS
Annapolis, Maryland

Library of Congress Cataloging in Publication Data
Rausa, Rosario.
  Gold wings, blue sea.
  1. Rausa, Rosario. 2. United States. Navy—
Aviation—Biography. 3. Air pilots, Military—United
States—Biography. I. Title.
V63.R38A33   358.4'14'0924 [B]   80-26954
ISBN 0-87021-219-2

Unless otherwise indicated, all photographs
are official U. S. Navy.

Printed in the United States of America

To my wife, Neta, and our children—
Anna, Zeno, Emily, Rachel, and Michael—
for their patience and perseverance.

Contents

Acknowledgments

The author is indebted to many for their help in producing this book. I wish to express my abiding gratitude to the following:

The folks at the *Naval Aviation News* and History office. Headed by Captain Ted Wilbur, and part of the Deputy Chief of Naval Operations (Air Warfare) staff, this unit has been a consistent and reliable source of information for authors for many years. This story, incidentally, emanated from a series of articles that appeared in *Naval Aviation News*. Some illustrations accompanying this narrative were originally published with those articles and are creations of the very talented Bob George, former art director, and Charles Cooney, incumbent art director at the magazine.

Continuing, the author is most grateful to Commander Bob Brewer, USN (Retired), executive director of the U.S. Naval Institute, who examined the first draft of the manuscript and made invaluable suggestions; Carol Swartz, talented editor at the Institute, who applied her expertise in fine-tuning it; R.G. Smith and his capable assistant, Norma Bert, of the McDonnell Douglas Corporation, who lent their support. R.G., a configuration engineer and aviation artist of international renown, reviewed the manuscript and created the drawing of VA-25 Spads on a night combat mission that appears on the jacket; Harry Gann, also of McDonnell Douglas, aerial photographer without peer, who provided technical information and photographic help; Peter Mersky, author and artist, who reviewed the manuscript; Major John Elliott, USMC (Retired), author and aviation buff, who examined the text and made helpful comments; and Lieutenant Commander Bob Nedry, USN (Retired), who supplied the picture sequence of Training Command T-28s in the FCLP pattern.

Although they did not contribute in a direct way to this project, I am especially appreciative to three gentlemen who were important sources of inspiration: Mr. Robert Osborn, whose Grandpaw Pettibone illustrations in *Naval Aviation News* and "Dilbert the Pilot" and "Spoiler the Mechanic" posters have enlightened and entertained the naval aviation audience for generations; Vice Admiral William I. Martin, USN (Retired), one of the Navy's most illustrious and dynamic leaders and a great carrier pilot who personifies the very spirit of naval aviation; and Ed Heinemann, "Mr. Attack Aviation," one of the most gifted aircraft designers of our time, who led the Douglas Aircraft Company's El Segundo team that gave us the Skyraider, the Skyhawk, and many other durable and hard-hitting combat machines.

To the flight leaders, wingmen, and other fellow officers who shared the journey and made it such a memorable one, the author extends a special thanks. I also want to salute that indispensable assembly of people who determine the real strength of any military unit—the enlisted troops—particularly those who labored tirelessly on the flight line, in the hangar bays, and on the flight deck, night and day, to keep the airplanes in the sky.

Profound admiration and gratitude go to my mother and father, not only for all those trips to Griffiss Air Force Base, but for supporting naval aviation in their own special way.

Above and beyond all others, however, I am forever grateful to my wife for her enduring support and the multitude of sacrifices she has made in my behalf.

Gold Wings, Blue Sea

The helmet lies deep in the attic now, stuffed inside a scuffed and warped metal footlocker that somehow survived the journeys aboard the flattops. The three log books, bound by rubber bands, are also there, a frayed package of statistics many years in the making. A pair of forest green flight suits, laundered but permanently wrinkled from the sweat of countless sorties, are folded and stacked in one corner. On top of them lies a bent and burnished knee-board, its spring-loaded clips still firmly clasping a note card from a final briefing.

These are the things of a still life, a naval aviator's still life, a picture that tells me my flying days are over. While there is sadness in that, a deeper message comes through: abundant are the memories and for them be grateful.

one

The Way to Wings

"Yew idjut!. . . . . Yew cain't even fix a hat. How can yew fly a plane if yew cain't fix a hat?"

Marine drill instructor addressing an aviation cadet from Class Thirty-Nine Echo, September 1957.

I was a junior in college, a substitute guard on the basketball team, and in Hartford, Connecticut, on a bone-chilling January afternoon in 1956 when naval aviation curled its summoning finger at me for the first time. We had a game with a near-by university that evening, but the coach released us for a few hours with the proviso that we not get lost in the big city. We had come from Middlebury College, a lovely but small school in a lovely but small village in the Green Mountains of Vermont.

A group of us wandered through the gray and windy streets of the insurance town. We were soon compelled to seek sanctuary from the cold, and for this reason, more than the lure of the title on the marquee, we filed into a movie house showing *The Bridges of Toko Ri*. Based on James Michener's novel, the film focused on a Navy carrier pilot during the Korean War.

I'm sure that the cut of his handsome, blue-black uniform and the bright gold of the wings pinned above his left breast pocket and the braid that circled his sleeves had something to do with igniting a spark of interest in naval aviation. And there were the enchanting interludes in Tokyo with his lovely wife, balanced appropriately against the combat-action theme, which propelled the plot briskly along to a solemn and memorable conclusion.

The most impressive attraction, the part of the movie that captivated me, however, was that which depicted a man, alone at the controls in a jet-powered aircraft, guiding his machine toward the narrow, seaborne runway that heaved in gentle unison with the

1

ship and the sea. In what seemed to me a challenging—if not perilous—endeavor, he flew onto the flight deck, struck it with considerable force, and roared ahead a few feet until the tailhook, which hung down from the tail of his fighter, snagged an arresting cable and brought the jet to a violent halt.

For a moment this evolution, the landing of a fast-moving airplane on such a small platform, was paralyzing. Something deep inside me took hold of that scene and registered it in permanent ink in my mind. As I left the theater, I had a vaguely discernible feeling that my life had taken a turn. What an exhilarating experience that must be, I thought, replaying that landing on the high seas. Surely it would satisfy any man's instinct for adventure and accomplishment.

In the days, weeks, and as it developed, months that followed, I became steadfastly fascinated with thoughts of pursuing the gold wings of a naval aviator. I read Michener's book and spent hours at the college library reading whatever I could about naval aviation, much of it historical stuff about carrier battles in the Pacific. I found a periodical called *Naval Aviation News*, a monthly published by the service. It was too technical for the most part but had plenty of pictures of airplanes and flyers and featured a character called Grampaw Pettibone who, with flavorful language and a foundation of flying expertise only experience could provide, chastised pilots who made mistakes in the air.

I contacted recruiters, savored the literature they sent, and officially applied for the aviation officer candidate program. Midway through my senior year I had passed a battery of tests and met the preliminary physical requirements that were an essential first step on the journey to Pensacola, Florida, the cradle of naval aviation.

Thoughts of becoming a Navy flyer began to dominate my life. I wasn't anxious to get into a fray with the Russians, mind you. I just wanted those wings. In my final year at Middlebury, while we were enjoying football and the eye-pleasing brilliance of autumn in Vermont, the Soviets crushed a revolt in Hungary. Israel and Egypt were fighting, and the United Nations had established a peace-keeping force in the Middle East. But except for a few less-than-intense discussions about such issues, I concentrated on preparing for end-of-the-semester comprehensive exams and dreaming of one day wearing a leather flying jacket.

Before graduation I traveled from my home in Hamilton, a picturesque and tranquil piece of America in central New York, population 2,000, to the Naval Air Station at Niagara Falls at the western end of the state for a final physical before being assigned a reporting date.

There were a half-dozen of us being processed in the medical examination rooms, and I was waiting my turn for a comprehensive eye test when the prospective trainee ahead of me, with whom I had chatted earlier, came out of the doctor's office. He was a personable, nice-looking guy with a Charles Atlas physique. Like myself, he wanted—more than words could suitably express—to become a Navy pilot. I thought, with some envy, that he was the type who could decorate a recruiting poster once he won those wings.

But something was wrong. Moments before, he was buoyed with anticipation. Now he was deflated. His eyes were moist, as if he were holding back tears, and he wore a vacant expression. He seemed to be gazing into an eternal distance.

"Astigmatism," he muttered. "Never had eye trouble in my life, but an astigmatism is gonna keep me on the ground." He walked away, leaving a cloud of apprehension suspended over those of us remaining.

Wow, I worried silently, if a man who is the picture of health and strength gets canceled out, what unknown malady will the medical men discover in my case?

Lady Luck smiled on me, however, and with a proud sense of optimism I left Niagara Falls certified OK for flight training. That day I said to myself that it would be wise to remember the fellow with the astigmatism, and be grateful.

My proud sense of optimism vanished shortly after arriving in Florida, when for the first time in what I was quickly convinced had been a sheltered life, I faced a United States Marine Corps drill instructor. I was assigned to Class Thirty-Nine E as in Echo and our DI was a muscular, fireplug of a sergeant with creases everywhere—in his Smokey-the-Bear hat, the short-sleeved khaki shirt, the green trousers, even his face. It was angular in construction, as if it had been hewn from oak with a razor-sharp hatchet.

He did not talk. He bellowed. He reminded me of a factory siren's gaping mechanical mouth out of which spewed invective under great pressure. In those first days I existed in a state of bewilderment, insecurity, and acute fear. The sergeant and the others in supervisory capacities stripped us of our identities, which was the whole idea, of course.

Busy barbers sheared our hair, the supply types issued us khakis, and before long we all looked alike, down to our book bags.

These were brown satchels in which we carried the written matter that had to be mastered before we could even consider leaving the ground.

And we marched. Everywhere. Platoons of us from the many classes passed en route to and from the imposing red brick buildings of the flight school. We were moving rectangles of khaki-colored robots.

President Eisenhower and the nation were having horrendous problems with school integration. There was a confrontation in Little rock, Arkansas, involving Governor Orval Faubus that reached historic proportions. The President ultimately ordered federal troops into the area to see that the integration process continued. That was in September. In October the Russians launched Sputnik I, the first man-made satellite, beating us into space. But my fellow aspirants and I had little time or inclination to consider such matters, as important as they were.

Each waking moment was controlled, monitored, and held up to judgment by either an instructor in the classroom, an athletic officer in the gym, or the DI everywhere else. We studied at night and, after lights out, stole from our beds clandestinely to the head, where illumination was permitted, to perform a critical chore that our ferocious schedule seldom left time for—spit-shining shoes. This became an art. We wrapped cloth around our index fingers, dipped them into water-filled lids of polish cans, and painstakingly rubbed and rubbed and rubbed. I believe it was during these furtive gatherings, as we worked polish into the leather and buffed it vigorously to avoid punishment for unglossy shoes next day, that I began to feel a part of an important group. Ludicrous, I suppose, that a head in a barracks building in the middle of the night was a place for fomenting esprit de corps. But in an unspoken way, it was.

Because my mechanical and mathematical aptitudes were less than impressive, ground school was very difficult for me. The navigation course, for example, nearly terminated my flying career before it began. It took endless hours, including special Saturday morning sessions that we called "Stupid Study," before I could halfway comprehend the labyrinth of lines, angles, digits, and triangles.

If the challenge of the books wasn't enough, there was always the DI, who, incidentally, could not—or would not—pronounce the letter *R*. In our quarters, immediately upon hearing the click of the intercom through the amplifiers, my stomach churned and my body groaned. The inevitable, albeit usually unexpected, muster was at hand.

"Class Thutah-Nahn Echo mustah on the quatah deck him-meedyutlee!"

We scampered as if a bomb had exploded in our midst, pulling on uniforms, affixing collar devices, and blurring down the passageway with our bodies barely under control, careening off the bulkheads as we ran. In the vestibule of our barracks, which served as the quarterdeck, we slid to a collective halt, quivering momentarily like plucked guitar strings before stabilizing at the proper stance of attention.

One day, as our quivering subsided, cadet Al Kelty, Fordham '57, had been fixing his bridge cap but was unable to slip the cloth cover onto the circular frame. Rather than stand there dumbly, the skeleton of a hat in his hand, he elected to place it on his crewcut head.

The sergeant was on him instantly. A well-built six-footer, Kelty towered over the Marine, who was nearly half a foot shorter. But the Marine eyed him and the hat contemptuously, and in theoretical terms their sizes were reversed. Kelty went pale. I trembled. I fully expected that the New Yorker was about to undergo bodily harm and that the furious DI would grind him into gristle.

"Yew idyut!" spat the sergeant. "Yew cain't even fix a hat! How can you fly a plane if yew cain't fix a hat!"

Kelty was not supposed to answer that question and wisely did not.

"Yew betta go home to Momma," warned the Marine venomously. "Yew don't belong heah!"

Kelty stood firm. Bone white, but firm.

"Well?" cried the DI, glaring at the would-be flyer. "Dew you think you belong heah?"

The vestibule was uncomfortably quiet for ten or so seconds during which we wondered intensely if our comrade would crumble. He did not.

"Yes, sir!" he declared forcefully. He withstood the challenge, and the DI was constrained to accept Kelty's determination as a positive sign. He ordered him to his room to correct his hat. We cheered in silence. I think the DI did, too, but you could never tell it from his expression, which was as implacable as a sphinx. Kelty was not about to go home to Momma, and we all took pride in that.

Boxing smokers were regular affairs during preflight, and those who volunteered to fight were given weekend liberty, win or lose. I volunteered to box. It was one of the less astute decisions in my life. In the first place, my experience with gloved fisticuffs, ungloved as well for that matter, was limited to a single match as a high school sophomore—three one-minute rounds during which my opponent bloodied my nose and I, his. The referee called it a draw. We had cider and doughnuts afterwards.

My seconds, Terry Ward, a halfback from Marquette, and Jerry Simonson, my roommate, for reasons unknown to me thought I could win. Ward was a redhead with the fresh, midwestern looks of the All-American boy. I had the feeling that he should be going into the ring rather than I. Simonson, a compactly built Oklahoman with a boyish face that would give him a perpetual image of youth, looked as though he could handle himself in there as well.

Anyway, I was slated against a fellow from one of the advanced classes and knew I was in trouble the minute I entered the gym and saw the ring, professionally rigged with ropes, timer, and bell. A throng of boisterous, khaki-clad cadets, tiered in the fold-out stands that nearly reached the overhead, seemed like patrons at an ancient Roman arena. This was a far cry from Booster Night at Hamilton High School where fifty onlookers were a crowd.

Someone pointed out my opponent. He was a deeply-tanned, handsome cadet with a weight-lifter's physique, complete with washboard midsection and a look of grim assurance that seemed to beam out from his entire form like a sonar pattern. He was about two inches taller than my slim six feet.

Ward and Simonson wore expressions as ominous as mine, as if they had just come upon a gallows, until they saw me looking at them. At which point their jaws snapped shut and they rapidly fabricated tremulous smiles of sham confidence.

"You'll kill him," they said jointly, slamming me robustly on the back.

Ours was the third bout. While the crowd growled and cheered and yelped and whistled, I gave myself a pep talk. It was about as effective as my seconds' fragile attempts to placate me by denigrating my opponent. Our time came. Limbering up in my corner I said to myself, "You've got to be tough to be a naval aviator. So be tough."

"You'll kill him!" cried Ward and Simonson.

A crescendo of cheers rose from the sloping walls of cadets as the bell rang. A prickly brush whisked around my stomach, and my knees wobbled momentarily. But I puffed up, muttering "tough it out, tough it out." I jogged to center ring. So did the weight-lifter, his look of grim assurance replaced now by one of sheer menace.

It was no contest. I saw a lot of leather that evening. It came at me repeatedly, fast and furious, in bulbous form. It stung. It altered brain cells.

In between the three rounds, Ward and Simonson insisted, "Go after him! Go after him!" I was so exhausted I could only bob my head feebly. I may have gotten in a punch or two but, in the end, I was declared the unanimous loser. I was still on my feet, however, the bruises were short-lived, and I had two days off. It was some consolation when, a little later, I learned that my opponent had been on the boxing team of a Big Ten university. Less consoling was my discovery that Ward and Simonson, for their efforts, also received bonus liberty.

That was the last time I volunteered to box anybody, weekend pass or not.

At the end of our four struggling months at mainside Pensacola, we were forged into superb mental and physical condition. We had been steeped long enough in the sea of naval knowledge to be commissioned ensigns and therefore gathered for ceremonies that authorized us to wear the single gold stripe around our sleeves and the single gold bar on our collars. In accordance with tradition, I gave a dollar to the first person who saluted me. It was the Marine, of course, our beloved DI. We all wanted him to be the first.

It was incongruous to compare my circle of gold, which seemed quite naked, to his dozen ribbons tiered in technicolor on his chest. In the mere four months of preflight school we had gone from a status resembling servitude, in relation to the DI, to one of superior rank over him. He had fought in two wars that we had only read about. It was a paradox.

But I was too pleased to have this instructional hurdle behind me to long contemplate that mystery. It didn't occur to me at the time that those scrambling musters equated to general quarters drills I would experience on board ship. Or that the constant emphasis on punctuality and immediate response to orders was designed to accelerate reactions in an airborne emergency. At the same time we did have a vague understanding that the harassment our DI imposed on us had an important purpose and we were, in our own way, grateful to him for it. In any event, it was time now to get into a cockpit and get off the ground.

The pathway to wings, which would require another fourteen or so months, was clearly laid out for us. The first stop was Saufley Field, also in Pensacola, for primary training. There we would

Division of T-34 Mentors.

learn the rudiments of flight in the T-34 Mentor. There were a dozen dual hops (flown with an instructor), a safe-for-solo check, the solo itself, and after that, a few more dual and solo sorties before going on to basic training in T-28 Trojans. This phase, conducted farther up the road at Whiting Field, included familiarization flights, acrobatics, formation work, instrument—or all-weather—instruction, air-to-air gunnery, and the major challenge of carrier qualifications.

Advanced training followed, hopefully through the pipeline—or type of flying—the student desired: attack, fighter, patrol, anti-submarine, transport, or helicopter. From the beginning I had requested jets, which meant the attack/fighter pipeline, but confirmation of orders would come later based on the phrase, which is a haunting and constant undertone to life in the military—"needs of the service." In the meantime, while I occasionally let visions of high-flying jets streak through my mind, I concentrated on the T-34. I had never flown before, except in a commercial airliner once or twice, so I had to start out from scratch, literally.

The Mentor was a diminutive, low-wing, low-powered machine just under twenty-six-feet long with a thirty-two-foot, ten-inch wing span. It weighed under 3,000 pounds and had a Continental engine that provided 225 hp and a maximum speed of 162 knots. Most of our maneuvers were flown at far less velocity than that, although overhead, or acrobatic, maneuvers gave us an opportunity to accelerate and gain a reasonably good sensation of speed. Built by the Beech company, the plane could be slowed to a little over forty knots before stalling. It was quite forgiving of human error, a rather necessary attribute since it was subjected to unintentional but inevitable abuses in the hands of fledgling aviators. It could sustain the aerodynamic force of ten Gs (gravitational forces) on its airframe, although we weren't supposed to and dearly tried to avoid exceeding four or so Gs. It was an ideal plane for teaching the ABCs of flight and wore a cheerful coat of bright yellow paint with black tail letters—2S—on its vertical stabilizer and three-digit numbers on the fuselage and wings. Our call sign, or side number, for radio communication purposes, was "Two Sierra," plus the three numbers. When an airborne student became confused or inaudible in identifying himself by the proper call sign, a controller in the tower would make a radio transmission that became very familiar: "Station Calling Saufley, Say Again Your Side?" I liked its rhythm.

Shortly after we were issued flight coveralls, boots, helmet, gloves, and the coveted leather jacket, we were ushered out to the ramp and a T-34. It was rigged specially for ground-training purposes with a canvas mat on the starboard wing so that we could practice bailing out. It is only in retrospect that I look upon this as an accentuation of the negative. Seems that our inaugurating exposure to the flight line should have stressed the more optimistic nature of aerial activity.

My turn came and on signal I rose from the seat and felt the rush of wind from the spinning prop. I executed a pull and crawl maneuver and rolled down the fuselage onto the mat. I was then directed to another T-34, which was washed clean and parked by itself well away from the other machines. I fell in line behind other students, then noticed a photographer loitering near the plane. Each of us was directed to pose, one knee down, in front of the aircraft.

"What's going on?" I asked the cadet in front of me.

"Glory stuff for the home-town newspaper," he said. "You know, 'Local Boy Takes to the Air,' that sort of thing."

I am no more superstitious than the next man. But I won't deliberately walk under a ladder perpendicular to the path of a black cat to prove it. I did not like the idea of glory before it was earned.

"Why don't they wait till they know we can hack it?" I asked, reasoning that it was unwise to play with destiny.

"Don't ask me," said my comrade, "I'm just goin' along with the program."

I went along with the program too, of course. This public relations stuff was a bit unsettling, but I figured that if I did wash out, the photo would at least prove that I gave it a try. Earning the wings, that is.

It was only a few days later that I had my indoctrination ride. This was the first flight on the syllabus, and all I had to do was relax in the front cockpit and enjoy the experience while the instructor did the flying from the rear seat. He put us through several acrobatics and a few touch and go's, keeping a wary eye on me to see if I got sick or otherwise acted adversely to this first exposure to flight.

A classmate, not more than ten minutes airborne that same day on his first sortie, came to grips with himself and demanded that the instructor take him back to earth. "I was frightened when we took off," he confided later, "scared going through two thousand feet, and terrified by the time we leveled off at altitude. Flying is not for me." I admired his honesty, was most happy that my reactions were opposite to his and thought, I wonder what he'll do with his picture?

The holiday was over after that first gratis hop. To the seasoned flyer the Mentor was a tame animal, but to me, especially in the beginning, it was an unruly beast. I knew the flying would not come easily, but I had no idea how difficult it would be to make a machine obey the manipulations of my hands and feet. Flying became a matter of intense work, study, and concentration.

My instructor looked like Abraham Lincoln without a beard. I felt like a midget trailing him out to the trainer, which he "wore" like a glove. He was very deliberate, thorough, and unemotional in his briefings and wonderfully patient with me in the air. I was no Smilin' Jack at the controls, but this gangling lieutenant took matters in stride. At the end of each of the dual flights preceding the safe-for-solo check, he inked an awful lot of check marks in the "below average" column of my grading record. I floundered along uncertainly. I was safe, he indicated, but had questionable basic air work—that ability to smoothly maintain altitude and airspeed and to transition from descents and climbs to level flight. In short, I was rough with the stick and throttle. Nevertheless, he OK'd me for a safe-for-solo check.

For this test I drew a lieutenant named Krazinski. He wore his

"My instructor looked like Abraham Lincoln without a beard." (Drawing by Bob George)

hair in a crew cut, had enormous shoulders, muscular arms, and thin lips. He looked like a linebacker for the Chicago Bears. It was springtime in the South, but I shivered through the briefing and the first forty-five minutes of flight, climbing, descending, turning, negotiating the T-34 through a series of loops, barrel rolls, aileron rolls, and wingovers. He hardly spoke as I went about the routine, and I had no idea whether I was destined for a "down," a gut-twisting word that translated to failure and meant extra instruction was required, or an "up," a terse, joyful phrase that spelled success.

At "Eight-Able," a practice training field that was hardly more than a huge grass plot with a wind sock, I made several touch and go's under special scrutiny. Other elements of the primary syllabus were critical but none more so than the landings. These had to be mastered, a dictum based on the simplistic theory that it was not difficult to get into the air but coming down to earth, safely, was another matter. After the fourth circuit he directed me to land and

The author in photo taken before solo. Note fearless—or is that fearful—look in the eyes and, sigh, the hair on his head.

park the aircraft, keeping the engine running. I did so and after we came to a stop, he said matter of factly, "All right, I'm gonna get out now. Make four landings then come back and get me."

I taxied into position, scanned the area ahead to make sure it was clear of other flying objects and pushed the throttle full forward. Speeding across the grass runway I restrained the urge to shout. As the plane and I rose slowly above tree level, I glanced back at the empty seat as if to ensure that I was, in fact, alone.

I was.

"I can fly!" I yelled. "I can fly!"

The exhilaration stayed with me through the four landings and the rest of the flight after I picked up the instructor. Later, on the ground, my linebacker, who was really more like Old Saint Nick, said, "You've got an 'up'. Good luck in your next stage." I was soaring with joy and pride. It was a victorious moment in my life.

A few flights later I completed the primary course at Saufley. With a haughty tilt to my chin I packed my car, a second-hand

Chevy that I had bought, and drove the short distance to Whiting Field in Milton, Florida, for basic training in the T-28 Trojan. I checked into the BOQ—bachelor officers' quarters—as another student was checking out. Sharing his newly acquired experience and wisdom, he told me, "The difference between the T-28 and the T-34 is like that between a Cadillac and a Volkswagen."

The Trojan sat higher off the ground than the Mentor, and manning it was like mounting a huge steed. In the cockpit, with the canopy slid back and the prop sending a rush of wind along either side of the fuselage, I felt a sense of power and command not available in the primary trainer.

The T-28 was built by North American Aviation and introduced in the Navy's syllabus in 1952. It had about six times the horsepower of the T-34 and weighed more than twice as much. It was seven feet longer and had a forty-foot wing span, seven feet greater than the Mentor, and cruised in the 150-knot range.

The familiarization stage went well, and despite the larger dimensions of the bird my basic air work improved. I was able to keep the altimeter and airspeed needles fairly steady—in level flight and gentle turns, that is. I was even learning to keep the ball in the middle, the ball being a balancing device, like the bubble on a carpenter's level. It worked in conjunction with, and was located on, the same instrument gauge as the turn and bank indicator, a key guide for the pilot along with the all-important attitude gyro.

We were taught to "step on the ball," a basic precept that applied to all the planes we would fly, for an uncentered ball meant

T-34 in foreground with T-28 in background.

the aircraft was in aerodynamically unbalanced flight. If the ball slid out of the middle of its glass tube to the left, application of left rudder brought it back. Additionally, adverse aerodynamic pressure on the airframe was "trimmed" out by tabs that were located on the external control surfaces. The rudder trim tab, for example, was controlled by a knob, about the size of the palm of a hand, located on the port console. It was grouped with wheel-type handles for the aileron and elevator tabs, which performed similarly. When the tabs were properly adjusted and the ball was centered, the aircraft was trimmed up—"stabilized," so to speak. This had been true in the T-34, of course, but the forces involved with the T-28 were greater, especially because of torque—the twisting effect created by the action of pistons, shaft, and related components at work in the engine. Torque tended to pull the aircraft to the left when power was added. Therefore, changes in throttle setting, in addition to variations in flight attitude, caused the ball to move.

A lyrical phrase favored by the instructors echoed in my earphones throughout those sessions in the sky at Whiting: "Keep her trimmed up, check the ball; keep her trimmed up, check the ball."

During the instrument flight-training stage I rode in the rear seat under a canvas cocoon, which I pulled over me when directed to do so by the instructor. It was a dreaded device that separated the student from the bright, clear world of VFR—visual flight rules flying—and forced him to concentrate solely on the gauges arranged vertically before him on the instrument panel. We learned to scan these rapidly, reading the information they provided, interpreting same, and responding with the necessary control and power corrections. It was work, all work.

Always there were the classes and the books on every aeronautical subject from meteorology to navigational aids, from tactics to hydraulic systems. Still, I was getting the hang of flying the T-28 and felt good about it. Until I reached formation stage. Confidence and what skills I had gained seemed to begin to disintegrate when it came to flying alongside another machine. From the ground it looked easy enough, but in the air it was incredibly difficult to accomplish. It was a matter of mastering relative motion, anticipating power changes, and pure concentration. As a wingman, our eyes were never to leave the leader, never.

At the outset an instructor told us, "You're being trained to fight, and in naval aviation when you're operating carrier-type aircraft, you work as a team with your fellow squadron pilots. You'll be flying in formation most of the time. You must learn to function with each other in the sky." In other words, if we could not hack formation flying, we were in the wrong line of work.

Keeping the ball in the middle, holding altitude and airspeed, maintaining the proper angle of bank in rendezvous turns—the whole spectrum of tactical maneuvers—were as physically exhausting as they were mentally demanding, especially in the notoriously hot and humid skies of the Southeast in summer.

We progressed from two- to four-plane work. Stacked in stair-step echelon we "broke" from each other—peeled away—at a previously decided interval and, maintaining altitude, lined up after 180 degrees of turn. The number-four man, or tail-end Charlie, clicked his mike button twice when the column was formed, signaling the leader to commence his turn back to the original heading. As he did so we observed the visual keys we had studied, turned toward the leader and worked feverishly to establish the proper line of bearing and join up with him without jostling precariously all over the sky. Then we would change the lead and do it all over again so that we gained experience in every position in the formation. In the years that were to come, formation flying and making rendezvous would become routine, second-nature activities. But in those fledgling days at Whiting they made even some of the above-average students sweat and wonder what they had gotten themselves into.

There were other tactics as well, like the exciting tail-chase routines in which we flew in close column formation, snuggled up beneath the tail of the man ahead. We hung on for dear life as the leader took us through steep turns, rolls and—whoopee!—loop-the-loops. These were "confidence builders," and I felt very good when they were over, not so much because my confidence had been fortified but rather that I had survived without slamming into a fellow student or instructor.

One day, Joe Martin, a Class Thirty-Nine Echo pal, returned from one of these excursions. He was disheveled from the heat, the aerial antics, and the frustrations inherent in the student naval aviator's day. "Wow," he exclaimed, "it's a roller coaster out there! When I was tail-end Charlie I felt like I was on the end of a whip!"

In air-to-air gunnery training we flew out over the beautiful blue Gulf of Mexico and tried to spray fifty-caliber bullets through the red bullseye on a long white banner that was towed by an instructor in a T-28. From a "perch" a couple of thousand feet above and parallel to the target we rolled in, swooped down, and fired the ammo in staccato bursts, which produced a fine, deep sputter—our first exposure to the sound of ordnance delivered by airplane.

I remembered World War II movies and grimacing pilots squinting through gun-sight reticles, firing long bursts into enemy planes. It looked easy. Ah, but in real life if that ball wasn't in the middle and if you didn't lead the target with the proper number of mils, or measurement angle, you would not come anywhere near the bullseye, much less the elusive strip of cloth streaming defenseless in the sky.

I got through these and the related phases of basic training somehow and moved back to Saufley Field for carrier qualifications, carquals or CQ as they were called. Members of Class Thirty-Nine Echo were by now widely dispersed throughout the training command, some having progressed faster than others due to weather or other factors. But new acquaintances were made on an almost daily basis. We were all bound up in the mutual pursuit of a coveted goal, and because of this, friendships developed easily.

Yet friendships, no matter how abiding, did not make field carrier landing practice (FCLP) any easier. Learning to fly the Navy way was still a one-on-one matter between me and the airplane. And the airplane was winning. It wasn't long before I felt like a prizefighter on the ropes.

In the CQ pattern, which simulated the approach to the carrier at sea, we flew low to the ground, power on all the way to the "cut," that critical point over the ramp, or touchdown point, where we "chopped" the throttle, cutting engine power, and flew the plane onto the runway with an aircraft attitude that allowed the tailhook to snare an arresting cable. Of course we didn't extend the tailhook during practice sessions ashore. The first time we would use it would be at sea on a genuine flight deck.

The philosophy of normal field landings was to "grease" the plane smoothly onto the runway, steadily reducing power in the process. In FCLPs more precision was required for obvious reasons, but we used the "cut" technique, which constituted a rather radical departure from gentle, roll-on landings. Some called the carrier landings controlled crashes, which I always considered a gross exaggeration of the issue. True enough, the planes did appear to drop abruptly out of the sky, crunching onto the runway in a less than genteel fashion. In any case, it was essential that the aircraft be set down in the center of the simulated flight deck landing area, which was outlined in white.

In a ground school briefing an instructor—perhaps weary of the overworked word *precision*—said, "Gentlemen, what you're after is *exactitude*." Enter "Paddles,"— the LSO, the landing signal officer, the man who stood alongside the touchdown point at the edge of the runway and helped us achieve exactitude. In either hand he held signaling devices that resembled tennis rackets—thus the sobriquet, Paddles. Although the days of the landing signal mirror, a far more automated system, were at hand, we were required to learn the paddles method. At that time, it was used in the fleet both as a back-up to the mirror in the event of mechanical problems and occasionally when the sea was whipped into a frenzy and produced a pitching deck.

As I skimmed low over the ground in the FCLP pattern, I lost a sense of dimension. I simply could not get the picture. I would have done better if the wind was straight down the runway or nonexistent. Days with such conditions are rare, however, so it was necessary to compensate for the cross and quartering winds that pushed me off the oval approach course that I needed to follow in order to arrive at the cut in good enough shape. But those cross and quartering winds became my formidable enemies. The T-28 was flying me rather than the other way around. The LSO had to wave me off more often than not. After more downs than I cared to count, and a second extra-time hop, one of the instructors called me aside and socked me with the words I would never forget: "I don't believe you can hack it, dad." His voice was matter-of-fact and altogether ominous in tone.

"I used a chair and a desk for a cockpit, coke bottles for throttle and control stick, and 'flew' the pattern in my room." (Drawing by Bob George)

I was long-jawed all Friday afternoon waiting for the commanding officer of the carqual unit to make a decision in my case. Should I be terminated from the program or be allowed to continue? I feared the worst, but the CO must have been a relative of Old St. Nick at Saufley.

"Look," he said earnestly, "get away for the weekend. Raise hell some place. Forget about the Navy. Loosen up. Come back Monday morning ready to go!"

I wanted those golden wings more than anything else in life, and charged with the spirit of unbridled ambition and hope, I boomed "Yes, sir!" At the same time I contemplated the catastrophic consequences of failure. If I could not win those wings, I truly believed I would carry the defeat with me for the rest of my life.

I didn't take the CO's advice. I moped around the BOQ, but I also studied the approach and landing sequence. In what might have been viewed as a weird training method, I used a chair and desk for a cockpit, coke bottles for throttle and control stick, and "flew" the pattern in my room. I made the required radio transmissions to myself and imagined adverse winds trying to push me all over the sky while I corrected for them accordingly. Fortunately, no one inadvertently interrupted me, otherwise my personal behavior might have been brought to the medical officer's attention.

This endeavor helped, but not much, and after a dismal exhibition of flying on Monday I felt sure the axe would descend upon me. I must have shown something, though, because the instructor decided to give me one more chance. His must have been a good weekend.

Happily, I improved just enough to be continued in stage and a few flights later I was OK'd for a crack at the boat—two touch and go's and six arrested landings, or "traps," on the carrier. If I could master these, I would be carrier-qualified and sent on to advanced training.

In retrospect, despite the frustrations and sleepless nights, those were good days. We'd bus out to Bronson field, an auxiliary training facility near Pensacola, not far from the Gulf of Mexico. Stripped to the waist, veteran LSOs, their torsos bronzed by day after day in the sun, brought out rods between flights and fished in the near-by waters. Rusted and empty gas drums were stacked in fields of weeds not far from the runway, and blackjack pines had overgrown all evidence of a former bustling activity. A romantic in our group likened Bronson to a way-stop on the Burma Road, circa World War II.

Lined up for Field carrier landing practice in T-28s.

LSO gives launch signal.

Approaching simulated flight deck.

"On glide slope, but you need right rudder."

"On glide slope."

"You're high."

"Cut!"

We were organized into flights of four students each for the showdown with the ship. We would rendezvous with the USS *Antietam*, the training carrier, as she plowed through the waters of the Gulf of Mexico. We felt some degree of anxiety, to be sure, but all of us also had haughty tilts to our chins by then. Still, they were far less dominant than those on the pilots returning from successful sessions at the carrier. The blue Pensacola skies were filled with canary yellow T-28s shuttling back and forth to the flattop. It was a grand open-air arena, and the stakes were very high for someone who could not envision life outside the naval aviator's world.

On the big day we plodded across the ramp to our birds, parachutes slung low on our backs. A student had dismounted his T-28 after qualifying and flashed us a jack-o'-lantern smile. He tossed a hearty thumbs-up and bellowed, "Piece of cake!"

Sure.

In finger-four formation—the leader flanked by two wingmen with a fourth trailing one of them—we crossed the sandy coast of Florida. It occurred to me that this would be our first flight over the sea. It was a little unsettling not to have that familiar column of smoke from the paper mill north of Pensacola for a reference. It had served us well as a navigational guidepost on earlier flights over land.

At first the *Antietam* looked like a toy boat in a wading pool. We arrived overhead and began a holding pattern to await our turn while others went about qualifying below. It seemed to last an eternity. I snuck glances at the ship as we arced by. The carrier became the Coliseum and I felt as though I were going up against the lions. I was as nervous as a poker player letting it all ride on a pair of nines.

Finally, the air boss in the ship's control tower, the officer who was responsible for all flight deck operations, gave us a "Charlie," the signal to let down and come aboard. We maneuvered into a four-plane echelon and, like a flock of birds winging toward their nest, descended.

Up close, the *Antietam* was a gargantuan creature of dark steel cutting effortlessly through the sea, in total domination of it. This was high drama, and as we swung past the carrier my heart was pumping like a jackhammer. We sped to a point well ahead of the ship where, in interval, we broke away from each other to enter the necklace-shaped landing pattern already occupied by several other T-28s. In the next few moments I would know, unequivocally, whether or not I would stay in the running for those golden wings. So, in a sense, I was at a turning point in my life.

I could not speak for the others in my flight, but for reasons beyond my comprehension, as soon as I banked downwind and began to concentrate on driving the bird on speed and altitude, my jitters dissipated. Like steam from a teakettle after the flame has been turned off, they were gone. I was totally caught up in the reality of an evolution that heretofore had been played time and again only in the imaginary theater of my mind.

The ship was on my left, an enormous profile of power proceeding in the direction opposite to mine. It looked all at once beautiful and forbidding. "This is the big leagues," it seemed to say, "welcome aboard if you can hack it."

It was nearly a thousand feet long, about three football fields in length, but the landing portion was roughly half of that, extending from the island superstructure aft. The runway itself was angled about ten degrees to the left in relation to the bow, a modification from the straight decks of World War II carriers. This reduced the danger of planes landing, possibly missing the engaging wires, and colliding into aircraft parked forward.

"Two Sierra Four Zero Five, abeam, gear and flaps down," I reported to Paddles, the LSO, before commencing the approach turn. This and the next approach would be touch and go's, a sort of preliminary exam. I would be allowed to drop the tailhook and make an arrested landing only if these were performed satisfactorily.

T-28 near touchdown point, USS Antietam.

A casual voice from the ship said, "Roger, Four Zero Five, keep it comin'."

I glanced back and forth between my instruments and the flight deck, working to stay within the altitude and airspeed parameters that I had to maintain in order to get a "cut." The T-28 ahead of me was seconds away from touchdown, so I was at a comfortable distance from it. I searched for the figure of Lieutenant Commander Van Winkler, the LSO. He would be standing on a platform at the edge of the stern, port side. He was the most experienced of the landing signal officers in the carqual training squadron and more often than not was elected to "wave" the new students aboard. I had never met the man, but by reputation knew him to be one of the best in the business.

At the ninety-degree position, half way through the final turn, I found him. He was a puppet-like figure in khaki coveralls emblazoned with strips of bright cloth. In his outstretched arms he held the "rackets," illuminated by panels of brilliant orange and red fabric. The puppet's arms fell to his knees. I was low. I added power and adjusted the nose sightly to nudge the machine back up on the proper glideslope. The puppet's arms rose slowly until Van Winkler and the paddles formed a "Y." I overdid it. Now I was high.

Talk to me, Van Winkler, I muttered to myself, I need all the help I can get!

He had a transmitter available but spoke to me with his body instead. His arms lowered as I made my corrections. The flight deck loomed larger. I dipped a wing for line-up, drawing closer, still a bit high but on speed. The moving runway waited. It was alarmingly naked, free from all diversions, a flat stretch of gray with bright white stripes outlining the touchdown area. The thought was fleeting as it raced through my mind, but for a microsecond or two as I descended, I felt like a wide receiver all alone downfield, the football spiraling high toward me. I had to catch it if for no other reasons than because everyone in the stadium was watching. Except for the puppet at my ten o'clock position slightly below me, I could see no one else, but I knew many people were observing. There was the captain on the bridge, the spectators along vulture's row—the walkway that encircled the island—and the flight deck personnel waiting in the recesses at the edge of the flight deck. To them I was the immediate focus of attention. They knew I was a student performing in the real world of carrier aviation for the first time.

The deck filled my entire sphere of vision. I could make out Van Winkler, who seemed to be leaning toward me. Suddenly, as if swatting a fly, he whipped his right arm cross his chest. He had given me the cut!

Instantly, in fact hardly before Van Winkler's arm had completed its full stroke, I chopped the throttle. I made an abbreviated high dip, allowing the nose to drop momentarily then bringing it up again to establish the landing attitude.

We sank to the deck, the T-28 and I, and struck it roughly. There was no time to savor the moment, though. This was a touch and go, a bounce and go, really. I rammed the throttle forward and rose quickly off the deck. Out of the corner of my eye the superstructure and an audience of human figures capped by oval faces blurred by. I felt a hundred pairs of eyes on me as I roared away to set up for the next approach. What must have been a surge of adrenalin flooded through me. The wide receiver had caught the pass and raced cleanly into the end zone.

The next touch and go was neither better nor worse than the first, but Van Winkler's voice boomed in my head set. "Ok, four oh five, drop your hook!"

Approaching ship in T-28 with other T-28s orbiting in distance.

Joy! He was going to let me trap—make a bona fide carrier landing. I drove around the pattern gathering confidence. I was a football team with momentum on a long drive.

At the cut for the arrestment, I slammed onto the deck. It was like watching a movie when a sudden break in the film freezes a single frame on the screen. I felt a hefty jolt against my shoulders as the seat harness held me in check against the abrupt cessation of movement. I raised the tailhook lever on the cockpit's right side, shoved the power up gently and tapped the right brake—all in response to visual commands from a flight deck director.

Quickly, my plane was lined up abeam the island aimed toward the bow. The director passed me off by pointing toward a tall-sun-tanned man wearing a yellow jersey, and my attention switched to him. "Flight Deck Officer" was printed across his chest in large black letters. He wore a faded yellow cloth helmet tightened by a strap beneath his chin and in his right hand held the black and white checkered launch flag. The engine was at idle power, chug-ging steadily in what seemed like near silence compared to the more deafening noise level that prevailed at approach power set-tings. To my astonishment, the flight deck officer was looking up at me and laughing robustly. Why was he laughing? What was so fun-ny? He formed words with his mouth which, like a lip reader, I tried to interpret.

"Welcome aboard!" I think he said, "you're a carrier pilot now!"

Despite the realization that I had to make five more landings to qualify, I was so charged with the spirit of the moment that I let go of the stick and gave him a thumbs up. Then I laughed, too.

The elation gave way to the business at hand as the officer raised the checkered flag, looked forward to ensure the way was clear, and waved it furiously. In response, I advanced the throttle and the engine wound up to full power, a snarling animal ready to pounce. The T-28 shuddered beneath me. I felt as if my feet, stif-fened on the brakes, would tear through the cockpit floor. With a fluid, ballet-like motion, the flight deck officer sprang toward the bow, halting in the fencer's an garde position, the checkered flag his foil. My feet came off the brakes and the T-28 lunged forward, gathered speed quickly, and rolled along the deck.

The superstructure disappeared from my peripheral vision, and ahead of me was the expanse of the sea and the square-edged tip of the bow which, at the moment, emitted the perilous aura of a mountain precipice. But I was soon enough airborne, above and beyond it, with the calm sea below me as blue as the field in the American flag.

There followed five more arrested landings, each as exciting as the first. I was far from perfect and was even waved off twice, once because my technique was poor, another time because the aircraft ahead of me was delayed "in the gear," getting its tailhook unsnared from the arresting cable.

The others in my flight also qualified, and each of us felt a victorious inner glow as we joined up to return to home base. We resisted the temptation to clutter the airways with radio transmission attesting to our accomplishment. There would be time later for a jubilant release of the happiness we felt. Full of contentment we flew our T-28s back to Saufley. I was so elated I think I could have made the trip without a plane.

Later, walking toward the hangar after shutting down my aircraft, I saw another group of qualifiers heading for their planes to go out to the *Antietam*. I gave them a thumbs-up but was not about to say "piece of cake."

That night, sated with the success of the showdown, I relived the moments at the carrier. Those first landings on the ship in an aviator's life cannot be fairly compared with any other physical or intellectual experience. There is too much drama, too much action, too much concentrated exultation taking place all at once. I suppose there are other pursuits—somersaulting through the upper atmosphere of a circus tent, whipping by slalom gates on a ski run, climbing the vertical face of a mountain—that equal the personalized adventure of flying an airplane, by yourself, onto a moving runway at sea. But for me it was a crucial test of human ability, and I was very, very happy to have passed it.

It was time to load up the Chevy again. Happily, I received orders for jet transition training in the F9F Cougar at Chase Field in Beeville, Texas. The Chevy and I made the trip in good time. Unfortunately, on arrival I was told that a student overload had plugged up the pipeline and that about a dozen aspirants, including myself, would have to stay in a stand-by pool of student aviators until the pipeline was unclogged and we could be inserted into it. As a result we were forced to endure idle days attending an occasional briefing of one sort or another and watching the sweptwing fighter-trainers takeoff, streak overhead, and land. We were like race horses pawing the ground—raring to go, but held in check by forces beyond our control.

In a few weeks time the overload, coupled with some aircraft availability problems, conspired against us, and the powers above

Getting the checkered flag for takeoff on USS Antietam.

decided to send us elsewhere in the training command. This meant I would not get the jets after all. We wore long faces the day we were summoned before a sincere and sympathetic captain from the staff.

"I'm sorry, gents," he said. "We just can't hold you here at Chase Field any longer. We'll give you two options. You can go into multi-engine training, which would lead to patrol plane, antisubmarine, or transport flying duty. Or you can have AD Skyraiders and become attack pilots." I bolted for the Skyraider, as did the majority.

I was not acutely aware of it at the time, but naval aviation was experiencing a period of change greater than any since it came into being in 1911. Guns were being replaced by missiles; aircraft were carrying nuclear weapons; airspeeds jumped from subsonic to supersonic; new emphasis was placed on research; and space flight was a focus of major attention. The AD seemed caught in a sort of time warp. We weren't quite sure what to make of it.

The aircraft had one engine, a single-seat cockpit, carried bombs and a generous assortment of other weaponry. Even so, it was slow, far less attractive than a jet, and seemed old compared to other machines. No doubt about it, I was extremely disappointed. My dreams of becoming a jet pilot and experiencing the romantic and glorious perquisites I thought were associated with life in that capacity were dashed. With great reluctance I accepted the reasoning that life is a compromise and left Chase Field. I motored an hour down the road to Corpus Christi and checked into Aviation Training Unit Three Zero One.

The A in the Skyraider designation stood for "attack," the D for Douglas Aircraft, the company that built it. (Nearly twenty years later I would meet Ed Heinemann, the man who headed the El Segundo Division of Douglas Aircraft and led the engineering team that designed the AD and many other planes. It wasn't until I got to know Heinemann that I fully appreciated the ingenuity and skill that went into the making of the AD.) I was fascinated by the nicknames it had earned over the years. At various times it had been identified as The Mighty Machine, The Pedigreed Pulverizer, Old Faithful, Able Dog, Workhorse of the Fleet, and a few others. It had not yet earned its most popular sobriquet. That would come a few years later when, in affectionate regard to a World War I fighter, the Skyraider would become known as the Spad.

I saw the plane for the first time in a scene from *The Bridges at Toko Ri*, a movie that started me down this particular path. A jet pilot had crash-landed in enemy territory and for a time was protected from North Korean troops by a flight of ADs. They swooped down and spat lethal rounds from their twenty-millimeter cannons. The shells tore into the ground and the enemy with fierce effect, keeping the troops away from the American in jeopardy. The Skyraiders emitted an unusually loud and powerful roar. I was left with the impression that it was a sturdy and tenacious machine. It reminded me of a heavy-weight boxer—tough, hard-hitting, and capable of absorbing punishment.

Chatting with fellow students in Corpus Christi, I was told the story of an AD squadron aboard the USS *Princeton* in Korea. To prove that the Skyraider could carry anything, the crew attached a real kitchen sink to a 1,000-pound bomb, and both were dropped on the enemy near Pyongyang in 1952.

A student who had just earned his wings and was heading for the fleet told me, "Going from the T-34 to the T-28 is like changing from a Volkswagen to a Cadillac. Going from the T-28 to the AD is like trading in your Cadillac for a Mack truck."

Meanwhile, at about this time, we had a break for the Christmas holidays. Two friends at Corpus Christi were Charlie Kehoe, a lieutenant (junior grade) and Ed Curtiss, a second lieutenant in the Marine Corps. We all lived in central New York State and were calculating a way to get home and back without going into debt. Flying commercially was pretty much out of the question. So we decided to hitch a ride to San Antonio and catch an Air Force flight out of Kelly Air Force Base. Another friend was driving north and dropped us off at the operations building.

No sooner had we checked in than we were told that a C-130 Hercules transport was just now taxiing out. "Where's it headed?" I asked. "Eastbound to Loring," answered the duty officer. Would they take us? Could they hold a minute for us? The word was relayed through the tower and a generous Hercules pilot said sure he'd wait, come on along. East was the direction we wanted to go, and a bird in hand is worth two in the bush.

We were hustled out to the approach end in a pickup truck and climbed aboard. It was a long, uncomfortable, hungry journey. We sat on canvas "benches" that folded out from the bulkhead. There had been no time to order box lunches, and time en route was seven hours. After an eternity, the C-130 touched down in a world of white. A storm had blanketed the terrain with several feet of snow.

As the hatch swung open, the temperature plunged and a frigid wind wrapped itself around us. We were wearing overcoats but they failed to ward off the brutal chill. We hurried inside to the transient waiting room and checked a wall map.

Loring Air Force Base, we discovered, lies in the far eastern corner of Maine, a few miles from the Canadian border. We had overshot our mark by three or four states. Taking that flight was a rather impetuous move for three aspiring naval and marine aviators.

"Well," said the sergeant behind the desk, "there's a B-25 going to Syracuse. The heater doesn't work and you'll have to ride in the cold for about three hours."

We took a collective look at the arctic expanse surrounding us and the fast fading sun. We nodded to each other silently, then grabbed our bags and jogged across the frozen turf to the B-25. We piled into the modified World War II, twin-engined bomber, and settled into what represented a passenger compartment but was really an improvised bomb bay.

Oh it was cold, cold, cold. We felt like refugees from one of Robert Service's tales of the Yukon. We rode through the evening skies cramped, restless, and numb. We were westward bound, which was a plus, but as we sat there hunched in our seats wearing vacant expressions, I thought painfully of the comparative warmth of the great American Southwest.

Finally, late in the evening, we landed in Syracuse and fled into the cheerful—and warming—embraces of families who had come to meet us. (We had telephoned from Loring.)

It was worth the effort, of course. We were home for the holidays, and the interlude gave us the opportunity to recharge our mental batteries for the final run to the wings.

As soon as we checked into ATU-301, we were told we had to earn "green cards," that is, instrument ratings. We therefore were temporarily assigned to another Corpus Christi-based unit for all-weather type flight instruction wherein we had to learn how to fly "on the gauges," using the instruments to get from point A to point B without visual reference to the world beyond the cockpit. We had had some basic instruction in this area earlier, but the advanced course was far more demanding and complex.

In any event we had to put the Skyraider out of our minds for a time while we concentrated on flying the twin-engine SNB built by Beech. A small personnel transport with limited seating, it had been around for generations. It was a fine, well-instrumented machine and was reasonably stable in the air. It was also as laboriously slow as it was reliable.

I was paired with Larry Murphy, a tall Californian with a sharp wit, lively Irish eyes, and a nonchalant demeanor that belied his fiery determination not only to win his wings, but to win them in style. Our instructor was a decent fellow who flew very well and grew ecstatic whenever weather moved in and clouds hung low over the field. "We can get some *real* GCAs, today!" he would exclaim, referring to ground-controlled, or precision-type, instrument approaches. Murphy and I plowed through the course, propelled along more by our enthusiasm than by our skill under the "hood."

This dreaded device, the hood, resembled a poker dealer's or vintage bank teller's light shield. We didn't wear helmets in the SNB, so it fit snugly around our heads, separated us from the outside world, and constrained us to fly the plane purely on the information we obtained by scanning the attitude gyro, airspeed, turn and bank, and heading indicators, and a variety of other engine and navigational gauges.

One-upmanship flavored the relationship between Murphy and me, so whenever either of us could best the other, in the air or on the ground, the challenge was relished.

The instructor rode up front in the right seat while students

32

alternated in the left seat of the SNB. The standby flyer observed from the passenger station behind the student. It was essential that the observer call out other aircraft traffic on his mike and monitor events over his headset.

Shortly after takeoff one day, with Murphy driving the machine, my radio in the observer's seat went dead. Failing quick repair we'd have to abort the mission, which would bring instant and prolonged chagrin to our mentor. He was vying for instructor-of-the-month and needed ever minute of flight time he could muster to help him toward that goal.

"Can you fix it?" he asked over the drone of the 450-horse-power Pratt and Whitney engines, looking back at me with hope in his eyes. I detected Murphy's snickering. He knew that my mechanical skills were on a par with those of Donald Duck. I was about to be "one-upped" for certain.

"I'll try, sir," I cried. I pulled off the earphones and mike and forlornly examined the apparatus.

"How ya comin'?" the instructor asked anxiously every few minutes. Not only would an abort cause him dismay, it would impose an aura of failure on Murphy and me, mostly me.

"Still workin' on it, sir!" I would answer. Murphy would snicker.

I was about to confess defeat. I could neither locate nor correct the malfunction. Angrily, I clutched the device and with a violent surge twisted the cords and plastic covers, and slammed them into my lap. I started to give a thumbs-down to the instructor, signaling my inability to make repairs, when I heard the crackle of an open line. I rapidly donned the earphones and keyed the mike. It worked! Hooray!

"Observer checking in, sir!" I proudly reported in the deepest baritone I could contrive. The instructor flashed a bright smile. He'd bag another three hours after all.

Murphy glanced back at me. He was grim, tight-lipped. Holding a thumbs-up below my chin I sent a voiceless message to him: "Log one, one-up for me!" Our Bug Smasher, as the SNB was often called, charged contentedly through the sky.

A few weeks later, green card in hand, I was back at ATU-301 ready to get acquainted with the Able Dog. From close up or afar the Skyraider was a rugged looking piece of hardware. It was a little under forty feet long and when its wings, which could be folded up, were spread, they spanned a distance of fifty feet. In addition to three main pylons on the wings and fuselage, there were twelve racks on the wings to hold weapons and fuel tanks or other stores.

33

It also had four twenty-millimeter cannons. The breech mechanism and ammo loading system for these operated inside the wing, but their black barrels poked out ominously from the wing's leading edge. In the beginning, however, I was more concerned with simply being able to fly the plane than with its ordnance capabilities.

Before my first hop, which, incidentally, would be a solo, there being only one seat aboard (an instructor would follow me in another AD), I stood in front of the machine one day. As I gazed up at the enormous four-bladed propeller, which was nearly sixteen feet high and which swung through an imposing arc more than thirteen feet in diameter, I felt like a rather frail child.

Driving that propeller was a powerhouse of an engine designated the R-3350, built by the Wright Company. It could produce 2,800 horsepower and was notorious for the mighty torque effect caused by the action of its eighteen cylinders. These were in two rows, or banks, of nine each in a radial arrangement, like spokes on a wheel.

The dictionary defines torque as a force or combination of forces that produces or tends to produce a twisting or rotating motion. Automobile engines have it to a minor degree. But for me, torque was very simply the R-3350's propensity to pull the AD's nose to the left when throttle was added. To counteract this, it was mandatory to apply right rudder, especially on the takeoff roll. A crudely drawn cartoon made the rounds among Skyraider flyers. It depicted a weary, if not grubby-looking, AD pilot with his right leg swollen three times the size of his left. The caption said something to the effect: "The price you pay to pilot the Pedigreed Pulverizer."

It was not uncommon for a student new to the Skyraider to drift off the runway on takeoff because he failed to use the proper amount of right rudder to compensate for torque. This phenomenon was a two-edged sword as well. On takeoff, right rudder was the answer. On landing, the reduction of power tended to sway the nose to the right, calling for left rudder. I remember one student halfway through his takeoff roll who motored off the runway to the left kicking up a cloud of dust that engulfed the AD. I feared the worst, but when the dust settled the Skyraider and student were intact and hardly the worse for wear.

So, with deep respect for torque and the R-3550, I taxied onto the centerline of the runway for my first episode with the attack bomber. I opened the throttle to thirty inches of manifold pressure, quickly reviewed the gauges, and released the brakes. I moved the throttle on up to fifty inches, releasing all the might and energy of the 2,800 "horses." A deep-pitched, strong bellow rose up from the nose of the machine as the Able Dog charged forward. Luckily, I held the right amount of pressure on the right rudder and the aircraft obeyed by steering nicely down the center of the runway. I was pleasantly surprised at the liftoff. The AD seemed to have a life of its own, as if it were determined to get into the sky where it belonged. But it did so smoothly, like a mature thoroughbred who left clumsy and jolting departures from the earth to inexperienced colts.

I raised the gear handle, and the wheels folded up into the wings. This reduction in drag gave the plane a boost, and the rate of climb jumped enough that I had to roll in a little nose-down trim with the wheel-shaped trim tab handle on the port console.

I think I am going to like this aircraft very much, I said to myself, climbing into the sky. This initial encounter was like a blind date. Neither party was quite sure what to expect from the other. But early on, a level of conviviality and respect was established. The Able Dog and I would have our differences in the years to come, but this first flight marked the beginning of a grand and memorable affair.

At Corpus Christi I crossed paths with preflight pals Terry Ward and Al Kelty, who were going through multi-engine training. A pair of lively Irishmen, Ward was the footballer from Marquette; Kelty, the New Yorker. They told me a story, which went this way.

The Irishmen were dedicated to the pursuit of wings and were sharp enough, as evidenced by their respectable flight grades, to maintain a slight irreverence toward the curriculum. They were navigating their way through a check ride in the dual seat—side by side—instrument flight simulator. This was a completely enclosed, mechanical device that looked like a real cockpit and was operated by electrical and hydraulic forces to emulate a a genuine aircraft in the air. It responded somewhat like a real plane to control inputs, but was used mainly to teach students how to improve their scan pattern—reading the gauges rapidly—and to refine instrument flying procedures.

The first couple of legs on their check ride went beautifully and an en route approach was executed with fluid skill. The civilian instructor, who sat at a control console immediately outside the trainer, was lulled into a state of distraction by a combination of the students' fine performance and the lure of magnificent legs that belonged to a lady instructor across the aisle.

Inside the darkened chamber of their cockpit, Ward said something inane, which evoked a robust charge of laughter from Kelty.

Which prompted a sharp guffaw from Ward. Which sent the pair reeling. The trainer shook momentarily, as if an earth tremor had struck the Southwest. Concentration disintegrated, and the students were helpless to correct the uncontrolled spin that they had forced on the trainer. The instructor, meanwhile, continued his study of contours.

Kelty: "We're in trouble."

Ward: "You're tellin' me?"

Needles spun, gyros toppled, and the controls, which resembled automobile steering wheels, swayed like a rudderless ship on a stormy sea. At the instructor's station the flight path etched by a tracking pen on the card-table-sized navigational chart resembled the blade pattern of an inebriated figure skater.

Kelty: "If this were for real, what would we do?"

Ward: "Hit the silk, of course!"

A knowing smile was exchanged between the young flyers. Whereupon each man opened the door on his side of the simulator and stepped gingerly from the box. Engrossed with flesh-toned curves, the instructor did not immediately notice the students suddenly poised like marionettes beside him.

"What the . . . ," he began, startled. Were they dressed in toyland red, white, and blue with rouge on their cheeks, the marionettes could not have looked more obedient and innocent. They exuded the sure-eyed confidence of someone who has aced an examination and knows it. Superb thespians, this pair.

Gambling that their reputation would carry the day, they explained how the trainer inexplicably went out of control. Whether mechanically or instructor-induced, the malfunction dictated emergency egress. Therefore they bailed out.

Fortunately for them, the instructor had no axe to grind and felt constrained to buy the explanation. He'd examine the device later. He glanced furtively at those soft and gentle lines across the way and eyed the marionettes who remained diplomatically at attention, clear eyes shining.

"Well, ah, yes," said the instructor. "You fellows did the right thing. You can secure now. You have an 'up.'"

Is that what they call the luck of the Irish? If so I would have welcomed some. After my first few AD flights I began to realize I might make it all the way to those golden wings. There were occasional doubts, however, and though I preferred to rely on personal skill rather than luck from any ethnic source, I secretly hoped that some of whatever Kelty and Ward had would rub off on me.

I was among a small group who had a frustrating time learning how to dive-bomb. We would hardly be useful as attack pilots if we couldn't put bombs somewhere near the target. Enter Lieutenant Ken Moranville. He saved us.

He was a talented instructor with the rare ability to project his knowledge directly into a student's cockpit and make it pay off. He would circle low over the target, which consisted of concentric circles marked in white on dirt terrain, and look up at us 10,000 feet above. He literally talked us through our runs until we got the picture and could do it on our own. We'd roll in and mechanically respond to his commands. "Raise your nose five degrees," he would say, "drop your right wing. Release." It was as if he were sitting inside the aircraft with us, guiding our every move.

We certainly didn't become the Wyatt Earps of naval aviation, but we could put the practice bombs within a 300-foot circle, and for that stage in our careers, it was enough.

Another instructor was Lieutenant Ves George. He was a giant of a man who could have passed for actor-author Sterling Hayden's twin brother. He was also the resident expert and principal investor in the pinball machine. This was a recreational diversion that was permitted in the ready room and paid off handsomely to the rare winners. When he wasn't in the air, Lieutenant George was usually at one end of the machine feeding it nickels and intently manipulating its silver balls.

He led us on a formation flight one cloudless night. There were four planes altogether, and after several practice rendezvous he called on the radio, "All right, Alpha Deltas [another name for the AD based on the phonetic alphabet], turn off all your navigation lights. Fly on the exhaust flames." I sensed the collective question, What was that?, racing through the minds of my shipmates. What kind of a gambler was this guy George anyway?

We obeyed, extinguished the lights, and for half an hour were roaring phantoms in the Texas night. It was surprisingly easy to maintain position by using the glowing fingers of flame as they shot out from the exhaust stacks alongside the nose. "You might want to fly like that some evening," George explained later, "when you don't want someone to see you, perhaps, or just for the hell of it."

The other phases of the syllabus went well, and along the way I even received a silver bar for my shirt collar, having been promoted to the rank of lieutenant (junior grade). We began field-carrier landing practice, a prelude to carqualing on the USS *Antietam* again, this time in ADs. Another group that was ahead of us in

37

the program had completed its session aboard the flattop and was returning to the base when tragedy struck.

A lieutenant (junior grade) who was a very popular, if slightly flamboyant, individual did a slow roll at low altitude, offshore from a beach full of people. He lost control of the aircraft, plummeted into the Gulf of Mexico and was killed. He was to get his wings the next day.

The commanding officer summoned all hands to a meeting in the ready room. He made some sympathetic remarks in behalf of the deceased officer. But his solicitous tone then changed into one of controlled indignation.

"With all due respect to a fellow flyer," he said, "this accident should never have happened. It was a waste of human life, not to mention an airplane!"

"You've all been cautioned about flat-hatting—showing off," he went on. "Don't do it. No matter how much you're tempted. The price is too high. If you don't lose your life, you'll most certainly lose your wings."

One of my preflight classmates was killed in primary training when he and his instructor crashed into a heavily wooded area following an engine failure in their T-34. The solemn aftermath of that accident fixed permanently the specter of quick and violent death in my mind. It was a dark and unavoidable fact inherent in a flyer's life. This mishap at ATU-301 served as a grim reminder of that fact. Fortunately, the tendency was not to dwell too long on tragedy.

The carquals with the Skyraider went much more smoothly and with far less anguish than was the case with the T-28. I made the landings and shortly thereafter found myself wearing dress khakis in the unpretentious office of a staff commander to get my wings. Ironically, I hardly recall the event that I had been looking forward to for so long. There were a few wives at the ceremony who pinned wings on their husbands, and I believe it was the commander himself who did the honors for me. Anyway, the important thing was that I got them. I was as happy as I was anxious to get moving.

The Chevy was still operational, and with my flight gear stowed in its trunk and orders in a manila envelope at my side, I headed east for duty in Attack Squadron Eighty-Five, a fleet-going outfit home-based at Naval Air Station Oceana, Virginia.

two

First Tour

We were walking toward the island from the bow after a practice bombing mission. Lorfano was smiling from ear to ear. Suddenly, he stopped in his tracks. As if to embrace the carrier and its planes, he opened his arms.

"They're payin' me for this!" he shouted. "I'm doin' the thing I love most and they're payin' me to do it!"

NAS Oceana was one of many naval activities in the Tidewater area of Virginia. It was home field for jet-powered Skyhawk squadrons as well as for Skyraider and a few other units. Less than an hour away by car was the Little Creek amphibious base, Naval Air Station Norfolk—which hosted a large variety of flying activities—and a huge shipyard and pier complex, which accommodated all sizes of vessels, including carriers. Clearly, this was Navy country. The Atlantic Ocean was at its doorstep and beyond it was the Mediterranean. The squadron to which I had been assigned, VA-85 was one element of Carrier Air Group Eight, attached to the large carrier USS *Forrestal*. Together we would spent a lot of time in the next three years in both the Atlantic with the Second Fleet and in the Mediterranean with the Sixth Fleet.

The VA-85 insignia depicted a black falcon with its wings spread and a cobra-like tongue that jutted defiantly from its mouth. It had lethal-looking arrows in place of talons. This image was contained in a circle against a plain white background. I admired the simplicity of its design.

But before I could join these birds of prey I had to attend Skyraider graduate school in Attack Squadron Forty-Two at Oceana. It was a replacement air group, or "RAG," unit charged with honing the skills of newly designated aviators and revitalizing those of flyers who were rotating back to fleet duty from other assignments and needed refresher training. The instruction was vigorous and

VA-42 A-1 Skyraider over the Virginia countryside.

demanding, conducted under the tutelage of expert pilots, most of whom had recent fleet experience. It was like ATU-301 all over again, except that much more was expected of us and we were treated like bona fide pilots. I felt I still had to prove myself, even though I had the wings. A sagacious commander in the squadron told me, "In this business you have to prove yourself just about every day anyway. You might as well get used to it."

After four months with VA-42 I piled into a C-118 for a lumbering journey to Athens, Greece, by way of the Azores. The *Forrestal* was in port there for a respite between operating periods at sea.

By the time I got from the airfield to the pier at Piraeus, a coastal suburb of Athens, it was nearly ten P.M., 2200 military time. I jumped into a liberty boat, rode out to the ship, and somehow made the struggle up the accommodation ladder with my two parachute bags of gear. They weighed no less than seventy pounds apiece.

The bags plopped inelegantly to the deck when I released them to salute the officer of the deck. He returned the salute, welcomed me aboard, and directed me to ready room five, which was on the mess deck level below the hangar bay. He also reminded me that the ship would be getting under way at 0800 in the morning. A young sailor came up to me and said, "I'll take one of those, sir."

He grabbed a bag and led me across the cavernous hangar bay, down an access hatch, and along a passageway to the ready room. I thanked him and went into the dimly lit space, which was about as big as a decent-size classroom.

The ready room was empty but for the duty officer and a couple of enlisted men who were dozing in the high-backed, cushioned chairs that looked like family room recliners arranged close together. Row after row of these occupied most of the area. The duty officer was situated at a desk just inside the doorway and was making an entry in a frayed, green log book.

Mae West survival vests, flight helmets, and other gear hung from hooks on the far bulkhead. There was a wooden podium with the Black Falcon decal on its front, centered in the area between the front row of chairs and the bulkhead to my left. A three-deep series of sliding blackboards was rigged to the bulkhead. Adjacent to the blackboards was a huge teletype screen on which weather and other tactical information would be pecked out during flight operations. Next to it, mounted on a metal frame bolted to the overhead, was a television monitor about the size of a small portable set. This was PLAT—pilot landing aid, television. It would display all takeoffs and landings, day or night, live and by video tape.

The ready room had the smell of worn leather about it. Quiet as it was now, I sensed that it was more often a vibrant place that hummed with the movement and sounds of busy human beings.

The duty officer gave me a hearty welcome, arranged for some help with my bags, and assigned me to a stateroom on the 02 level, two "stories" above the hangar bay in the forward section of the ship where most of the VA-85 officers lived. My roommate would be Lieutenant (junior grade) Sid Wegert. He was apparently ashore, so I unpacked and stowed my gear in the empty drawers and what closet space was available. The ten-by-fifteen-foot room was equipped with over-under bunks, twin desks that were really chests of drawers with fold-out panels that formed writing platforms, dual closets, and a pair of straight-backed chairs. There was hardly enough room for two grown men, but the furniture, all of sturdy, metal construction, was so well designed that it was surprising how much clothing and other items could be stashed away. The walls and furnishings were entirely gray in color except for the bed coverings. They were light blue. The floor was of marbled black and white tiles. Overhead an air-conditioning vent droned softly.

I was a bit keyed up and uneasy in the manner of someone suddenly cast into a new environment with unfamiliar people. I didn't feel like sleeping so I shed my blue uniform, heavily wrin-

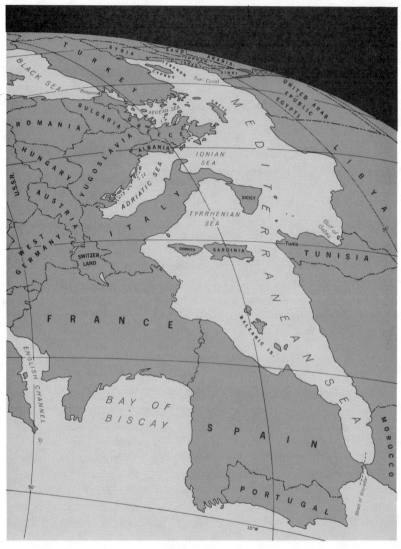

The Mediterranean Sea—VA-85 tour with the Sixth Fleet.

kled from the trip, and slipped on khakis, leather flight jacket, and fore-and-aft cap. I walked through officers' country, traveling clumsily over knee-knockers—the lower sections of oval-shaped hatches that could put painful dents into shins if you didn't high-step properly over them—and found my way outside to the cat-walk. From there I climbed a set of steel steps, about as high as a common stepladder, and went out on the flight deck.

It was a clear, chilly night. Lights hung from cables that extended from the peak of the island structure forward to the edge of the bow, and aft to the fantail. More lights outlined the huge letters, CVA-59, *Forrestal*'s hull number, which was painted white against the gray of the island. I thought of James Forrestal, the carrier's namesake. He had been a naval aviator and later became Secretary of the Navy and the first Secretary of Defense. Quite an honor, I said to myself, having something so mammoth and powerful bearing your name.

The lights provided enough illumination for me to make out the silhouettes of the airplanes. There was an armada of them parked along the full length of the flight deck. The Skyraiders, their wings folded as if in quiet supplication, sat tail-down on the after half of the deck. Along the perimeter were the Skywarriors, the "Whales," as they were called. The giants of the flattop, they were twin-engine, heavy-attack bombers. They were parked nose-in so that their tails extended beyond the deck's edge over the water. Amidships and forward were two squadrons of Skyhawks, diminutive, subsonic jets that packed a solid punch with their weaponry; F4D Skyray fighters with manta-ray-shaped wings and an astonishing ability to climb to altitude in a hurry; supersonic F8U Crusader fighters with long slender fuselages, (also photo-reconnaissance type Crusaders with small "windows" on their sides for cameras); a pair of H-25 helicopters for logistic and rescue work; and E-1 Tracers, also called Willie Fudds, based on an earlier WF designation. These had flying-saucer-shaped radar domes and were driven by a pair of piston engines, which allied them with us and the helos as having reciprocating power plants in common. In fact, the E-1 unit was a three-plane detachment with a small number of personnel and shared our ready room spaces. Outfits like theirs were called splinter groups, an appellation that was never clearly defined to me and which, although it wasn't intended to be, I considered rather unkind. It was as if it implied they weren't full-fledged members of the carrier-air wing team.

I wandered through and around the silent planes. Several miles away the city of Athens, its lights radiant and alluring, looked like an enchanted palace on the night of a gala ball. I thought of my home town and how small it was and how small I now felt. There were about 5,000 people on the *Forrestal*, more than twice the number in the village of Hamilton where I was reared. And here I was exposed to the splendor of Greece while standing on a warship with an awesome capacity to fight any enemy on earth. But no matter how small I felt, it was 1960, I was twenty-four years old, and right where I wanted to be.

43

The next morning began with a foot race. The general quarters alarm, a clanging assault on the ears, sent us scurrying. Sid Wegert, who was a six-foot, 200-pound hulk of a man with a baritone voice and an Arkansas drawl to go with it, said "Follow me!" It was nearly 0800 and most people were dressed, but as we galloped down ladders and wove our way around various obstacles, such as airplanes and small yellow vehicles on the hangar deck and people everywhere else, many individuals were in some degree of undress, pulling on shirts and what-have-you without losing stride.

"We've only got three minutes to get to the ready room before they close the hatches!" cried Sid as we ran. I tailed him like a halfback following the lead blocker through the line of scrimmage.

It was inexcusable to be caught somewhere other than your general quarters (GQ) station during such exercises. Their purpose was to simulate preparing for immediate combat operations. Specified sections of the ship had to be sealed off primarily to minimize the effect of possible damage inflicted by an enemy. Although as pilots we were assigned to the ready room for the GQ drills, we had access to the flight deck and could reach the planes by way of an escalator, the entrance to which was nearby.

Each of the *Forrestal*'s 5,000 members had a place to be, whether he was a cook in the galley or an air controller in the combat information center, a boiler technician in the engine room, or a phone-talker on the LSO platform. Everyone was critical to the defense and operation of the floating city.

Memories of those exasperating muster calls in preflight days flashed through my mind. But we made it on time, and I found myself safely inside the door of ready room five breathing heavily. The same place that last night was as tranquil as a cathedral now bustled with wall-to-wall people and animated conversation. I was introduced to so many individuals so quickly that their names blurred by. I'd have to study a roster sheet later.

The world stopped spinning after a few moments, and a compactly built commander wearing dress blues who had been sitting in the near-corner chair of the front row caught my attention. As we shook hands he said, "I'm Hedge Lee. We're glad to have you with us." His was one name I did recognize. He was the skipper.

His grip was firm and hardy, but what struck me immediately were his eyes. They were blue, set deep in a craggy, Marlboro-man face, and as clear and lively as a mountain stream. They had the glimmer of youth along with the cool, don't-tread-on-me look of a warrior.

"I hope you like to fly," he said. "We do a lot of that around here."

I had heard about Lee's airmanship. The year before, he had won "top gun" honors at the Navy's nationwide bombing derby held at Yuma, Arizona. Not only was his marksmanship unsurpassed, the word was that no one could fly the Skyraider better than he in any phase of flight. I do not know if it was this knowledge, the way he shook hands, the eyes, or a combination of all three. But this stern-looking man with sandy, crew-cut hair, who in reality was half a foot shorter than me, seemed at least ten feet tall.

"The *Forrestal* is like the *Antietam*," he cautioned, "except it's newer and bigger all the way around. In this outfit we earn our reputation by solid airmanship. No fancy stuff. That means good interval [maintaining proper spacing between aircraft] in the landing pattern; a minimum, if any, goof-ups on the flight deck; and good-looking formations, especially when we're within sight of the ship. Got it?"

"Yes, sir," I said. I told him I sure looked forward to the flying and retreated to a seat in the rear of the room. The words of a commander who was in the RAG at VA-42 came to mind. "I love flying in the Navy," he had said, "but what appeals to me more than that is being *around* the people who love to fly."

The squadron flew in the afternoon after the *Forrestal* cleared the Greek coast and got some breathing room at sea. I was given indoctrination lectures and had to wait till the next day, when I completed a rather tame tactics flight with one of the lieutenant commanders. Then the following day I was put on the schedule for a practice bombing hop with the CO, Lieutenant Gene Teter (pronounced Teeter), a lanky, personable veteran with many hours in the AD, and Lieutenant (junior grade) Jim McNally, a conscientious, cheerful officer from Rochester, New York, who was to become a great friend of mine.

At the end of the briefing, despite Lee's formidable reputation as a marksman, I was unfazed enough to suggest that we bet a quarter per bomb to liven things up a bit. Teter and McNally looked at me queerly. Skipper Lee smiled. Was that a flicker of satanic delight I saw in his eyes?

"Better not, pal," Teter whispered.

"Not a good idea," said McNally.

I was what was called in aviation vernacular a "nugget"—a rookie—and as such was filled with a sort of blind exuberance not uncommon in such creatures. I persisted about the bet. The CO ahemmed and we all looked at him.

"You're on," he said with finality. Teter and McNally cringed.

An hour later we launched and proceeded to an assigned section of the sky called a working area. The skipper released a smoke light that would serve as a target, and we broke up into the bombing pattern, giving ourselves space from one another so that each could concentrate on his diving runs. I was on Commander Lee's wing as the number two man and had a good view of him as he rolled his AD onto its back, pulled the nose through, flipped upright and dove at a steep angle toward the water. He dropped his right wing quickly, brought it back, and continued steady as a dart tossed to the ground. The wing-drop was a corrective measure to help his alignment with the target, which was now marked by a lone column of smoke rising from the sea. He released his bomb and pulled up.

We used Mark 76 practice bombs. These were about the size of a bowling pin, were blue in color, and had fins and tapered shapes like life-size weapons. They contained a ten-gauge shotgun charge that exploded on impact producing a miniature white cloud for spotting purposes. Skipper Lee's cloud erupted approximately fifteen feet from the smoke light, a nearly perfect hit.

I rolled in, took aim, pressed the "pickle," or bomb-release button on the control column, and hauled my Skyraider upwards. Teter called my hit: "Two hundred fifty feet, six o'clock."

Teter was next and planted one seventy-five feet at twelve. McNally hit ninety at nine. On his second run the CO scored a bull's-eye. My next one was three hundred at eleven. Teter and McNally hit within a hundred feet. And so it went.

The Navy's top gun had two more bull's-eyes, and four other hits inside fifty feet. My closest strike was a hundred seventy-five feet from the smoke light and it was a generous call. I would lose a few quarters today.

After the bombing runs we split up into two, two-plane sections for some navigation and formation work. Flying on the skipper's wing was extremely easy. I'd never been in the air with anyone so incredibly smooth at the controls. I needed very few throttle and control corrections to stay with him, and when he turned or climbed or descended, he did so with such finesse that I began to think I was a part of his plane. He said little, content to motion me into proper position with brief hand signals.

Three and a half hours after we had taken off, we recovered aboard the ship and convened in the ready room for a debrief. Teter, McNally, and I hovered anxiously around the landing signal officer who had just come down from his platform on the stern of the ship. Each landing aboard the carrier was carefully graded and the LSO personally counseled us on our technique, good or bad. Our Paddles was Lieutenant (junior grade) Kit Carson Saunders

from Texas. He was an ebullient individual and wore a perpetual
Halloween pumpkin smile. Even when an approach was a pitiful
exhibition of airmanship, Saunders wore that smile. It served to
ease the pain after a bad show coming aboard. I appreciated it.

I noticed that the skipper stood apart from our huddle, quietly
removing his Mae West and seemingly oblivious to us. Kit read
from a well-worn, green notebook about the size of, but not as
thick as, a typical Gideon bible. It was an important volume and
contained detailed accounts of every one of us. It was a record in
pencil of our performance in the landing pattern. The LSO customarily dictated his remarks to a "writer," an enlisted man
assigned to assist on the platform. Professional reputations were
based in part on the data collected in that book.

Saunders described my pass in the succinct language of his
trade, deciphering a string of hieroglyphic abbreviations next my
name as he did so: "High start, overshoot, low in the middle," he
began. "Rough nose, fast, a little dive-for-the deck, number four
wire." Clearly a bad approach and landing. Teter's and McNally's

USS Forrestal *(CVA 59) at sea.*

were significantly better and then Saunders called out to the CO "Ok, number three, skipper!"

An "OK, number three," was a perfect pass. The OK implied an onspeed, on-the-glide-path-all-the-way approach. The three stood for the third of four cross-deck pendants, or arresting cables, and was the one that ideal approaches were geared for. The first was nearest the stern, the fourth, the last one available up the deck.

Jim Reid, a lieutenant (junior grade) who would become one of my closest friends, took me aside that evening. He'd been in the squadron months before I joined it and was qualified to explain a few things to me.

"Listen," he said, "nobody bets with the skipper on a bombing flight. He never loses. He flies the AD better than anybody else around. When he leads, it's like going fishing with your grandfather. He's so good he could turn you upside down and you wouldn't know it. He's the complete aviator, all the way into the number three wire at the end of a hop."

My confidence level plunged that day. Some wind was taken out of some proverbial sails. In the long run, it was a good thing.

One of the wonders of operating at sea for long stretches is that in retrospect there is a tendency to remember the better times and forget those less pleasant. On the bleak side were: endless hours standing conflagration (fire) watches in a booth overlooking the hangar bays; the interminable sessions as squadron duty officer throughout a day and night of heavy flying when you are asked more questions, give more answers, and make more decisions than the average high-level executive does in a week; the occasional flare-ups between individuals, a natural consequence among humans working and living in close quarters; the longing for companionship with someone soft and gentle and of the sex opposite to yours; the list could go on. Still, life on the *Forrestal* was adventuresome, eventful, and brimful of more positives than negatives.

I was assigned as line division officer, an excellent job for one of my comparatively low rank because it gave me responsibility for the largest group in VA-85. I was in charge of about thirty sailors. They were called plane captains and were tasked with servicing, cleaning, and making minor repairs on the planes. In effect they watched over the machines day and night in all kinds of weather. Fortunately, I had Chief Petty Officer Johnson and Petty Officer First Class Fountain to supervise the troops on an hour-to-hour basis. Experienced veterans with numerous deployments behind them, they were used to the twelve- and fourteen-hour working days and knew how to get the most from the men.

As a youth I had worked on construction gangs. I dug ditches, carried mortar, tore down old structures, that sort of thing. But mine were summertime jobs, and I knew that no matter how weary or bored I became with the work, I had school and less back-breaking pursuits to look forward to. So, I could not help but be empathic toward the line crew. They were young men who didn't have autumn semesters to look forward to.

With weighty tie-down chains draped over their shoulders, they walked from one end of the flight deck to the other, often in the face of twenty-five-knot winds. They toted cumbersome parking chocks, helped lug serpentine refueling hoses, and occasionally had to push airplanes into position. They labored in an arena of spinning propellers that could slice a person to pieces in an instant; jet intakes with lethal suction power; and wind blasts from both jets and propeller-driven machines that could sweep a man overboard into the sea, a long one-hundred feet below.

Compounding the physical hazards was the pressure of meeting launch times, ensuring that aircraft were ready to go precisely as scheduled. In concert with their counterparts in the other air wing squadrons and personnel from the ship's own air department work force, our plane captains were at the very heart of carrier operations and always under the scrutiny of the captain and other senior officers.

The troops had a damp, cramped, and dimly lit chamber immediately below the flight deck where they stacked chains and chocks and took rare breaks. During an in-port period I bought a small popcorn machine and turned it over to them. The great smell of freshly popped corn did not permanently nullify the heavy odor of grease, fuel, and human sweat in that chamber, but it helped and the troops appreciated it.

Interval in the landing pattern around the carrier was important. It was a sign of professionalism to be able to "recover" large numbers of aircraft aboard ship efficiently and with a minimum number of wave-offs. Wave-offs usually meant delays and forced the captain to keep the ship into the wind, which was undesirable, because even in the spacious Mediterranean the fleet had tactical boundaries inside of which it was supposed to remain.

So, each of us tried to keep a proper distance from the plane ahead and the one behind while in the approach and landing sequence. For purposes of uniformity it was essential that we fly precisely on the proscribed altitude and airspeed. The jets were intermingled with us in the pattern and flew at different speeds, but we compensated for them. Squadrons competed against each other to demonstrate their proficiency, and the air wing commander railed when timing was off and for one reason or another the pattern was botched up. The CAG (as he was called in reference to Carrier Air Group, former title of Carrier Air Wing) would get on the backs of the squadron COs, and the COs would get on the backs of their pilots.

Skipper Lee never seemed to get a wave-off, and one evening in the ready room—surrounded by a group of us junior pilots—he was asked why that was. "Even when you look as if you're too tight on the next guy and a wave-off for close interval seems inevitable," one of the officers said, "you get aboard."

"Well, boys," he allowed, sipping from his mug of coffee, "you can do it, too." Like pups at the master's feet, we listened.

"Airspeed is the answer," he began. "Let's say you're coming around the corner at eight-seven knots and Dilbert is ahead of you." (Dilbert is a cartoon character created by eminent illustrator and satirist Robert Osborn during World War II when Osborn was an officer assigned to training duties. A chronically error-prone pilot, Dilbert's goof-ups were depicted on posters as safety aids. The main message was: "Don't be a Dilbert." Osborn also helped create Grampaw Pettibone, a character who has been promoting safety in aviation since 1943 when he first appeared in *Naval Aviation News* magazine. He still appears in that publication monthly, and Mr. Osborn still draws him.)

"He's long in the groove as usual, messin' everybody else up. But he's not so long that Paddles will wave him off and send him around. What you do is ease the nose up just a tad, tickle the throttle a bit, and slow to eighty-five, maybe eighty-four knots. That's below what the book says so be on your toes."

"Hold that speed for a second or so," he went on, "and keep an eyeball on your pal Dilbert up ahead. You'll gain precious feet of interval. Get your nose back down, massage the throttle again, get back on speed and drive her on in. Fly the bird with everything you've got. Concentrate. Stay with it all the way. You can hack it."

I had a couple dozen traps under my belt by then and tried his system one day. It worked! It was neither a recommended nor an authorized procedure, but when the master talked we listened— and learned.

The early sixties were played out under the somber shadow of the cold war. Therefore, tactical planners inserted frequent long-range, simulated nuclear strike exercises into the training scenarios.

For us in the ADs it meant flying lengthy, low-level navigation flights called "Sandblowers." Masked by the terrain from the probing sensors of radar, or skimming low over the ocean to avoid detection, we sped to simulated targets like airfields and oil storage facilities, made practice bomb delivery maneuvers, and returned to the carrier. These journeys were normally flown at less than 200 knots and often required six to ten hours to complete. A few warriors exceeded that extreme, logging marathon distances involving a dozen hours and more in the saddle.

Although these excursions were ruinous to the backside, they set us apart from all other air wing types. If our flight suits were more greasy and unkempt than our counterparts who flew the air-conditioned jets, and if our flying boots were scuffed and lusterless because we spent our spare time in the air rather than with a buffing cloth, (or elected not to promote our image through glossy shoe tops, which was more likely the case), then it was more power to us. This behavior gave us and the fraternity of Skyraider pilots throughout the Navy a special identity. Other aircraft drivers flew low-levels, to be sure, but none remained aloft and alone and in such delightful agony as we did.

We were off the Sardinian coast steaming in the Mediterranean night well along on my first cruise when a typical strike exercise was under way. The sequence of events went like this:

0200: The stateroom telephone rang and I fumbled for it in the darkness, knowing already who would be at the other end.

"It's me," a tired voice said. "Your friendly air intelligence officer." Lieutenant (junior grade) Chuck Watson sounded as if he hadn't slept in days. He was a Virginian with impeccable manners, a keen intellect, and a tremendous capacity for hard work. He knew his stuff and was highly respected in the wing. On such exercises he played a key role in that he gave us overall briefings and coordinated much of our activities with the strike planners a level above in the chain of command.

"When's the launch?" I asked bluntly.

"Oh four-thirty. You're off to Italy," he replied.

I plodded my way to the shower, which partially awakened me, shaved quickly, and pulled on a flight suit. The passageways were bathed in the dull red light of "darken ship" conditions, a precautionary environment in warships. I stumbled my way to the air intelligence spaces. My body was still in first gear but my mind was shifting to second. I had an hour and thirty minutes to plan the route, have breakfast, and perform the one-hundred-and-one functions necessary for a carrier launch.

Watson was nearly punch-drunk with fatigue, having been on the go since the exercise began nearly a day and a half ago. But he dutifully had charts and kneeboard cards waiting, and I set to work building a map on a table cluttered with pencils, scissors, plotters, trimmings, and other remnants of target planning. A few pilots and aircrewmen assigned similar missions crowded the area, shuffling between tables, asking questions, and examining the overlay chart of NATO's southern flank and the Mediterranean, which covered one bulkhead.

0245: After a final glance at the map I was satisfied I knew where to go and how to get there. The route would take me over miles of ocean and a good portion of Italy. I would make a landfall at Sorrento and then swing southeast to the heel of the boot before turning north and slicing up through central Italy. My target was a small, abandoned airstrip east of Florence and after hitting it, I would go "feet wet"—that is, depart land—at Livorno, cut to the island of Elba and then proceed south to rendezvous with the ship. The route promised mountains, valleys, and flatlands. It would be a respectable challenge to navigational ability. Presumably there would be some easy-on-the-eyes scenery as well.

There was a hitch, however. The flight would be a butt buster; time en route would be nine hours and fifteen minutes. I thought of the jet jockeys, especially the fighter pilots who seldom flew more than single-cycle, one and one-half hour hops, and for a moment despised them. Most of those fellows will have launched and recovered twice in the time it would take me to complete a single mission. I reconciled myself with the thought that there is distinction in being able to solo an airplane for a period as long as an average businessman's eight to five day at the office.

0310: In the wardroom I loaded up with scrambled eggs, bacon, home fries, and fresh coffee. But there was no time to savor an extra cup. Mentally, I was in third gear and cruising. Check-lists were cycling through my mind.

0315: The ready room teletype pecked out the ship's position and area weather as I flipped through flight logs once again. Three other VA-85 pilots plus the duty officer were milling about, preoccupied. Chatter was limited. A messenger appeared with a stack of box lunches and at oh four hundred on the button, the squawk box came alive. A voice from air operations ordered, "Pilots for the oh four-thirty launch, man your aircraft." Then, in deference to our friends who flew the E-1 Tracers, also known as the Willie Fudds, "and fill the Fudds!"

I zipped up the G suit, checked my pencil flares and other emergency equipment, and pulled on the yellow Mae West. Systematically, I scooped up the hard hat, the nav bag, and the checkerboard-sized plotting board, tucking it under my arm. I was through the doorway when the duty officer tugged at my shoulder and shoved a box lunch under my other arm. On the escalator that led to the flight deck, the same old jibes flowed forth from the jet pilots riding with me.

"Where's the picnic?" boomed one.

"AD pilots lead the world in hemorrhoid disorders!" cried another.

The brisk night air whiffed away some of the perspiration as I emerged onto the catwalk. There was no moon, and against the grey-black sky the Skyraiders on the fantail were awkward silhouettes, their folded wings like inverted Vs over the canopies. A twinge of envy went through me as I looked at the slim-lined Skyhawks, Skyrays, Skywarriors and Crusaders. But it was quickly gone. The Able Dog would win no beauty contests, but it was still the most versatile airplane on the ship.

0415: The preflight took longer than usual because of the darkness and having to poke into joints and crevices with a red-lensed flashlight. By the time Airman Prothro (pro' throw), my plane captain, strapped me in, the air boss spoke through the bull horn and cracked the hush of early morning.

"Start the ADs," he ordered, "stand by to start the jets!" We fired up the engines and the crescendo of sound became a powerful roar. The flight deck came alive, like a waking animal.

0430: The jets were poised on the catapults, and a green beacon outside the island pri-fly (the primary flight control) tower flicked on. The launch officers at their stations on the bow and waist (angled deck) catapults swirled their slim wands and the launch began. The entire carrier felt the rocking, thrusting force of the steam-powered sling shots as jet after jet was kicked off into the darkness. The heat from their exhausts, as engines labored at full power, cascaded down the deck and flooded over my machine. The temperature soared momentarily in the cockpit.

0440: I was connected to the cat and the launch officer waved his wand. I slowly moved the throttle full forward and reviewed the red-lit instruments. Everything was vibrating, the aircraft, the gauges, me. All the needles were where they should have been. I snuggled back into the seat and pressed my helmet firmly against the head rest. I felt like a bronco straining at the gate. I flipped on the master light switch, located outboard of the throttle quadrant, illuminating the Skyraider's exterior lights, which signaled that I was ready to go. Then I waited the one or two seconds that preceded my "shot."

Then it came, like a good solid sock to the behind, and I was hurtled into the night. I raised the gear handle and the wheels folded obediently into the plane. At 500 feet I leveled off and throttled back to a cruise power setting, which brought the tumult of sound down to a reasonable level. I transmitted to the ship using the squadron call sign, "Buckeye five oh four, departing on course."

0530: The horizon was a blue-grey swath between the dark of both the sky above and the sea below. I could make out wave patterns, however, and changed heading five degrees, correcting for the wind. Landfall, the "feet dry" point, was an hour away, and except for an occasional freighter there was little to see. Fuel pressure from the external tanks was steady, the autopilot was holding nicely on a northeast heading and I settled back to enjoy the solitude, my hand loosely on the control column. The engine hummed deeply.

0620: The sun was up a good angle so I descended to the daytime altitude limit over water, 100 feet. Discomfort was already setting in, especially in the buttocks area, but once land was sighted the distraction of having to navigate carefully over the hills and plains would lessen the pain, if only in mind. I twisted in my seat, the Skyraider pilot's massage.

0634: Sorrento passed under the left wing in all its crystal blue and white beauty. I had lost two minutes along the way, but that wasn't bad considering that the ship's position may have been off a few miles at launch time. The real estate was post-card pretty, especially along the coastline, but it was soon enough behind me and I was over land pointed southeast toward higher ground. Up ahead mountains seemed to have sprouted unexpectedly, so I added power. The engine rose anxiously, drawing the aircraft with it. I shook away complacency, replacing it with aggressive concentration. I remembered the stories from low-level training about flyers who found themselves boxed in by canyons with no way out. I did not want that to happen to me.

0700: I flew into a wide valley between jagged mountain ranges that paralleled the course. It was as if the earth had opened up. On the right appeared a small city at the edge of a finger-shaped lake. I checked my map. So far, right on course.

0750: I hit the southern coastline of Italy a minute late. No sweat, though, I could make it up later. There was no chase pilot behind me to check my expertise, and this was only an exercise, but pride is a fine motivator and I wanted this strike to be as real as possible. Timing accuracy was vital to that realism, so I maintained my navigation log with close attention to the elapsed time of the mission in minutes and seconds.

0930: Before me was a plateau, flat, sienna-colored, desolate. Not even a farm house was in sight. The sun grew hotter and beat down through the plexiglas of the canopy. The cockpit seemed smaller. My anatomy ached. Same old symptoms. A can of pineapple juice from the box lunch was warm but refreshed me a little bit anyway. I tried not to think of the endless hours ahead but it was unavoidable. My hind quarters would remind me anyway. If this were a road trip, I'd pull over and walk around for a few minutes. One of the pilots told me he unfolded a map and draped it over his head on really hot days as a shield against the sun. "It cooled the temperature a few degrees," he said. I did not consider myself dexterous enough to try that, especially at such low altitude.

0945: I was two minutes overdue at a checkpoint. A railroad bridge should have been easy to see, even from my height, the proscribed 200-foot limit over land. There was a city dead ahead, but according to the chart there should have been two of them united by a highway. OK, I figured, maybe I was lost. A thumb rule hammered down our throats ever since we started Sandblower training came to mind: "Hold your course and if the checkpoint doesn't come up, turn on time anyway."

So I swung left twenty degrees to my planned heading and anxiously checked back and forth between land and map, map and land. I was over rolling hills and to the left saw two sharp peaks that formed a crude V rising from the earth. I couldn't pinpoint them on the chart. Then suddenly, directly below, appeared a strip of brown in sharp contrast to the green of the countryside. Running diagonal to my course and projecting vertically from the strip like enormous robots, were steel towers supporting a network of power lines. These I could locate on the map. I found myself ten miles east of course and banked the Skyraider to intercept the route.

1050: Smooth going now, I thought to myself. I had picked up the lost minutes by eliminating a short leg and was a few seconds from the crucial run-in to the target. There could be no mistakes from here on.

I passed a U-shaped bend in a river and accelerated. The ground swept by faster and faster as the AD bucketed along at 240 knots of airspeed. I could feel the growing pressure on the machine as it sped through the air mass. The road I had selected to follow in the approach led to the Initial Point, the IP, a seventy-five-foot-high water tower, conveniently visible because of its bright, white coat of paint. I made final checks. Harness tight, mixture rich, fuel boost pump on, all other switches set. Then I glanced at the timer setting on the automatic bombing gear to ensure it was correct. My speed was now 260 knots.

The tower, a huge ball on struts, whipped by the port wing. I depressed the pickle on the control stick and held it down. The carefully calculated and preset sequence of seconds began clicking away, and a warning tone sounded in my earphones as the red timer light illuminated on the instrument panel. This was the moment of truth, the time of attack.

I pulled back on the stick and hauled the bomber upward, my eyes shifting to the gauges. Airspeed fell off rapidly and the stress of four and a half Gs inflated air pockets in my anti-gravity suit. These held my blood in check, preventing excess flow of the precious fluid from the brain. Otherwise, I might black out. The light and tone stopped as I passed through the near-vertical position simulating release of the bomb. On top of the maneuver the altimeter pegged at 1,900 feet. The world was upside down but I pulled on through the horizon, completing three-quarters of a loop before righting the aircraft and descending to tree-top level for my escape out the run-in line.

I had performed many of these maneuvers, called medium-angle lofts, but each always paid off with its own special kick. On this day I was pleased with my on-top altitude and the G schedule. I was nice and tight and believed that my "hit" would have been reasonably near the target.

1230: The Italian coast was behind me and I took a long look at Elba. It was the last land I would see for the day. Discomfort began to dominate once again. (Try sitting in a chair without standing up for eight hours some day.) To offset the gnawing fatigue, I finished the box lunch. There was another hour or so to go.

1320: I was still at 100 feet when I saw the grand profile of the *Forrestal* in the distance. Coming home to the carrier is one of the great and exhilarating sensations in naval aviation. Minutes later I joined three other Able Dogs in the holding pattern above the ship. I sucked some 100 percent oxygen directly from the supply tube to help revive my mental faculties in the struggle against exhaustion. I began to feel a bit punch-drunk like Watson. But it was uplifting to be in formation with the other squadron flyers who had gone through the same evolution.

1355: The jets finally got aboard and I double-checked gear, flaps, and hook down as I turned off the abeam position. On final, the ball on the signal mirror stayed frustratingly high and I corrected downward too abruptly, close in. This was not going to be a good pass. Safe enough, but no cigar. Our LSO, Kit Saunders, knew that we had been up in the air for hours and, as a pilot himself, identified with us. He was slightly more tolerant than usual.

I drove the Skyraider down the slope and bumped onto the mobile runway catching the number four wire. The firm tug of the harness straps against my shoulders told me I was home. With an economy of movement that never ceased to amaze me, the yellow-shirted flight deck directors guided me forward to the bow where Prothro waited, tie-down chains draped around his neck. When the last aircraft slammed aboard a few minutes later, the bull horn wailed "Recovery complete!" By the time I climbed out of the plane, the carrier was quiet but for a few commands barked by the directors and the sputtering of a tow truck here and there.

I took a moment and faced into the wind. There was satisfaction in this endeavor, the sort that is appreciated silently, personally. As much as I believed that my partners and I could do the job if the real bell rang, however, I hoped that time would never come.

Two of VA-85's most experienced pilots were Lieutenant Commanders George Carlton and Joe Bingham. They launched together one day, flew individual Sandblower missions, and joined up overhead the ship after an incredible eleven hours and forty minutes airborne! They had covered more than 1,800 miles and were obviously ready for an immediate landing and some rest.

"Your signal—delta," said the air boss laconically. Delta meant hold—wait your turn. George and Joe said nothing over the air, but they must have felt as incredulous as I did. The jet drivers, who had been aloft a fraction of time compared to them, were given priority. Inferiority complexes have been born over such discriminatory decisions. But Carlton and Bingham took things in stride. They accepted the situation far better than I would have.

After another half-hour they were cleared to land, did so with veteran efficiency, taxied up to the bow and shut down their engines. I was on the flight deck with the line crew and very curious to see how two old pros reacted after a half-day in the cockpit *and* a delta signal at the end of it. I expected them to be fuming.

But they weren't. They were sitting in their cockpits, canopies slid back, laughing! They were limp-eyed, bone-weary, and as flaccid as banana peels, but laughing heartily. I was confused.

I mounted Carlton's wing. "Good lord," I said, "I figured you'd be spittin' fire, getting a delta after all that time in the air."

Carlton threw up his hands nonchalantly. "Ah well," he sighed, "under the circumstances, laughter is the best medicine."

Night carrier operations impose demands on flyers that are unprecedented in any other type of flying—commercial, civilian, sport, or military. They call for extraordinary instrument flying skills, relentless concentration, and confidence in individual abilities. One night a Skyhawk pilot from the air wing had some problems. He was on his approach and for reasons never determined, flew into the water. A lieutenant (junior grade) with a wife and two young children, he was lost without a trace.

When word comes through that a plane has gone in with its pilot, mourning commences immediately, but in an invisible way. I never saw tears when such tragedies occurred, although some may have been shed privately. The grief is there, nonetheless, confined to individual minds where it creates its own brand of turmoil and solemn contemplation. It lasts for varying lengths of time, ultimately subsides, and is worked out of the system. Life goes on.

A number of us were in the ready room when we learned of the crash. After a time I rose to leave and paused in the doorway. "Why does it happen to the married guys?" I said. "Why not one of us bachelor types without a family?"

Chuck Watson, who was my age but far wiser than me, grabbed me by the arm. "Don't talk like that," he said adamantly. "Be happy that you're alive. Feel sorry for the other guy and his family, sure. But be glad it wasn't you."

I was stunned by his candor and said nothing. Later, in my stateroom thinking about it, I realized he was right. My words had been immature and unintelligently composed, not to mention emotionally charged. I didn't know it then, but Watson's remarks were to stay with me. So were those of John Donne, a man of wisdom from another age. He wrote that "No man is an island . . . any man's death diminishes me."

We may not have voiced such thoughts but we felt them. Like my shipmates, when one of us was lost, I mourned in a private way. But I was also silently glad that it wasn't me.

There was a rhetorical question occasionally asked aboard the *Forrestal* directly relating to flights from the flattop: What is like a game of three-dimensional chess with all the characters weaving wildly through space in a style worthy of a Freudian dream sequence? The answer to that question was always the same: Night carrier controlled approaches (CCAs), of course.

I recall a cloudless, moonless evening in the Mediterranean when six of our Skyraiders were tiered in two-plane sections, flying oval-shaped holding patterns fifteen miles behind the carrier waiting for clearance down out of the black. A pair of jets had to get aboard before we would be summoned. Moments passed, and finally we were cleared to commence the approach. Like an unraveling necklace of lights, we left the holding points and in one-minute intervals descended toward the carrier.

In situations like this pilots have a rough idea of who is where and in what plane, even though the aircraft are little more than a vague display of wing and tail lights. All was well for us until an unsettling voice belonging to the air controller in the ship captured our attention *and* our imaginations all at once.

"All aircraft, we have an emergency in progress, return to your holding points immediately!" This implied a mad dash to where we were moments before.

Six "Oh my Gods!" were muttered in six individual cockpits.

The last jet had boltered—had missed the arresting cables and become airborne again—and reached a low-fuel status. The air boss didn't want half a dozen Skyraiders cluttering up the airspace as the Skyhawk tried to get on deck.

Our heads began to swivel with rapid frequency from one side of the sky to the other and up and down it as well. It was a little like a free-for-all as each of us tried to get back to the assigned position. Pilots turned, climbed, descended, and in some never-to-be-admitted cases, temporarily spun out, in the return to the holding ovals. Hearts skipped beats, perspiration bubbled on foreheads and other places. Lights criss-crossed in the night.

I was somewhere in the middle of what was fast becoming a fiasco and saw a briefly illuminated outline of an AD blur by, right to left. I had the prickly feeling I was in the very depths of the ocean and a shark had passed by, sizing me up.

"Is that you, Sid?" I asked meekly, wondering if the shark was my friend from Arkansas.

"It's me all right," Sid answered.

"Where are you, Gus?" a high-pitched voice questioned.

"As far away as I can get," replied Gus Schuster, one of our seniors, who was obviously demonstrating wisdom in the face of adversity.

"Jim, are you still at my six o'clock position?" asked another. Since both Jim McNally and Jim Reid were in the air that question could have no satisfactory reply.

"No," said a voice, "but I am at somebody's three."

Thankfully, the Skyhawk short on gas got aboard safely and order was restored within the aerial ranks. We started down again.

Over the years media types who have viewed the flight deck of an aircraft carrier from aloft in the daytime have compared it in size to a "postage stamp," a worn-out phrase but one of some merit. At night the flight deck is invisible except for two rows of lights outlining the landing strip, one marking the centerline, and the Fresnel lens, or landing signal mirror, located on the port side of the ship. The LSO still "waved" us aboard in a sense, but, as in daytime, used his radio instead of paddles. Meanwhile we listened and tried to keep the bar of yellow light reflected on the lens between the rows of green datum lights that extended from the three and nine o'clock positions of the lens. When the bar or ball of light was below or above the green lights, you were too low or too high, accordingly.

Coming down in the dark, CCA controllers tracked us on their radar screens and funneled us toward the final approach course where we were turned over to the direct control of the LSO. So we got a lot of help. At the same time it was a little like floating in an ink well. Once visual contact with the mirror and the landing lights was made, however, I felt "connected" to the carrier. From there on in it was a matter of maintaining line-up and staying on the glide slope all the way into the arresting cables.

The sense of relief after landing at night exceeds that of daylight operations, and on this fretful evening the relief was darn near intoxicating. We convened in the ready room where fright stories, which would be embellished in years to come, careened across the space with rifle-shot intensity. Everyone seemed to have had a worse time of it than the next guy in this game of chess in the sky. Still, we had conquered the elements, albeit not with much style.

One of the flight surgeons dropped by to dispense bottles of medicinal brandy, which was an authorized custom after night recoveries in those days. We convinced him of the need and consequently received double rations.

One of the reasons I envied the jet drivers was the delta-wing "Fords," the F4D Skyray fighters. Although destined for retirement after the first cruise, they were great performers for the air wing.

They were the glamorous stars of air-power demonstrations that were held with some frequency for both American and foreign VIPs. I used to watch the shows from vulture's row on the island. (It would be a while before I earned a participant's status.)

For a typical show, four Fords were strapped onto the bow and waist cats, and when the launch signal was given they cracked in their after-burners. The hands of observers quickly went to unprotected ears. The roar was absolutely shattering. The ship seemed to tremble until, in short interval, the Skyrays were fired into the sky by the mighty mechanical slaps of the catapults' steam-powered pistons. Instantly the fighters began near-vertical climbs and on the way up displayed their manta-ray outlines as they converged toward each other. They were so high, so fast, I was breathless with awe. Their tails were blowtorch bright, and as they disappeared into the upper heights, they looked like blazing comets.

The Fords flew from sea level to more than 20,000 feet in a matter of seconds and I thought, that must be some ride. I would have given a tidy sum to trade places with a comet rider for at least one of those pursuit climbs.

R.G. Smith depicts the aircraft of Air Wing Eight, USS Forrestal. *Left to right, Skywarrior, Skyray, Skyhawk, VA-85 Skyraider, and Crusader.*

Ah well, the Skyraider was no bat-wing beauty but it had heart and personality. And is it not true that heart and personality are more durable than beauty?

Our CAG, Lawrence Heyworth, flew with us once in a while, although the Skyraider was a departure from the jets in which he collected most of his flight time. He handled all the air wing's machines masterfully, befitting a man in his position. Commander Lee, in a not so subtle ploy to ensure that Heyworth fully appreciated the rigors we AD pilots went through on Sandblower and routine three-and-a-half-hour sorties, convinced him to fly a modest six-hour low-level mission, a sort of compromise between the two.

Commander Heyworth launched and flew the route that equated to four short jet hops, the type he was more accustomed to. He returned to the ship and in deference to his rank was given landing priority by Commander Joe Garafalo, the ship's air boss. The senior pilot in the air wing was waved off, however. He was a little ragged coming in, perhaps due to fatigue. On his second try he was slightly erratic again and told to go around again. Meanwhile, all other aircraft got aboard, and the air wing commander found himself alone with a very interested audience—including people on the captain's and flag bridges, in the pri-fly tower, vulture's row, and along the recesses of the flight deck.

Garafalo, who had a fine sense of humor—a desirable, if not mandatory, attribute for those whose nerve-racking job it is to oversee flight operations aboard ship—saw an opportunity to jab the CAG. As Heyworth flew the Skyraider through the turn onto final approach, Garafalo keyed his transmitter so that all hands on the flight deck as well as the lone AD pilot approaching the carrier could hear.

"OK, CAG," said the air boss, "just hold her right there and we'll back the ship down to you!"

Rejuvenated, if not angered, by this verbal slam at his professional flying abilities, the CAG summoned the powers of experience and determination and flew smoothly all the way down the glide scope to a successful landing.

In hockey when a player scores three goals, the feat is called a "Hat Trick." On occasion, when a carrier pilot is waved off three times, the phrase is similarly applied. As he was taxiing toward the bow a voice radioed to Heyworth from the tower. "We thought you were going for the old Hat Trick today, CAG!"

Author in VA-85 Skyraider.

The air wing commander tilted his head back and leered at pri-fly and all personnel who were in the tower. "I'm going to pretend I didn't hear that," he said.

We left the Mediterranean for the good old U.S. of A. after a long half-year with the Sixth Fleet. After an interlude of reduced operations at Oceana, which permitted extended leave periods and time with families, we commenced a cycle of training that would prepare us for another deployment across the Atlantic. We would have about six months of shore duty, intermingled with brief at-sea deployments, before leaving again in early 1961.

We also got a new commanding officer. Skipper Lee's tour was over, and as much as we hated to see him go, we were happy with his replacement—a man aptly named for tailhook duty, Bill Carrier. In fact it wasn't long before we were called "Carrier's Pigeons." A quiet, intelligent, and dedicated individual, he was easy to work for and highly respected. He also had a fairly liberal cross-country policy. This allowed us to take an airplane for a weekend to build up some flight time.

Naval Air Station Quonset Point on the Rhode Island coast was a popular stopover. In nearby Warwick there was a fresh seafood outlet store called Wickford's Shellfish. When I traveled in that direction I carried with me orders for fresh lobsters, which I purchased at Wickford's and brought back to Oceana.

I entered the establishment late one October Sunday and noticed there was a commotion in progress. Around a holding tank that was about the size of a pool table and a foot or so deep, a group of people were marveling at something.

"He's a granddaddy all right," someone cried.

"Biggest I've seen in ten years," said another.

"My goodness!" exclaimed an elderly lady.

I squirmed my way through the onlookers to the edge of the tank. At first glance it looked like nothing more than a placid pool of water. Speckled dark green crustaceans were lounging there like the hard-shelled denizens of the deep they were. Suddenly, there was a splash of water. A large claw tore up through the surface, scissored in the air, and plopped back down. Several observers jumped back dampened by the spray.

"Twelve pounder, I bet," uttered one gentleman.

"At least!" wailed a youngster.

The proprietor, a stubby man in heavy rubber apron, broke through and fearlessly reached into the water in the vicinity of the portentous claw. He probed for a moment while the rest of us worried about the well-being of his submerged hand. Then, from the drink, he hauled, dripping, the largest lobster I had ever seen. Spread, the claws would measure three feet from tip to tip. The tail was as thick as a salami. The lobster waved those claws angrily and the sheer weight of it compelled the owner to lower it into the tank.

"Sir," I asked the man in the apron, "how would that giant taste if broiled properly?"

"The tail'd be a bit tough. Claws OK. Overall not bad."

Usually I purchased a load of one and a quarter-pound chicken lobsters at sixty-five cents a pound (those were the days!). These were succulent and of manageable size. But this monster was a rarity and the boys back at the hangar would get a kick out of it.

"How much?" I inquired.

"Ten bucks," said the proprietor.

"Sold," I said.

It and a dozen of regular size were crated up and secured nicely in the hellhole of my AD. A storm was stirring off the coast, but I figured to beat the worst of it. It was dark when I made a climbing turn out of Quonset Point toward the south. Because of the droning engine noise I couldn't hear the rolls of thunder in the billowing clouds to the west. But the crackling lightning, patterned like rivers on a map, was vivid enough.

Over Long Island the weather continued to percolate and the plane began to buffet against the unruly winds at the edge of the storm. As the Skyraider dipped and rose uneasily through the turbulence, it occurred to me that it was October. Halloween and goblin time were only a day or so away. Behind me in the hold was an ungainly, if not grotesque-looking, creature, who would fit right in with those goblins, not to mention broomstick-borne crones, bubbling caldrons, and things that go bump in the night. I was thinking of the twelve-pounder, of course.

What with the rocking aircraft, the black sky, and the flashing charges of electricity, I began to believe the witching hour was at hand. Abeam of Atlantic city I aimed my flashlight on the port wing. I was only at eight thousand feet, but the temperature outside my AD had dipped and there was enough moisture in the air to encourage formation of ice on the leading edges of the wings. Sure enough, it was there but not in sufficient quantity to drastically change the airflow over the machine.

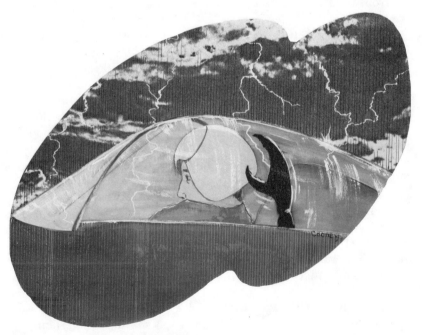

Leo the Lobster. (Drawing by Charles Cooney)

As I twisted slightly to place the flashlight back on the starboard console I was stunned by a cold, clammy substance rubbing against my neck. My pulse quickened. My body stiffened. My eyes blossomed into coat buttons. If anything felt like a lobster claw against the flesh, that was it. More in fear than anger, I cursed and against all reason reached back slowly behind my neck, fully expecting to shake hands/claws with a twelve-pound grandfather lobster.

There was nothing there but my imagination—and a loose harness clamp, which was the villain. I shook my head vehemently then shoved the mixture to full rich and the prop and throttle to normal rated power. This gave me 240 knots. I was going to hurry on home as fast as those eighteen cylinders would get me there.

In about an hour I was on the flight line at Oceana where the duty crewmen unstrapped the box of lobsters and set them on a flatbed trailer alongside my traveling bag. Inside the hangar we pried open the crate. By some weird instinct I had decided to call the mammoth lobster Leo, and I was happy to see that he and his companions were there, groggy but alive. Relieved that it really was my imagination up in the brooding sky over Atlantic City, I bravely grasped the huge denizen and held him up. Leo had grown lethargic from the flight but was greeted with admiring remarks by the crew.

The other lobsters were collected by their owners, but I kept Leo around for a couple of days during which his notoriety grew. He was a showpiece, and visitors came from around the base to see him. However, there was a point at which I felt I was exploiting one of nature's magnificent creations. It was time to end the affair. I was tempted to return him to the sea but reasoned that the local waters would not sustain him. I tried the Virginia Beach seafood restaurants figuring Leo might make an attractive display, but he was rejected by all. Finally, I sold him to the BOQ manager at Oceana, who converted Leo into a luncheon salad. I managed to dine elsewhere in the next few days until I was certain that that particular salad had been consumed.

Now and then in late October, when others look for black cats on the back fence, full moons, and trick-or-treaters, I think of Leo, an unnerving touch on the neck at eight thousand feet, and the unanticipated wonders of flying the Navy way.

By early 1961 we were fully involved in Sixth Fleet flight operations in the Mediterranean, and I was sharing a stateroom with Jim Reid. George Carlton, our operations officer, was one of the best flyers and officers I ever knew. He had a way with words and nicknamed Jim "Short, Squat, and Dynamic," which he was. The title stuck. Reid accepted it because of his unflappable nature and the veracity of the three adjectives.

But he worried me nonetheless. Jim was as healthy-looking as a Marine recruit and an excellent aviator besides. What worried me was his blood pressure. It was on the low side of the safe range—testimony, I suppose, to his extraordinarily low-keyed outlook on life.

"I may be short, squat and dynamic," he told me once, "but I try to stay loose." A Naval Academy graduate, he admitted that the Army-Navy football game managed to excite him. But that was only an annual affair. He slept as blissfully as a dry, well-fed baby, but when he woke up and with typical lethargy struggled to his feet, he wavered like a prize fighter wobbling against the ropes.

One morning he got up oh-so-slowly, swayed, and toppled to the deck, his head narrowly missing the sharp edge of an extended flip-down desk top. That low blood pressure again. He shook away his grogginess and sat down on the edge of his bed.

"Would you care to comment on the hazards of life aboard ship?" I asked.

"Well," he philosophized, rubbing his eyes, "just let it be said that if an airplane doesn't get me, the desk in my stateroom will."

Beneath Reid's unruffled demeanor lay a subtle wit. We were in loose cruise formation over Spain one day. Rays of late afternoon sun filtered through a golden curtain of haze that hung over the countryside. It played visual tricks with the rolling, tawny-colored landscape. The city of Granada passed below, its cathedrals, plazas, and fountains rising in unison from the land. For a precious moment it was like a vision from Shangri La. Reid keyed his mike.

"That's a nice lookin' town," he said, "somebody ought to write a song about it."

Bob Dugan was a gruff-looking, cigar-chomping, stevedore-strong mechanic who headed the power plants division in the maintenance department. A petty officer first class, he wore his salt-and-pepper hair in a crew-cut. He was tough as a bear on the outside, gentle as a doe underneath, and wise as an owl all over. He knew the R-3350 engine better than anyone else around.

We became close friends and I was intrigued by his personal history. He was a South African and left his native country as a youth when the drums of World War II began beating on the dark continent in the form of Italian troops fighting in Ethiopia.

"My mother was worried about the future and thought I could make a better life in America," he told me. "I got a job as a cabin boy on a steamer. I had absolutely no money and neither did my family. At the dock my mother gave me a penny. 'Just so you don't leave with completely empty pockets,' she said."

He journeyed to the U.S., became a citizen, joined the Navy, married, began a family, and built a new life for himself. He was ingenious with mechanical things and always sought more efficient ways to get the job done. He also surprised people with his knowledge and love of classical music. Before the second deployment he scrounged around salvage yards in the Oceana area, found spare pieces of hardware, and designed and built what became known as Dugan's Dolly.

The apparatus had a long handle and could be pulled into position under the AD's pylon-mounted fuel tanks. By pumping a simple hydraulic jack, a support platform could be raised up to the tank, which was then detached and lowered to the deck for maintenance and repair purposes. Without the dolly the tanks had to be purged of fuel, a laborious task, and raised and lowered manually, which required about six grunting troops.

The dolly was in demand by other units as well for the simple reason that it prevented many a backstrain. It also saved time, a precious commodity in the hectic world of carrier operations.

But most important, Dugan knew engines. One day I was strapped in abeam the island for a test hop and had turned up to thirty inches of manifold pressure to check the magnetos. Dugan was standing alongside the aircraft holding his "Mickey Mouse" ear protectors slightly away from his head, presumably listening for any adverse sounds. According to my instruments the mags checked satisfactorily. I gave him an emphatic thumbs up signifying all was OK.

He gave me an emphatic thumbs down. And when Dugan tells you not to go, you don't go. I secured the engine and climbed out. "She checked out OK, Dugan," I said, "what's up?"

"There's somethin' wrong with that engine, sir," he replied. It was a statement of fact, devoid of conjecture.

He and the crew labored through the night until they discovered incipient metal fatigue near one of the engine mounts. I will never know if that engine might have failed that day. But I have a lingering feeling that Dugan saved me from going into the drink. In a way he was like a doctor who had detected an infinitesimal heart murmur, one that others might miss. It occurred to me at the

VA-85 A-1s approach British carrier during Mediterranean operations, 1962.

time that if the Navy had people like Bob Dugan, I had certainly joined the right outfit.

Another fascinating personality who helped keep the planes in the air was pipe-smoking Maintenance Chief D. T. Krupski. A rotund, hard-working man with boundless energy, he was a human computer. These were the days before automated record-keeping and sophisticated visual display systems. Krupski monitored the machines as if they were his own children, however, and somehow always knew the detailed condition of each of our dozen birds.

"How do you keep track so well?" I asked him.

He tapped his head then his rear pocket, pulling from it a green, wallet-size memorandum book. He flipped through its pages, which contained a myriad of notations that only he could understand.

"I've got the dope recorded in those two places," he said.

His methods would succumb to the advances of technology, but I always thought that Krupski's total devotion to the machines was as admirable as it was old-fashioned.

Part way through the second cruise Mr. Zanuck of Hollywood came to the Mediterranean to film *The Longest Day*, a story about the Normandy invasion in June 1944. Our ADs were asked to participate for a few days. It was all at once a compliment and a dig, since our aircraft were considered the only ones in the fleet that resembled types flown in World War II, twenty years ago. He wanted Skyraiders to make fly-bys over a convoy, as well as attack runs on a Sardinian "beachhead." Lieutenant Jack Fellowes, a spirited officer, and I collided at the doorway of Gene Teter's stateroom. Gene was the schedules officer, and Fellowes was as much a ham as I was. We both wanted "in" on the Hollywood hops.

"OK, boys," said Teter, "if it means that much to you, you're on."

So Jack led and three of us followed on several tail-numbing, multi-hour flights. We swept back and forth repeatedly over the task force. We protected the "Allied troops" with devastating attacks on the "Hun." Time after time we dove on the enemy and, wearing John Wayne grimaces, pulled our Skyraiders up into the sky to dive again. All the while the cameras recorded the drama.

I liked to believe it was Zanuck himself in the whaleboat that was located a few yards offshore directing us. "Move it over to the right a few yards," a voice would say over the radio, "and this time bring those planes in lower!"

I must jump briefly ahead a few months to the time the film was released. I sat in a Virginia Beach theater pumped up with anticipation, savoring the fame that surely lay ahead. The film began, and droned on and on until the invasion finally started. I just knew the ADs would steal the show. At a certain point I figured "here we come." It was like sitting on the catapult waiting for the piston-stroke to boot you into the air.

And there we were! Four combat-primed Skyraiders winging proudly over the convoy as it plowed through the English Channel. Abruptly, however, we were gone. There was a quick cut to General Eisenhower on the bridge of a ship. I waited, believing we would return for the assault on the beaches. I waited a long time. Alas, we did not appear again.

Our film debut consisted of approximately two and a half seconds on the screen. The rest of our labors lay on the cutting room floor. It was a very long drive back to the BOQ that night.

Sid Wegert was a wizard in the air. A natural in the cockpit, he could coax the Skyraider down the slope during ragged weather, day or night, and still score an OK Number Three Wire pass. A likeable bear of a man, he was talkative enough on the ground but silent as a snail in the sky. It was a sign of professional airmanship to keep radio transmissions to an absolute minimum.

Nevertheless, on those excruciatingly long night navigation flights over the Mediterranean, far from lighted landscapes, I yearned for conversation to relieve the tedium of flying steadily, uneventfully, along on Sid's wing. Even a succinct, "I'm comin' left," from the wizard would have been welcome. But he specialized in silence, and I motored through the night dutifully clammed up. He was so smooth I hardly had to hold the throttle as I followed him through turns and descents and a practice approach pattern now and then.

The silence grated on my nerves, while the seat cushion frayed another portion of the anatomy. The wizard cruised on in his taciturn fashion.

"Look," I said to Sid one night in the ready room, "I'm all for zipped lips and no unnecessary chatter, but when we have to drive around up there in the black for hours, couldn't you say something once in a while? Like, 'It's bleak out tonight,' or, 'I'm descending 500 feet,' or just 'hello out there.' Frankly, when I'm with you I feel as though I'm flying with a phantom, and I don't mean the F-4 type." (F-4 Phantom fighters had replaced the Skyrays in our air wing.)

"This carrier operatin' business," he explained, "is violent, earshattering, and not very conducive to relaxation. So when I get up there on those nighttime patrols to nowhere and back, I take all the peace I can get. Lord help the guy who transgresses on that solitude."

He spoke with such outright conviction that I retreated from the issue. I contemplated his reasoning for some time and felt it best to honor his tranquility.

The sea was churned into foaming swells by angry winds one morning as we launched for a practice bombing flight off the Italian coast. A high overcast colored the world gray but for the meringue-like whitecaps. I had fired a rocket on what was called a low-angle-loft delivery. This entailed skimming low toward the target (a smoke light) at high speed, pulling up at a specified point, "tossing" the rocket, then making an exaggerated wingover recovery. I was in the escape turn, banked 120 degrees and pulling hard when I felt a severe vibration accompanied by a sickening thud. The rpm and other engine gauges stuttered and the needles fell off momentarily. The engine in effect had coughed but immediately spurted to life again.

I brought the nose up, began a climb, and instinctively took up a heading for the carrier, fifty miles to the west. The sump warning light flickered, then came on to stay. This was a red beacon centrally located on the instrument panel that detected any metal chips that found their way into the oil sump area. Metal chips could portend disintegration of engine parts. At the same time it was not uncommon for a metal sliver or two to adhere to the magnetic sump plug and cause the light to illuminate by way of an electrical signal. This did not necessarily signify a serious problem, especially in the case of newer engines being broken in. In such cases the sump was checked, the metal removed, and the engine turned. If it checked out satisfactorily, the aircraft was returned to flying status.

We were taught, however, to assume that whenever the sump light came on, engine failure was imminent. In my case there was no doubt that I had more than a sliver to worry about.

So I continued my climb and suppressed the lump in my throat long enough to report, "Buckeye five oh six has a rough runner and sump light. I'm headin' home."

Swiftly, flight leader George Carlton was on my wing. He directed the other two members of the flight to stay clear and continue their mission.

"All the gauges are normal, George," I said. It would have been more professional to stick to side numbers but this was a moment of stress, and George had instantly become a source of hope and guidance—a friend in need. It was easier to use his first name rather than a number, and less formal.

"Roger," he said flatly.

Suddenly, the Skyraider trembled as if it wanted to stop in mid-air, made another thud sound, then smoothed out.

"She just quit again," I said, my voice rather tense.

"Roger," acknowledged George, "The ship's straight ahead, thirty-nine miles."

Oddly, my mind swung back in time to my youth. Thirty-nine miles. That was the distance from my home in Hamilton to Syracuse, a good hour's drive. And an hour is a long time. Of course by air in a 180-knot aircraft it was only a matter of minutes. I looked down at the sea. It was very rough.

"If it quits," I said to George, "I'll try to ditch on the back side of a swell."

"Roger," said George, "let's do the check list, just in case."

I locked my shoulder harness, ensured the mixture was in rich, reported same to George, and then scanned emergency procedures on my flip cards, the ones listed under "Engine Failure."

The engine stopped again then erupted back to life. (Carlton told me later he saw smoke belch out of the exhausts and the nose shake violently each time the engine seized. "I did not believe it would hold together," he said, "but I felt it would serve no purpose to tell you that." He was right.)

George checked us in with the ship, declared an emergency, and asked for immediate landing clearance.

"Unable," responded a voice from the carrier. "The deck is re-spotted for launch and the landing area is covered. Bingo to Pisa." Bingo meant divert.

George amplified the serious nature of my problem, but the decision stuck. We both knew the deck could be cleared although it would take a few minutes and assuredly foul up the schedule. I suppose the reasoning was that the R-3350 would hold together for the seventy-mile trip to Italy where a long, stationary runway was waiting for me.

I felt powerless and insecure in that moment of my life, and the major reason was the water below. I feared its tumultuous con-dition and the late spring temperatures, which were cold although not brutally so. Had the sea been more calm, a controlled ditching into the wind could be made with excellent possibilities of success.

We had aboard the *Forrestal* a small detachment of AD-5, multi-crewed, early-warning Skyraiders. The unit shared the ready room with us along with the Tracer people. One of the AD-5 pilots had an engine failure earlier in the cruise and made a controlled ditching on a beautiful sunny day in clear view of the ship. The pilot and crew escaped unscathed and were rescued almost im-mediately by helicopter. But the wind-whipped ocean below me now looked far from accommodating. I was concerned that I would be flipped over abruptly or that the plane might be torn asunder on impact like so much kindling if I didn't hit the swell just right. On top of that if I did get out of the machine, it would be a chore waiting for the helicopter in the choppy waters.

In any event we turned toward Pisa and with unsettling regu-larity the engine spat and shook for a second or so every two to three minutes. We flew eastward for what seemed an eternity. Eventually I noticed the clouds breaking up exposing patches of blue. If this raised my spirits, the sight of land sent them soaring. And land lay straight ahead.

"You're gonna make it," Carlton said.

I gave him a thumbs up.

We crossed the beach at 8,000 feet, an altitude that I main-tained until we reached the airport at Pisa a few miles inland. George took care of the reports to tower personnel, and when I had the runway in sight I began a gentle, spiraling approach.

There was nothing more he could do at this point, so George detached to return to the ship.

"Thanks, five one oh," I said.

"Enjoy yourself," George said, banking steeply away.

The landing was uneventful and I taxied off the runway to a hangar adjacent to the control tower. It was a small, tidy airfield with several commercial planes and a number of military training types. I shut down, and in the welcome silence removed my helmet and breathed deeply, feeling the sunshine on my face.

I did not want to go swimming today, I said to myself, so thank you, airplane, thank you, R-3350, thank you very much.

Not long after I settled down, an Italian airman who spoke English told me a COD (carrier on-board delivery plane) from the ship was on the way with help. This would be the *Forrestal*'s support aircraft. It was similar to the Tracer without a radome and accommodated both passengers and cargo. A few hours later it came and when its hatch swung open, the lanky figure of Petty Officer First Class Virgil Hughes appeared at the opening. He surveyed the premises as if he were the President alighting from Air Force One, then jumped down to the ground. He was followed by another mech, a second class named Roland. They carried tool kits and hastily packed duffle bags.

Hughes was a sandy-haired, ruddy-faced southerner who wore his blue ball cap on the back of his head, its bill about ten degrees off center. Roland, who was in dungarees like Hughes, was a muscular man of medium size with black hair and the hardy good looks of someone who has spent a lot of time on the range. He came from a small town in Texas. Hughes was in his late thirties, Roland in his twenties. They had a reputation for working well with each other, and both were known to be superb with a wrench.

"Understand you got a sick airplane, sir," said Hughes.

"Very sick," I said.

"Not to worry," Hughes announced walking directly toward the Skyraider, "we'll fix her up."

Several hours later Hughes was wiping his hands with a rag and staring at the engine, which he and Roland had partially dismembered.

"She's sick all right," said Hughes. "Gonna have to take off that engine. How she held together I'll never know. She's thrown a rod and a few other things. You were lucky, sir."

Next day an electrician and a metalsmith from the squadron joined us, and I was directed to stay with the group to supervise the engine change. Thus began two weeks in another town, an unexpected and gleefully appreciated tour of shore duty. We stayed at a small hotel in town, about thirty harrowing minutes away by jeep. Our driver was an Army private who was absolutely fearless behind the wheel. We were at the mercy of a frustrated Mario Andretti who treated any obstacle in his path, human or otherwise, with contempt.

But if those twice-a-day journeys were detrimental to our nervous systems, we were placated every noon hour at the Italian Sergeants' Mess Hall.

My family is Italian, and although both my mother and father were born in America, their forebears hailed from Sicily and northern Italy, respectively. No one mastered Italian cuisine better than my mother. For years she was encouraged to bottle up her spaghetti sauce and go into business. She was too busy working and raising children to do so. The point is, I was raised on the delights of Italian victuals unsurpassed in their quality.

I must say, however, that the food we enjoyed in that mess hall was so fragrant, so delicious, so bountiful, and so appealing to the eye that those noon hours became excursions into a sort of wonderland for the stomach. For fifty cents apiece—yes, fifty cents—we opened up with large bowls of thick, steaming soup (varied daily) and fresh-baked loaves of bread. Next came the pasta course, with sauce if desired, followed by the entrée, which included fresh garden vegetables and generous slices of roast beef, veal, chicken, or steak. Fruit and cheese came after that and from beginning to end there were decanters of wine, all we wanted. Buxom ladies who wore white aprons and hearty smiles served the food and treated all of us like royalty. But it was Roland who brought an extra twinkle to their eyes.

Roland out-ate every one of us and never failed to clean every morsel from his plate. Although the ladies didn't understand English, they nodded and laughed as Roland extolled the virtues of the food. He downed bowl after bowl of soup and at least three helpings of spaghetti each day. He savored the food slowly, mannerly, and consumed it with perfect joy.

"Good lord, Roland," I said. "If I didn't know better, I'd say you hadn't eaten in years."

"Sir," he said. "My family was poor, and the truth is I didn't have that much on the table as a kid. One of the reasons I joined the Navy was to get three squares a day."

"And you're makin' up for all the chow you missed," interjected Hughes, "isn't that right, Roland?"

"I guess," said the Texan.

One day as Roland was finishing a fourth plate of pasta, I noticed a nearby group of Italian servicemen watching him in awe. Roland finished, leaned back in his chair, and patted his stomach. A look of total serenity came over his face. Then, the four Italians rose from their table and as if they had just observed a moving scene from an opera, they applauded. It was a spontaneous ovation, and although I'm not positive, I do believe that Roland's appreciation of the culinary offerings was looked upon as an endorsement of the very essence of Italian life.

Believe it or not, we did little carousing in Pisa. It was a quiet city dominated by the great Leaning Tower, which was only a block from our hotel. We made it a practice to have coffee or a nightcap at an outdoor cafe opposite the tower. Hughes, incidentally, held the unwavering belief that "It's gonna fall down one of these days."

Perhaps it was the overwhelming magnificence of the structure and the way it was lit against the night that induced what I thought was a phenomenon. We watched as along toward midnight, Italians came from all directions and converged on the previously uncrowded piazza that surrounded the base of the tower. They strolled for a half hour or so and then were gone. They were simply making a constitutional in the shadow of their very own wonder of the world, but it seemed like an almost mystical migration of human beings, lured willingly to a scene of enchantment.

"This is a very peaceful place," said Roland.

We did not miss the ship at all.

"All good things have to end," I told our group at the end of the two weeks. Under Hughes's unassuming but effective leadership, they had done an excellent job swapping the old engine with a new one that had been shipped in. I had test-flown the aircraft and was saying goodbye. They would wait a day or so for a COD, and I was to fly the plane to the ship.

I manned up and found a note signed by Hughes taped to the instrument panel.

"Sir," it read, "please tell them not to hurry to pick us up."

About a month after Pisa another Skyraider from VA-85 suffered engine problems, and the pilot was diverted to Palma de Mallorca, a city on an island paradise in the western Mediterranean. Mallorca was a haven for sun-worshipers and fun-lovers from Scandinavia, the British Isles, West Germany, all over. "The secretaries of Europe vacation there," a ship's company officer said, "and it's the only place I've ever been where women actually outnumbered men."

It was unfair but logical that Commander Carrier send me in to oversee repairs. After all, I now had the benefit of experience in such matters. There was envy in the ranks, and I *did* feel guilty about getting another plum. But not guilty enough to disobey the CO's orders.

An engine change was not required, but some major components had to be replaced on the aircraft. For a week we put in a full day at the field and cavorted rather conservatively at night, just to keep the blood circulating. On the negative side, we had communications problems that far exceeded those in Pisa, where I was in almost daily contact with the ship through the Italian's radio network. Each day in Palma, phrase book in hand, I climbed a ladder to the airfield's tower and with help from an operations clerk, drafted messages updating our progress and asked that they be sent to the carrier. The Spanish controllers shrugged as if I were intruding on their life style but ultimately obliged me. They typed the words on flimsy blue onionskin and gave me information copies.

Back on board the *Forrestal* at the end of the sojourn, I checked in at the ready room and was succinctly informed by the duty officer that the CO wanted to see me right away. The tone of his voice suggested trouble in the wind.

"Something wrong?" I asked.

"We haven't heard from you since you left," he said.

I stiffened. "Didn't you get my messages?" I asked with alarm.

"What messages?" he replied.

My heart sank. The Spanish had failed me. Everybody in the squadron, including the skipper, probably figured I was preoccupied with social matters and had neglected Navy business.

Commander Carrier was at his desk when I came in. His face reminded me of Mount Rushmore. "Well," he said flatly, "we were wondering what happened to you."

I reached down to the shin-level pocket of my flight suit, pulled out the crumpled blue onionskins, and handed them to him.

"Will this evidence hold up in court?" I asked, hopefully.

He read through the dispatches carefully, and except for the rustling of the paper, an ominous silence hung in the stateroom. Finally, Mount Rushmore faded and animation returned.

"Case dismissed," he said, "glad you're back."

I was born under the eleventh sign of zodiac, Aquarius, but I am no advocate of astrology. However, somebody told me that Aquarians tend to save things. Boy, am I glad I saved those onionskins.

I was a veteran of sorts on this second cruise and was assigned to the fire power demonstration team. Our new CAG was Commander Jim Ferris, an accomplished aviator and officer destined for flag rank, as was Commander Heyworth, his predecessor. CAG Ferris was as concerned about making the demonstrations effective as was Heyworth. The mighty F-4 Phantom fighters had replaced the Skyrays and got a lot of attention as the new aerial "stars" of naval aviation. But the ADs continued to leave their mark, although not always in a positive way.

Lieutenant Commander Dick Hartigan was a vivacious and articulate man in VA-85. He wore an almost perpetual smile that reflected a debonair outlook on life. One afternoon, with NATO visitors aboard to view a demonstration, Dick earned some notoriety he would have preferred to avoid. His speciality in the air show was dive-bombing with a full load of five-hundred pounders. Because his aircraft was at maximum gross weight, he was given the aftermost position in the column of Skyraiders aligned for deck-run takeoffs. He needed all the wind and traveling room he could get.

He had made several successful launches with his enormous cargo, but on this particular day he remarked in the briefing, "I really should have a cat shot. I've figured the estimated wind-over-the-deck, my weight, and plotted the distance required. There's just not enough margin for comfort."

He consulted the flight deck officer who told him, "We'll give you plenty of wind. You don't need a catapult shot. And besides, we have to get the jets in the air. It would foul things up if we had to shoot you off, what with the importance of air show timing and all that."

Hartigan pleaded fruitlessly and manned up, his normally sparkling disposition somewhat subdued. It was an overcast day, and an erratic wind had agitated the sea, which resembled soapy water on a laundry machine's wash cycle. The carrier heaved and pitched sluggishly. But the show went on. The jets were slung into the sky and the props lumbered off the deck to join them. Finally it was Hartigan's turn.

He ran up to thirty inches of manifold pressure, checked his gauges, and nodded to the flight deck officer. The flight deck officer nodded in return, twirling his upraised right arm, and examining the flight deck forward, which was clear. The man in the yellow jersey then squatted and swung his arm toward the bow. Hartigan came off the brakes instantly, advanced the throttle, and began the long ride from the stern to the front end of the boat.

He felt only slightly uneasy as the hulk of the superstructure blurred by on his right. A second or so later, however, a disturbing realization took hold of him. The machine was acting properly and serving up a full measure of pep. But that extra sense of perception vital to the well-being of a carrier pilot told him that he was not moving fast enough to proceed safely off the end of the ship. It may have been the reduced rate of passage of key signposts—like the island structure or the hulking, yellow crane, Big Tilly, parked forward of it—that told him this. In any event, it came to him with frightening impact that he was beyond the point where he could haul the beast to a stop. The appalling truth was that he did not have flying speed and consequently was destined to plunge into the sea. Which he did.

He left the bow like a fledgling nudged prematurely from its nest and sort of fluttered in space before sloshing into the swells. Fortunately, Hartigan was a savvy flyer. He had jettisoned the bombs before impact and kept the aircraft pointed straight ahead without trying to raise the nose, risking a stall. The captain of the ship alertly swung the stern away from the disintegrating attack bomber to prevent the carrier's screws from chewing up the pilot. Hartigan unbuckled and scrambled out of the cockpit as the Skyraider sank beneath him. He was plucked promptly from the churning waters by a helicopter and delivered to safety on the flight deck.

George Carlton used to call Hartigan "The Silver-Tongued Dissenter," because the latter gentleman invariably protested almost any expenditure from the squadron slush fund—used to buy going-away gifts and the like. These protests were good-natured in tone and did not detract from his debonair outlook. Still, we weren't quite sure how this normally cheerful officer was going to react to his impromptu dip into the sea.

It was never quite clear to me who bore the brunt of blame for the accident, the flight deck crew or the pilot for some error in flying technique. To my knowledge, no blows were exchanged and although he was understandably angered at the outset, by nightfall Hartigan was able to laugh about the mishap. Happily, his reputation as an outstanding aviator remained intact.

I was orbiting overhead when Dick crashed that day. I recall feeling instant gloom followed by soaring joy when the air boss reported, "The pilot has been rescued. He's OK!" I was also very pleased that my event in the air show required the transport of a diminutive, ten-pound Mark-76 practice bomb rather than a full load of real-life 500-pounders.

Among the places we visited in the Mediterranean were Naples and Livorno in Italy; Palermo, Sicily; Palma de Mallorca, Valencia, and Barcelona, Spain; Beirut, Lebanon; Athens and Rhodes, Greece; and my favorite, Cannes, in the south of France. There wasn't enough liberty, of course. Sailors have complained about that probably since before the days of the Vikings. But what shore leave there was had quality.

Lured by the intrigues and romances that surely awaited us at any of these ports, we rode launches from the carrier to the fleet landing full of anticipation. More often than not we returned without fulfilling those dreams of romance and intrigue, but the joy was in the quest for them anyway.

Cannes had a special enchantment. By day there were the beaches, beautiful slim-limbed ladies in bikinis, luxurious-looking yachts, and an unreal sensation of mingling with the very rich of the world. By night there were the casinos with their roulette and baccarat tables, night clubs brimming with sun-tanned vacationers, and restaurants serving fare that aroused the palate to new highs. Cannes, seen from the sea in the evening, was a magnificent spectacle. It was as if its gently rolling hills, which rose rather sharply behind the shore line, were covered with a black velvet cloth then showered with gems of every color that sparkled in the night.

Importantly, despite their abbreviated nature, these breaks from tiring work periods at sea gave the seven-month deployment its flavor. Adventures ashore provided the fodder for stories that augmented those that took place on the briny deep. Had it not been for the Navy, most of us would have never been exposed to the Mediterranean countries, met their people, and observed their way of life. Our own lives were enriched by the experience.

We returned to the U.S. in the summer of 1961 and were a couple hundred miles off the Atlantic coast on a picture-perfect day preparing for the flyaway launch. The entire air wing was departing the ship. We would fly the planes ashore and be followed by the carrier, which would tie up at a pier in Norfolk next morning. I was just senior enough to make the bottom of the fly-off list and was preflighting my aircraft as a song called "Mustapha," a Middle-Eastern melody with a belly-dancing lilt to it, carried loudly across the flight deck. It had become a theme song of sorts for the deployment.

I noticed that Attack Squadron Eighty-One pilots were conspicuous by their absence. Their Skyhawks were parked adjacent to our ADs on the fantail, and plane captains stood by to strap in the flyers who weren't there. I was about to say something when a voice from the loudspeaker interrupted the music.

"Now hear this! All hands attention on the flight deck." There was a pause then, "Presenting the pilots of the world's best attack squadron—VA-81!"

The music kicked back in and amidships, emerging from the catwalk like football players into a stadium, came a dozen men. Their flight suits were hardly noticeable because each of them wore flowing white turbans secured to their heads by black cords. The turbans flapped in the wind like an scene from an Arabian movie. The flyers quickly formed into two rows, one group kneeling, the other standing behind. They cradled their flying helmets uniformly in their right arms while camera buffs from all over the ship appeared to take their picture. It was a nice gesture to cap the cruise and when "Mustapha" ended and the turbans were removed, the haunting strains of "Till We Meet Again" filled the air.

An hour later the flight deck was empty and we were airborne, flying in waves by squadron to the beach.

Customarily, after a long deployment there is a substantial turnover of personnel—officer and enlisted. Such was the case with us as we began a nearly year-long training cycle before going overseas again. Lieutenant (junior grade) Stan Cobb was part of the new blood who joined us. He had what the ladies call Greek-God good looks. He was blond-haired, muscular in build, recruiting poster handsome, and wise enough not to let his natural gifts swell his head.

Stan was big with the ladies, but a girl from Sweden named Lee won his heart, and they decided to wed in Cobb's small home town in Ohio. The bride came from aristocracy and was gorgeous in her long white dress and a stunning silver tiara. Stan and the rest of us from the squadron wore choke-collar dress white uniforms.

The ceremony was held in a church before a packed crowd. The bridesmaids were visions of loveliness, and we were the Prince Charmings of the fleet with our gold buttons and wings shining brightly. I felt as if I were at Cinderella's ball.

Formality prevailed as the reverend recited prayers to the splendid-looking couple standing before him. When it came time for the bride and groom to kneel, they did so with a grace befitting the event. Then something happened.

It began with a snicker, spread to muffled chuckles, and stopped short of outright laughter. Seems a squadron mate or two had gotten to the white soles of Cobb's white shoes before Stan had dressed that morning. In bright, red ink the letters *H* and *E* were written on the left shoe followed by *L* and *P* on the right. The ceremony continued rather uneasily but ended on an upbeat note.

At the reception one of the local gentlemen, without malice, said to me, "You Navy flyers take things lightly, don't you?" Not having participated in this irreverent disruption to an otherwise lovely joining-in-the-bonds-of-holy-matrimony, I avoided the question.

Although we were shore-based at Oceana and on a schedule less hectic than that aboard ship, we did plenty of flying, working with each other in the air just as a football team practices on the gridiron. We had an ensign with us learning the ropes who was a capable pilot and very knowledgeable of the AD. I was involved with him in an incident during a training mission.

But first let me express a feeling I have. A naval aviator's reputation is like a fingerprint. His (or her) whorl pattern is similar to everyone else's, but nuances give it an individual character. Flyers share common qualities of determination, intelligence, dexterity, and a propensity for adventue. These are pretty much mandatory attributes for the winners of wings. But each has his own style, you might say—good, bad, or in between.

The ensign, for example, flew very well, but he tended to dramatize the undramatic and this was his nuance. He demonstrated little reluctance to call "Mayday," a distress alarm that was reserved for occasions similar in gravity to volcanic eruptions, quaking of the earth, or discovering a scratch on the new car. In other words, unless things were going really badly in the air, a pilot did not issue a Mayday because it called into play all kinds of emergency units. The idea was: alert them if needed, but be very sure you need them in the first place.

In his first few months he issued three such alarms, well over "allowance," and each of them culminated in a safe recovery. Minor mechanical malfunctions were faulted for his airborne trouble.

One afternoon he and I were on our way inbound to Oceana from a radar-tracking hop with a destroyer. We were about seventy miles out over the Atlantic when he keyed his mike.

"I've got a rough runner," he said.

"Roger," I said. His Skyraider looked healthy enough. There was no lamentable belching of smoke, no abnormal trembling of the power plant or airframe. But I gave him the lead so he could concentrate on his dilemma rather than flying wing on me.

"Better give the call," he said solemnly. "She's running rough."

What choice did I have? He was the captain of his ship and if he said he had a rough runner, I was constrained to believe him.

"Mayday, Mayday, Mayday," I declared in as resonant a tone as I could contrive. I followed this with an appraisal of the circumstances, and within seconds responses were flowing into our earphones. Had there been a telephone switchboard to handle such matters, it would have been lit up like launch time at Cape Canaveral. Everyone and his brother, including a proficiency pilot flying an SNB out of Andrews Air Force Base in Maryland, offered help.

But we made it to the beach while the radio chattered with talk from many aircraft wanting to assist. The ensign executed a very nice precautionary approach to the airport at Elizabeth City, North Carolina, the nearest suitable field. Rescue units that were converging toward us returned to their home bases.

There is a saying that flying consists of hours and hours of boredom interrupted by moments of sheer terror. I believe that emergencies like the ensign's actually served to relieve some of that boredom for all within listening distance. Fortunately, in this case, nobody got hurt.

A veteran pilot from the squadron was sent to collect the plane the next day along with a mechanic. After a thorough examination and a lengthy turn-up of the aircraft, no discrepancy was found. The pilot believed the aircraft was safe for flight and took off for Oceana.

Short of home base his sump warning light came on and he dutifully made an emergency landing at Fentress, an outlying field a few miles from Oceana. He rolled to the end of the runway and was about to turn onto a taxiway when to his amazement, the engine froze and the propeller came to a quivering halt. There was indeed something amiss in that power plant, and the ensign had detected it. It turned out that the engine had to be replaced.

There was a moral to be learned here, but I am not sure what it was. I thought about the episode for some time and concluded that aircraft can be as unpredictable as the predictable people who fly them.

The maxim about the boredom of flying interrupted by moments of sheer terror came home to me not long after the ensign's Mayday flight. I had flown to Naval Air Station Quonset Point in Rhode Island and was making a night takeoff for the trip back. Just as my Skyraider left the runway the port wing fell off sharply.

My heart stopped and I thought for certain I was going to cart-wheel into the ground. But with great force on the stick and maxi-mum rudder I was able to right the plane and keep on flying.

I settled down on the climb-out wondering what in the world had happened. Then it struck me like a hypodermic needle in the arm. The servicing crew had filled my port external fuel tank by mistake and left the starboard one empty. I had accepted a load that placed the aircraft beyond its aerodynamic limits. The port-side fueling coupled with the left-pulling torque effect could have been disastrous. Why I didn't realize the error at the time, I'll nev-er know.

Stupid, stupid, stupid! I slapped my helmet as if it would knock some sense into me. Then I scanned the figures on a per-formance card we carried in the air. According to them the air-plane should have been uncontrollable at lift-off. The statistics indi-cated I should have crashed. The title of a book by an Army Air Corps pilot passed through my mind: *God Is My Copilot.*

I vowed not to make the same mistake again.

During the year at Oceana we made several relatively short training cruises aboard the *Forrestal,* conducting operations with the Second Fleet in the Atlantic and the Caribbean. On one of these I was assigned a solo, low-level—or Sandblower—mission.

I was 200 miles at sea tracking inbound to a point of land on the coast from which I would jump off to the target, a rusting hulk of a derelict ship in a bay near Stumpy Point, North Carolina. I had carefully aligned the compasses before leaving the carrier, and the first sixty minutes passed in a routinely dull fashion. Flying be-tween an endless cloud blanket above and a monotonous scalloped sea below was less than invigorating.

As the time en route passed the one and a quarter hour mark, I felt an acidic stirring in my gut. I should have reached Atlantic coast real estate at least ten minutes earlier. My dead reckoning was in order, but there was no land in sight. I was in the gloomy embrace of the elements and without the sun, unable to verify my general direction of movement. I began to wonder if North America really was out there beyond my nose after all. If by catas-trophic compass or human error I had swung full around to the east, I might be destined for a "mysterious" disappearance in the Devil's Triangle.

I cursed and railed against my Skyraider, its compasses, and naval air in total, for imposing this predicament on me. I squirmed in my seat as if that would appease the twisting barbs of frustration. Finally, I eased the nose up, adding power. It was time to climb and confess. I was lost.

But joy! As I was about to punch through the grey overcast, I saw ahead of me a strip of pale brown stretching across the horizon. It looked like a brush stroke on barren canvas. It was a beach. Land Ho!

I zoomed down to the wave tops and pressed on. It was against the rules to use certain navigation aids on practice flights like this one, except in an emergency. But pride was at stake, and in my own mind I considered the situation an emergency of sorts. So, with swift and surreptitious switch-ons of the direction-finding and distance-measuring equipment, I learned I was approaching the northeastern edge of Georgia. I had missed my intended mark by a couple of states.

Some rapid calculations ensued, along with realignment of the compasses. I determined that they were off forty degrees, including the standby compass that virtually never fails. I doubted that the boys in maintenance would believe this, but I would worry about that later. With the zeal of a postman I went to fast cruise power and turned north in the hopes of making my TOT—time on target. I bucketed along on a mad dash over the seaboard feeling like the runner who has broken clear on a kickoff return. Fishermen and farmers scattered along the route were my audience and halted in their endeavors to look up at me as I raced by.

By flying a direct route I made the TOT and flew a three-quarter loop, tossing the practice bomb I had carried toward the derelict. I rolled out and eased back on the throttle to give the eighteen cylinders a reprieve. I glanced back to see a puff of smoke where the bomb impacted the water. It was within a respectable distance of the ship. Then, with some help from the Willie Fudds and their excellent radar gear, I received vectors back out over the sea to the *Forrestal*. The return trip was made without further complications.

The weather cleared toward evening, and after the final recovery I went topside and gazed at the becalmed, moonlit Atlantic as the carrier creaked slowly through the night. I contemplated the anxious moments of the day and the gratification of getting to the target on time, which offset them. "There may be other ways to spend one's youth," I said to myself," but I am glad I chose this one."

After the relatively brief deployment we returned to Oceana and I took off on two weeks' leave for a visit home. When you have been flying on an almost daily basis, half a month out of the cockpit is a long time. It was the practice therefore, upon returning from extended leave periods, to fly a comfortable, daytime refresher hop before taking on more demanding aerial duties.

I checked in a day early from my vacation. It was a gray and rainy Saturday morning, and the duty officer was suspiciously delighted to see me.

"My friend," he said with a little syrup in his voice, "how would you like some flight time?"

"I'm game," I answered.

"John Clinton's stuck in Jacksonville, Florida. His aircraft is grounded because he needs a new fuel pump. Our supply folks have one packaged and ready to go. Would you deliver it?"

The duty officer was apparently unfamiliar with the refresher flight regulation, and I chose not to remind him of it. It was wet and gloomy outside and Jacksonville was a long distance away, but I said sure, I'd make the trip.

So, a short time later I was in the soup, level at seven thousand feet, southbound. The weather front engulfed the eastern seaboard, so I did not expect to break out until final approach at the Naval Air Station in Jacksonville. Which is precisely how it went. I logged nearly three and a half hours to Florida, all but a few minutes in genuine instrument flying conditions.

Lieutenant (junior grade) Clinton greeted me after I shut down and eagerly accepted the fuel pump. "Thanks a lot," he said. "Wondering if you'd get through. Looks nasty out."

"You'll be on the gauges all the way to Oceana," I advised, "but it's smooth and there isn't much turbulence. Just sort of dark inside those clouds."

I waited until the mechs replaced the pump and Clinton's plane checked out before taking off myself. My return journey was uneventful, although I was dragging a bit when I flopped down in a chair in the ready room after another three and a half hours in harness.

"Mission complete," I announced to the duty officer. "One fuel pump delivered. Seven hours flight time. Six and a half of them in the glue."

"Six and half hours in actual instrument conditions!" he exclaimed, shaking his head in disbelief.

I checked Monday's flight schedule before heading to the BOQ. I was slated for an oh nine hundred launch. The schedules people, true to regulation, had the foresight to give me a back-from-leave refresher flight.

That Monday, George Carlton, who headed the operations department, decided that under the circumstances it would not be detrimental to me or the squadron if I missed that oh nine hundred flight.

He did not refer directly to my Saturday excursion, but a thought hung between us like a voice balloon from a comic strip. The message was: "Don't overextend yourself. If something had gone wrong, there would be heck to pay. And in the future don't check in early from leave."

About a week later I launched as Tail-End-Charlie on a three-plane practice bombing hop to one of the targets south of Oceana. It was a gloriously clear day. A cold front had pushed through and washed the sky clean. Visibility was unlimited.

As I rolled down the runway I thought I heard a slight change in engine sound, a sort of hollowing out of the normal timbre at takeoff power. My eyes swept the instruments. They were OK and airspeed was increasing properly, so I continued in trail behind the other two planes. A moment or so went by and the wingmen seemed to be pulling away from me. All my senses indicated that I should have been closing on them. I felt fine, just this side of giddy as a matter of fact. It was a beautiful morning for flying and all was right with the world.

Another minute or two passed during which I crossed over into the realm of incipient drunkenness. A voice—was it Lady Luck? a higher being? reached a sober corner of my mind and flashed a message: "carbon monoxide poisoning."

I squinted at the gauges, examined the throttle quadrant, and discovered that I had unknowingly reduced power. This accounted for the lapse between myself and the others. I could never catch them at this rate. I opened the canopy to gulp in some fresh air and radioed that I must land right away. It was most difficult to turn the machine. I was dizzy. I was a floating leaf. I felt like a baby trying to jam a square block into a round hole. I thought I was moving the stick and adjusting power but the aircraft simply would not obey my manual commands.

The fresh air helped sweep away some of the numbness and somehow I reversed the aircraft and swung in a wide arc full around to line up with the runway I had just left. It seemed as if I was drifting effortlessly in the air on a magic carpet. I shouted to myself: "Land it! Get on the ground!"

There was a chasm between the earth and my Skyraider. I was over an ever-deepening valley. I stomped my feet as if that would

87

help push the plane downward. The air from the glorious, clear day whipped around me, and I inhaled it deeply. Thankfully, it infiltrated the anatomy and ultimately purged the toxic invaders from my body. Sobriety had just about fully returned as I made the final approach and swooped safely onto the runway. The wheels screeched against the concrete surface, but it was a wonderful, soothing noise.

When the mechs dug into the engine they found a cracked manifold, which had caused the unusual sound on takeoff. They also discovered a small opening through which the harmful gases poured into the cockpit and nearly sent me into an eternal sleep. We were carefully trained for this sort of emergency. We had been briefed countless times on the telltale signs of carbon monoxide poisoning and how it could rapidly convert a flyer into a helpless state of being.

Perhaps it was that training that found voice and spoke to me in a moment of peril. I also believed Lady Luck and a higher being were riding along with me in the cockpit that day.

We went out on the *Forrestal* for another training cruise before a major deployment to the Mediterranean and operated primarily in the waters north and east of the West Indies. One day the carrier was north of Puerto Rico, and Jim Reid and I were directed to fly to the Naval Air Station at Guantánamo Bay, Cuba. We were to pick up some items and return to the ship a day later. We launched and took up a westerly heading with Jim in the lead and both of us blissfully thinking ahead to some cold refreshments—a rum swizzle or two—at the Gitmo officer's club. We broke through some dismal gray clouds that hugged close to the warm waters and settled into cruise formation above an endless lid of white ones. The sun bore down on us, but we were at a relatively cool 9,000 feet.

After nearly two hours, still above the weather, we failed to get a lock-on with our direction-finding equipment as anticipated and, in jest, Jim and I exchanged defaming remarks about each other's navigational skills.

Another half hour passed and the situation became very unfunny. We were lost. I was reminded again of the Devil's Triangle and the inscrutable tales of vanishing planes and ships in that part of the world. We didn't know it at the time but headwinds, triple the velocity of those predicted before takeoff, had slowed us substantially. When we thought we were beyond Haiti we were really along the northern coast of the Dominican Republic.

So we poked down through the overcast into a dim steel-gray

world without sun. Visibility wasn't bad, however, and we flew our planned course for a few minutes before coming upon a string of islets. Unfortunately, we could not definitely match them with anything on our charts. We were still lost.

Despite its tremendous range— "long legs" in aviation vernacular—the Skyraider had its limits, and fuel became a consideration. I felt very uncomfortable and insecure, but did not want to admit such emotions to Jim, who kept his cool much better than I. Then, in the distance to the south, Reid spotted a P-2 Neptune patrol plane, one of the most reassuring sights in my life.

Like children separated from Momma at the department store, we added throttle and scrambled quickly alongside the dark blue, twin-engine aircraft. Using hand signals, fingers extended to denote numbers, we established a mutual radio frequency.

"We're lost," Jim reported, a hint of resignation in his voice, "request a steer to Gitmo."

If the Neptune crew chuckled at our dilemma, it was their privilege. At that point we didn't care. We were embarrassed, slightly humiliated, but destined to remain dry. We weren't terribly off course, as it turned out, just substantially behind time along the route because of those dastardly winds.

We detached from the P-2 a few miles out from the airfield at Gitmo, extended our prolific thanks to the crew, and proceeded inbound to make our landings.

We slunk into the operations building and were told that a search-and-rescue team had been alerted and had very nearly commenced looking for us. We tried to find the helpful Neptune flyers and set them up with a few rounds of rum swizzles but regrettably couldn't locate them. Reid and I toasted them anyway and elected to keep the incident in the "flights to forget" file.

The cruise and its countless hours of general quarters drills, briefings, and flying wore on until we headed north toward Norfolk. At noon on the final day of flight operations, with clusters of clouds drifting lazily across a bright blue sky, tragedy struck.

All of the wing's aircraft had recovered except for the Skywarriors, the huge, heavy attack planes we had come to call the "Whales" in deference to their gigantic dimensions compared to other carrier-based aircraft. As with most accidents that occur on the flight deck, it happened violently and with mercuric swiftness.

I had just parked halfway up the bow on the starboard side and was loosening my parachute harness when a thundering "pop!" shattered the air. It was unlike any sound I had ever heard and conjured up the vision of a mythical giant cracking an enormous whip. I twisted up out of the cockpit and looked back. A Skywarrior was floundering helplessly off the edge of the angled deck at an incredibly slow speed. Both of its jet engines were roaring at full power in a defiant attempt to keep the plane aloft. Like a slow motion film sequence, the lumbering machine disappeared from view. I scrambled onto the wing of my Skyraider fully expecting to see a geyser of water and burst of flame off the port bow. The emergency horn, activated by the air boss, screamed, and crewmen instinctively rushed toward the side of the ship to witness the crash.

But there was no ball of fire, no gushing upsurge from the sea. The pilot of the Whale had somehow, miraculously, overruled the aerodynamics of flight and kept the aircraft in the sky. After several seconds it appeared ahead of the ship skimming along at wavetop level with its tailhook nicking the surface. It struggled for altitude and began a gentle climb. It was some piece of flying.

I swung around. More than a dozen men were sprawled about the flight deck, most of them abeam the island and along the juncture of the angle and bow. Others raced to their aid while the voice of the air boss boomed: "All available medical personnel to the flight deck immediately!"

At the stern of the ship, curled in lifeless outline like a colossal, dead snake, was the instrument of destruction. It was an arresting cable that had apparently torn loose from its port sheave as the Skywarrior was being brought to a halt. I hurried down from the wing feeling weak in the stomach and wondering what I could do to help. But it seemed as if the stricken were already being treated. Response had been instant by the able-bodied.

The air boss made another announcement, this one delivered in a subdued, ominous tone: "Chaplains report to the flight deck on the double!"

Several yards behind my Skyraider a young sailor, one of the blue-shirted men tasked with positioning aircraft between launches and recoveries, lay motionless, his expression wide-eyed with shock. A corpsman knelt beside him administering first aid while another waved urgently for a stretcher. The victim's right leg from the knee down was a shattered mass of blood and torn cloth. Nearby, another member of the flight deck crew sat in dazed silence cradling one arm with the other. Behind him, at the foul line—an alternating red and white stripe dividing the landing area from the bow—lay a flight deck officer and his chief petty officer assistant. Both were still, frighteningly so, like discarded rag dolls. Their yellow jerseys were splotched crimson with blood.

Lieutenant Joe Pursch, the air wing's flight surgeon, was there, having arrived seconds before from somewhere deep in the ship. I remembered that Jim Bransfeld, our other doctor, was ashore temporarily handling medical duties for another unit, so Joe had his hands full. He was bent in examination of the unmoving bodies. The officer's eyes were open but glassy. Pursch grasped the man's torso, pushed in gently and released the grip. He studied what was a chest wound intensely then said to a waiting corpsman, "He'll be all right." He then gave instructions to the corpsman on how to stop the bleeding, and as he was doing so an uninjured officer from the flight deck crew grabbed the surgeon by the shoulder. "Hurry, Doc!" he cried, pulling Pursch toward the unconscious chief whose neck was badly gashed. Joe gently took hold of the chief's hand and tenderly placed his hand against the wound.

"How is he?" asked the anguished officer.

Pursch said nothing for a moment then looked up. "I'm sorry," he said, "he's dead."

What at the outset was a scene of frenzy became one of orderly action. Eleven more men less seriously injured were being treated by shipmates. Some were able to stand and hobble about. Others waited in stretchers because of leg injuries. The chief was the only fatality. The flight deck officer was seriously hurt but would survive. The youngster behind my plane had to have his leg amputated below the knee. Most of the others sustained sprains and lacerations.

Next day in a jam-packed ready room I watched a video replay of the accident recorded by the PLAT (pilot landing aid, television) system. On the TV monitor the action was re-lived and showed how the Skywarrior, which ultimately diverted to a shore base and recovered safely, landed and properly caught the arresting cable. It was almost completely stopped when the wire erupted from the sheave and whipped low across the flight deck, releasing the trapped aircraft. The bomber plowed forward trying to fly while the cable swept relentlessly in a wide arc across the ship, all the way back to the end of the island structure. Most of the men in its path were caught at knee level or below, (the flight deck officer and his chief were near the end of the angled deck when the cable snapped and were stuck higher), and flipped into the air feet first like so many tenpins. They tumbled back down to the steel deck on their necks and shoulders.

Those who heard the horrifying "pop" and observed what one senior officer called a horizontal guillotine would not soon forget that day. However, if we derived anything positive from the calamity, it was a strengthening of the bonds that held us together as military men who depended on and supported each other, especially in the face of danger.

By late summer 1962 we were in the Mediterranean again with another skipper and the same old airplane with a new title. Commander Norvel Scott, a tall, slim Virginian with a quiet demeanor, crew-cut hair, and a high-pitched voice that distinguished him from other air wing pilots over the radio air waves, replaced Commander Carrier. At about the same time Secretary of Defense Robert McNamara ordered the redesignation of military aircraft, and the AD Skyraider became the A-1. It would be a while before we succumbed to the appellation, although I must admit the "A" and the "1" carried with it a ring of first-rate quality.

Fire power demonstrations continued to occupy much of our time, and one day Commander Scott was briefing five of us on a fresh wrinkle he had planned. Skipper Scott had lots of hours in the Skyraider and was a superlative pilot, but he raised some eyebrows when he described the maneuver he wanted us to perform.

"We'll be at 8,000 feet in right echelon," he began, "and fly parallel to the ship's course. The carrier will be off our right wing, and I'll position us so we have enough slant-range distance to make a thirty-degree dive. We'll treat the *Forrestal* as a target, the object being to roll in, simulate an attack on the ship, then pull up—all together—line abreast."

We were listening very intently.

"I'll call 'stand by to roll in,'" he continued, "and then—"

Dick Hartigan's arm shot into the air like a rocket. The Silver-Tongued Dissenter was annoyed.

"You plan a right-hand roll-in, sir?" he asked, incredulous, "*into* the echelon? All six of us?"

Turning into a stair-step stack of aircraft was routine stuff for the Navy's Flight Demonstration Team, the Blue Angels. But it was not a recommended procedure for others, even experienced fleet pilots. Such a turn forced the "inside" pilots to reduce power and make other rather uncomfortable adjustments in order to stay in formation.

"That is correct," said Scott firmly. "We're professionals. We can hack it."

After a pause he went on. "Keep your props at 2,000 rpms in the dive. As we commence the pull-up I'll call 'Buckeyes now!' at which point everybody shove your propeller control up to full low pitch and get your throttles on accordingly. Got it?"

We nodded in skeptical obedience.

"Good!" said the CO. "Our Able Dogs may not be streamlined, but when we charge by those visitors watching from the flight deck, they'll know they've heard and seen power in motion!"

Hartigan's knuckles whitened. Sid Wegert, who was sitting beside me, worked his jaw apprehensively, his lips sealed tight. Kit Saunders smiled nervously behind a clenched fist. Jim Reid, on my other side, jabbed me in the ribs and whispered, "This is going to be an MGM special."

We went into the air and joined dutifully on the CO. The time drew near for our event and half-a-dozen hearts—perhaps only five excluding the skipper—began to race in unison. We arced carefully around the ship, Scott masterfully guiding us toward the roll-in point. I glanced at the defenseless flattop, slow in the water below, and pictured the VIPs sitting calmly in their chairs enjoying a balmy breeze. Surely they were gazing up at the six airplanes above them, anxious to see what was about to happen.

Fortunately for me I was on the tail end of the whip, a much safer location than my comrades in positions two through five. They had to be concerned with Skyraiders in front of and behind them. Theirs was a predicament much like a person caught in a crowd hurrying from a stadium. There was no turning back, and they were compelled to follow the leader. I sympathized but did not envy them.

"Rollin' in," said the skipper in that sharp, tenor voice of his.

In the next few seconds our formation resembled a fast-moving python with broken ribs. We made our right-hand turns en masse, pushed the noses downward, and smoothed out, stabilized in a line-abreast disposition. We dove on the carrier, and I must admit feeling a nice theatrical charge of excitement as we did so. The ship grew larger as we approached, then Scott called: "Pullin' up," followed by, "Buckeyes now!"

We complied with prebriefed instructions. The rapid and collective increase in rpms and engine power as we transitioned to climbing flight, swooping low over the *Forrestal*, converted us from mere airplanes into roaring, fearsome assault bombers. Our "attack" constituted a mighty and magnificent piston-engine salute.

After shutting down later, my plane captain, Prothro, said, "You guys really got them foreigners shiftin' in their seats. Especially when you revved the engines and flew overhead!"

Scott was right. We could hack it. Mission accomplished.

The carrier was a floating city populated by an endless variety of personalities. Two favorites were the flight surgeons, the best in the Navy as far as I was concerned. They were colorful, dedicated, and skilled. They watched over us, fascinated by the world of naval aviation and those people who thrived in it. After night recoveries they circulated through the ready rooms checking up on us, their ears and eyes attuned to the state of our mental and physical well-being. They preferred to stay in the background—in the wings of the carrier-life theater. But inevitably, they became incandescent members of it. Joe Pursch and Jim Bransfeld were their names.

Joe, of course, led the medical force which, within seconds after the cable snapped weeks before, helped turn possible chaos into order. He retained his cool under pressure and did the best he could for those who were hurt. Pursch was a suave-looking man with thick black hair, dark skin, handsome Mediterranean looks, and a rich baritone voice. In lighter moments we called him Ezio— Eeetseeoh!— after Ezio Pinza, the musical star of *South Pacific*, not so much because of the physical similarities but for the gracious, virile demeanor of both men. Joe had been a starving youth in Europe in 1944 when Allied troops rescued him in the rubble of Northern Italy. Through an aid program, an American lady supported him with a little money and a lot of kindness. Although she died before they met, he worked his way to the U.S., struggled, studied, labored at a variety of jobs, and became a physician. Like another immigrant, my favorite mechanic, Bob Dugan, he chose the Navy for a career.

Jim Bransfeld was also an orphan, having lost his parents at a young age. He sweated his way up the educational ladder and earned his surgeon's credentials. He was a rugged-looking man with the strength of a farm hand but the gentle nature of a lamb. He had flaming red hair, wore glasses, and owned a sword-sharp wit. He was a workaholic. When he wasn't tending to duties, he studied encyclopedia-sized medical texts.

Jim Reid said once, "If I ever have to go under the knife, I want those two guys there."

Pursch stayed in uniform, contributing, excelling. He actually gained fame as a captain years later when he headed the Alcohol and Drug Rehabilitation Center at the Naval Hospital in Long Beach, California. Joe cared for the famous as well as the unknown and treated them the same regardless of their stature.

Bransfeld became chief of surgery at St. Frances X. Cabrini Hospital in Chicago. His is quite a success story.

From such flowers are beautiful bouquets made.

I was a lieutenant now, wearing parallel silver bars on my collar, colloquially referred to as railroad tracks. I was a full-fledged flight leader and considered one of the "old heads" in the squadron. We had a considerable changeover in personnel over the years, but many familiar faces were still there. The cruise was progressing nicely and we were flying actively. Then came October.

October was not a good time for us. It was not a good time for the world either.

Fidel Castro had brought communism close to American shores several years before. When Cuban exiles failed in their invasion try at the "Bay of Pigs" to oust Castro in April, 1961, the Russians and Castro had much to cheer about. Soviet prestige had been buoyed further, a few days before the attempted invasion, when their cosmonaut, Major Yuri Gagarin, became the first human to orbit the globe. U.S. Navy Commander Alan Shepard made a successful suborbital flight in May, but on earth, by late summer, the communists were building a wall in Berlin to prevent East Germans from escaping to the West. Tensions were heightened throughout the world. While the U.S. scored a success with Marine Corps pilot Lieutenant Colonel John Glenn's orbital flight in February 1962, events were taking place that would draw man's eyes down from starry heights and train them on an island off the Florida coast.

Missiles were discovered in Cuba, initiating an infamous stretch of days during which planet Earth was brought to the edge of nuclear war. It was cold and windy on the wine-dark sea. When we weren't flying, our planes were chained down against the weather but held in a state of readiness. We were on a war footing while Mr. Khrushchev of the Soviet Union, who put the missiles in close proximity to American shores, and President Kennedy squared off. Moods were as glum as the overcast skies in our corner of the Mediterranean. If fighting broke out, our strategic location dictated that we might very likely be a part of it. It was a solemn time for wondering and waiting and hoping.

On the wardroom television screen we watched a replay of the President's speech to the nation. His voice was determined and unwavering.

"I've got bad vibes about this situation," I said to Reid in our stateroom one evening.

"They'll move the missiles," he said with measured certainty.

"I'm not so sure of that," I said.

We had been trained for what might lay ahead. We were capable. The hours ticked by and grew into incredibly long days and nights. But the ordeal in anxiety finally ended. Reid was right. They moved the missiles.

The crisis over, flight operations returned to normal. Winter temperatures forced us into cumbersome, but necessary, exposure suits. These resembled diver's gear, like that which John Wayne wore in *Reap the Wild Wind*. Huge boots were sealed to the rubber suits, which fit snugly around our necks and wrists. We perspired dismally in the ready room until launch time, then got nicely chilled while preflighting our machines in the cold air. However, if we had to go into the water unexpectedly, the protection could save us from a frozen doom. If we didn't have to stay in the sea too long, that is.

I landed one night after a rain shower had thoroughly doused the ship and taxied carefully along the slippery deck to the bow. I was guided by a wand-waving director into position behind another squadron Skyraider. There was some confusion, and a plane captain was unavailable to chain the aircraft down promptly. So I had to stay on the brakes, a mandatory rule aboard ship; if you weren't moving, your feet had to be planted firmly on the pedals. What with the darkness, the disconcerting patterns of lights produced by wand movements in the periphery and the constraints imposed by the bulky exposure suit, I became quite uncomfortable. My feet grew numb from the steady pressure. The engine was chugging away in the night and even though it was at idle speed, there was a chance that the machine could move, especially with the treacherous mixture of water and grease lying between the deck and the rubber tires. I was an accident waiting to happen.

The aircraft inched forward so slowly that I had absolutely no perception of movement. I must have unknowingly eased up on the brakes. Suddenly, there was a terrifying, buzz-like noise. I knew instantly that I had plowed into the plane ahead and that my propeller had sheared its rudder. I chopped the throttle, secured the switches and unstrapped from the cockpit. I could see movement beneath the plane as someone shoved a pair of chocks against the wheels.

"My God," I thought as goose bumps blossomed on my flesh, "I may have killed somebody!"

I climbed out, jumped off the wing and nearly bumped into Airman Prothro, the plane captain. His face was recognizable in the dim glow of a red-lensed flashlight he was holding in one hand. In the other he grasped a jagged strip of metal about a foot long. A rivulet of blood ran from a tiny cut on his brow to a point just above his left eye. There was no pain in his expression. In fact his lips formed a trace of a smile.

"My God," I thought, as goose bumps blossomed on my flesh, "I may have killed somebody!" (Drawing by Bob George)

"Just grazed me, sir," he said calmly, "like in those western movies."

I took a deep breath. "Are you sure you're all right?" I asked.

"Yes sir," he nodded, wiping away the blood with a handkerchief. "I'll check it out with sick bay if it will make you feel better."

"It would make me feel better," I said.

The damaged plane required a new rudder (it could have been worse), Prothro was cleared for continued full-time duty by the medical folks, and because my fellow pilots recognized the perils inherent in long minutes on the brakes in those heavy exposure suit boots, there were no recriminations.

I felt badly about Airman Prothro, but he did not hold the mishap against me. He was a blond-haired, likeable, industrious midwesterner with the build of a linebacker. In fact, he was a standout on our squadron touch football team when we played in the base league at Oceana. On occasion, his misadventures got him into trouble, but they were superseded by his outstanding performance as a member of the line division. On this cruise, unfortunately, he got into a skirmish while on liberty and was placed on report. The charges were such that, combined with previous blemishes on his record, the skipper felt bound to give him a Summary Court-Martial.

This judicial proceeding is a formal, one-on-one affair between the offender and an officer, the Summary Court, conducted behind closed doors. I don't think the powers above wanted Prothro to suffer inordinately, but wisely, no one gave voice to that view. In any event, they may have felt I would not be too tough on him—I played on the football team, too, and in a sense, owed him some sort of debt for *my* misadventure that night on the flight deck—because I was assigned as the Summary Court.

Spiffed up in dress blue uniforms we convened in the XO's stateroom. We were both erect, stiff-chinned, and unsmiling. I had reviewed all the procedures to avoid slip-ups. I was determined that justice be served, and fortunately, Prothro was determined to be contrite. Even so, it was difficult, almost painfully so, to administer the proceedings. I had very strong feelings about the troops, those young men who worked so long and so hard to keep us flying, and Prothro was one of the best of them. Both of us lingered on the fragile edge of succumbing to informality. Complicating matters was the realization that I had the power of judgment against a man whom I nearly killed with a piece of shrapnel.

We got through the ordeal somehow, and for punishment I recommended four months restriction to the ship and reduction in rate to Airman Apprentice, which I surmised, and later confirmed, was more than what was expected by those in the upper echelons of command. The CO could reduce it, I reasoned, and my conscience was reasonably clear.

Oddly enough, Prothro was not surprised at the penalty's severity and indeed seemed to appreciate the spot I was in. I admired him for that. Outside the stateroom, the confrontation blessedly over, I pulled him aside.

"Look," I said firmly, "I don't want to go through that again."

"Neither do I, sir," he concurred strongly.

"Stay out of trouble," I cautioned, "please."

"Will do, sir," he declared, "will do."

He meant what he said and so did I.

The *Forrestal* paused in Livorno and some of us journeyed inland a few miles to the exquisite and colorful Tuscan city of

Florence in the northern half of the country. It was a place of cobblestone piazzas rimmed with statuary that pleased the eye and ristorantes that delighted the most discriminating palates.

We discovered one eating establishment called The Cave, presumably because of its subterranean location. It was reached by descending a flight of stone steps from street level. It consisted of a large dining room with a serving bar in one corner over which, suspended in string nets, were cheeses and salamis and bottles of wine wearing jackets of interwoven straw.

The tables varied in size, but each was covered with several layers of plain white tablecloths. The china was an austere white as well, the dinner dishes oversized. The stucco walls were off-white and barren. Here, the cuisine provided the color. The waiters wore dark trousers and white shirts with sleeves rolled to just below their elbows. Towels were draped over their shoulders. Like figure skaters they maneuvered with marvelous grace and economy of movement. Unobtrusively, they emerged from the swinging doors of the kitchen, adjacent to the bar, and dispersed to their customers, transporting bowls of steaming soup and plates heaped with pasta, vegetables, and assorted cuts of meat.

We were seated by the wall facing the steps that led into the restaurant and were soon savoring a luscious repast that was accompanied by ruby-red wine that arrived in a long-necked decanter the size of a basketball. We supped and sipped and flowed with the evening, enraptured by the atmosphere and the knowledge that we were in a place far, far away from home. The carrier and its world of steel grey, noise, and heavy hardware was, for the moment, a distant memory.

We had finished the dinner and our table was clear except for the wine and glasses when I saw her. She had stopped halfway down the stone steps. She was neither young nor old. She fit somewhere delectably in between. She was wearing a knee-length, camels-hair coat, and little makeup. But her high, distinctive cheek bones, the regal tilt of her chin, and the celebrated glitter in her eyes exuded a stunning presence.

I said to my companions, "Gentlemen, *there* is a beautiful lady." They looked. They liked. They agreed. Olivia DeHavilland continued her descent followed by a small entourage, including a handsome man whom I recognized as the Italian film star, Rosanno Brazzi. The group settled at a corner table and was immediately surrounded by waiters.

Perhaps it was the wine. Maybe it was the balmy enchantment of the evening. More likely it was a combination of both. But I gave

99

in to an immature instinct, rose from the table and proceeded across the floor, drawing to a stop directly abeam Miss DeHavilland's elbow.

After I was poised at her side for a moment ot two, she looked up at me. "I'm sorry to interrupt, Ma'am," I began, "but would you mind giving me your autograph?" She gave me a soft, endearing smile while accepting the slip of paper I held out.

"I'd be happy to," she said. "You're an American, aren't you?"

"Why yes," I said lamely.

"And I'll wager you're from one of the Sixth Fleet ships at Livorno as well," she added.

How did she know?

"Yes, Ma'am, we're from the carrier *Forrestal*," I said, nodding toward my companions who were looking the other way.

What a radiant face, I thought. She was the girl in *Gone With The Wind* all right. "Well," she said, "we were on your ship today, as a matter of fact. As guests of your admiral. We were very impressed."

I shifted nervously and mumbled something. Then the movie star introduced me to Mr. Brazzi who bobbed his head and resumed negotiations in animated Italian with a waiter. I thanked her and withdrew. My associates downplayed the achievement, far less than intrigued by this exposure to fame.

Olivia DeHavilland was wonderful in many motion pictures, but because of the circumstances my favorite was the one called *A Light in the Piazza*. She was making it in Florence the time we met. A year or so after the incident in The Cave I saw the film and, leaving the theater, smiled to myself and said, "Ah Olivia, I knew you when."

Fire power demonstration time again. Another flock of VIPs were due on board, and our new CAG (like his predecessors, also destined for flag rank) was a stickler for perfection. Commander Earl "Buddy" Yates was his name, and he worked us diligently. A flawless execution of the events was his, and our, goal. I was a regular on the VA-85 demo team, and one of my jobs was to join up with a Phantom for a flyby to graphically exhibit the "old," meaning A-1, and the "new," meaning F-4, of naval aviation. This was an affront to the Skyraider community but orders were orders.

I'm not sure of the Phantom pilot's name—a Lieutenant Benson, I think. But I remember his cherubic face and slightly rotund figure. He was a personable sort and had a reputation as "a good stick," meaning he was an excellent pilot. Behind him in the tandem seat F-4 was his radar intercept officer, the man who controlled the sophisticated array of electronic equipment designed to help Phantom crews pursue enemy aircraft and shoot them out of the sky.

Practices went well. Benson led and I flew close aboard him, both of us with landing wheels, flaps, and hooks extended—referred to in the colloquial as a "dirty" configuration. As we passed the ship we added power simultaneously, retracted gear, flaps, and hooks—"cleaning" up—our machines. Thus we demonstrated wave-off techniques. Importantly, as we did so, the announcer described over the loudspeaker to the guests how much more powerful the Phantom was compared to the aging Spad. To amplify the Phantom's might, Benson kicked in the afterburners on his twin-engine fighter, which accomplished two things: rattled the eardrums of the VIPs and other observers on the flight deck, and allowed him to zoom-climb away leaving my propeller-powered Skyraider in its wake as if it were standing still.

Before one rehearsal, Dick Hartigan took me furtively aside.

"Listen," he said, "you know as well as I that jet engines don't immediately accelerate faster than reciprocating types." This was true. Over a short haul, say a few seconds, an A-1 could hang right with a jet when both planes poured on the coals at the same time. After those few seconds, however, it was no contest. Hartigan had a devious plan up his sleeve and I figured in it.

"I'm listening," I said.

"The Phantom may be a world-class speedster, but for sprints the Skyraider can stay with anybody. Short sprints, that is. If you cheat a little—raise the gear a hair quicker than Benson and get that throttle on a second or two ahead of him, you can stay with that fancy fighter till you're past the audience. Don't let the Skyraider be humiliated out there! Besides, its only practice."

Hartigan could be very eloquent, and I was easily persuaded to comply with his suggestion. "I'll do it," I said.

So Benson and I approached the ship in formation at about 140 knots, dirty. We were an unlikely pair—a top-of-the-line, highly polished fighter and a grease-stained attack plane born at the end of World War II.

Witnesses later told me that the announcer's voice was most authoritative when he reported: "Now you will observe the F-4 going to full power. The pilot will demostrate the Phantom's ability to accelerate quickly."

Meanwhile, an air wing officer directing the sequence from the primary tower, transmitted a signal to us over the radio. "Event four" (which we were), he began, "commence wave-off now."

Before he had enunciated the word "four," I rammed the throttle forward and raised the gear, flap, and hook handles much in the manner of a mad scientist. So did Benson. But for the next five to six seconds I stayed right with him. *Together* we winged by the flattop. Benson's cherubic face registered a perplexed look and he flicked his hand at me as if to swat a bug from his shoulder. He was a bit late actuating his afterburners and we were actually beyond the carrier when the Phantom pulled sharply up and away into a high-performance climb.

Later at the debrief, the CAG was breathing fire. He singled me out right away. "Never," he said, "Never, ever do that again!"

Silence fell across the ready room. I wondered if my boldness was going to get me grounded. I searched for Hartigan as if I might transfer some blame to him. You could hear a pencil drop. Then the CAG smiled.

"At least not when the official audience is looking on," he said.

There followed a rousing cheer that built into a crescendo of laughter. When it subsided, Benson came up and shook my hand. Hartigan appeared and slapped me reassuringly on the back. Score one for the Skyraider!

Shortly before dawn one day during a prolonged, long-range strike exercise, the phone rang me awake in the stateroom.

"This is your friendly air intelligence officer," said a voice, "are you awake?"

"I will be in about thirty seconds," I said to Chuck Watson.

"What I have to say will step that up," he countered.

"Shoot," I said.

"If I told you that air operations wants to launch one A-1 on a four-hour, fly-anywhere, do-anything-you-want flight, totally without restrictions, would you believe it?"

"Nope," I said flatly.

"Believe it," he said. "If you can man up in one hour, the hop is yours."

Apparently there was a spare, up-and-ready airplane just waiting for someone to take it aloft and get some flight time. The hours would add nicely to the overall total of the exercise. I asked no questions and leapt at the opportunity.

It was a glorious, once-in-a-lifetime hop. We were north of Sicily, and I elected to sightsee along both the Italian and Sicilian coasts. It was daybreak as I approached a string of islets that extended north of Messina. Among them was Stromboli with its coal-black volcanic slopes—the subject of some notoriety when Ingrid Bergman and Robert Rossellini made a film there—and Lipari, the home of my maternal grandparents.

Lipari was a splendid-looking, emerald-colored place with a charming village of white houses at one end. These glowed ivory-white as the sun came up over the horizon like a burning copper coin. Then I flew to the peak of Mount Etna, over 10,000 feet high, where I circled its fiery mouth watching rocks spew from it. I viewed the numerous fishing villages along the way, and when a valley or a range of hills appealed to me, I proceeded to examine it as if I was on an exclusive Cook's tour. And so it went.

I did not take full advantage of my flight-without-restrictions. I could have buzzed low over the populated areas and raised a few heads, but it was enough just to see some of nature's wonders up close. The four hours passed quickly and after I landed, I felt like the kid who had seen two westerns plus a Tom and Jerry cartoon at a Saturday afternoon matinee.

I was reminded of Joe Lorfano, one of our lieutenant commanders. He was a vivacious, uninhibited sort who enjoyed flying as much as anyone I ever knew. We were walking toward the island from the bow after a practice bombing mission one day. Lorfano was smiling from ear to ear. Suddenly, he stopped in his tracks. As if to embrace the carrier and its planes, he opened his arms.

"They're payin' me for this!" he shouted. "I'm doin' the thing I love most and they're payin' me to do it!"

By early 1963 we turned for home and put the Straits of Gibraltar behind us. The ship needed to evaluate some radar gear, however, and an abbreviated flight schedule was authorized despite the paucity of divert fields along the Atlantic sea lanes. A few Skyraiders and Skyhawk sorties were ordered over a period of several days.

"You've got ninety-seven traps on this cruise," I was reminded by the schedules people. "We'll assign you the hops and give you a shot at one hundred if you want them."

I did not fall over myself volunteering, as nice and uniform as the century mark would be. The fact was, few pilots wanted these out and back, steady-altitude, drone-and-moan flights. They would be dull, debilitating, and occupy a mind-draining three hours plus to complete.

"Sure," I said. "I'll go for a hundred."

Meanwhile, there was Lieutenant Joe Martin, a friend from Class Thirty-Nine Echo preflight days. He was flying Skyhawks in the air wing's VA-83 and was also three traps away from one hundred. An aggressive, reputable flyer, Joe was very much interested in achieving the milestone and maneuvered himself on to the schedule.

It was a bit unusual for A-1 pilots to get more landings than the jet guys, because our hops were generally longer in duration. The latter types would often get two landings to our one. Over the course of the cruise it just happened that I was in the right place at the right time—namely hovering over the duty officer's shoulder—when an extra sortie was tacked onto the schedule. Single-cycle, post-maintenance test hops were the best plums, and I got a few of these. They added up.

Anyway, Joe and I joked about who would hit the magic decimal first and treated the event with calculated nonchalance. But beneath the facetious banter lay an acute compulsion to get there ahead of the other guy. Naval aviators tend to be competitive. We were like the hungry gent who says he can really do without a steak as he eyes an irresistible delmonico sizzling on the grill. While I may not have been excited about the hundred traps at the outset, I was now.

Two days later we each had ninety-nine arrested landings. On the third morning I went out on the first "go," and got the one hundredth. Martin was scheduled for the second launch. I had noticed on one of my tracking runs to the west that weather was building up. Nothing frightening. Mostly layered stratus clouds with a little precipitation inside.

By the time Joe was ready to man up, air operations called down to the ready room and canceled the launch. My pal from Class Thirty-Nine was furious. Magnifying that wrath was a subsequent announcement over the squawk box that *all* flight operations had been terminated for the remainder of the cruise. He was stuck on number ninety-nine.

I resisted all inclination to snicker in victory. In fact, to Joe I said, "Look, a hundred traps and a dime (this was 1963) will get you a cup of coffee anyplace."

I won't say there was smoke coming out of his eyes. I won't say he took it with a smile either. I will say that I was very careful not to bring the subject up again.

One of the magic moments in naval aviation is the fly-off from the carrier after having been away from home for half a year or more. It was a dramatic, if not romantic, way to rejoin loved ones not seen for what seemed an eternity. Although I was a bachelor without ties and expected no one to be waiting for me at Oceana, it was still a thrill to be a part of the aerial exodus of Skyraiders, especially when we went "feet dry" over the Virginia coast and flew en masse over the airfield.

We launched and grouped overhead in three divisions of four planes each. With a fine rumbling of engines we passed low over the ship in compact formation honed to precision by months of steady operational flying. Then we turned and drove on toward the beach. There wasn't an unexcited man in those dozen cockpits. I felt an emotional stirring inside that was a prelude to jubilation. The married men must have felt likewise.

As we made our landfall, the butterflies were really tickling my stomach. All the familiar landmarks were there in the countryside, but we were looking beyond to the Oceana runways. We thundered over them at 180 knots, stealing a glance or two at the assemblage waiting by the hangar to welcome us.

We touched down in turn. Happily, no one had to wave off, always a risk when trying to get twelve aircraft on the ground systematically. (Had somebody gone around, disrupting the sequence, he, or the party who forced him to do so, would be a marked man subject to recriminations for a long time to come.) We taxied single file toward our ramp in sufficient emulation of the Blue Angels.

Despite my steadfast admiration for them, I had to admit the Skyraiders were not comely looking machines on the ground. As tail-sitters, they angled awkwardly upwards, unlike the jets which, with their tricycle landing gear, were oriented parallel to the ground. Additionally, at taxi speed our engines chugged and expelled inelegant clouds of smoke here and there. Compared to the slim lines of the jets and the sonorous peal of their power plants, we were cosmetically, if not sound-wise, inferior. The fact that they had landed ahead of us didn't help either.

So, to compensate for such deficiencies, we relied on precise spacing and uniformity of movement. We also folded our wings in punctilious sequence as we entered the parking ramp area. This act, begun by the pull of a lever that brought hefty hydraulic forces into play, served us well. Unhinged, the wings rose up in a modestly impressive salute to the loved ones.

We parked, shut down, and disembarked, stuffing helmets into canvas bags that we slung over our shoulders for effect. We were on our own from that point and plunged into the crowd. At least the others did. I preferred to linger at the fringe, watching. There followed animated embraces, flashing smiles, unbridled tears and laughter.

And then I saw my father! He was standing silently, well in the back of the crowd, not even waving. He was just waiting there, barely smiling, looking for me to catch his eye. I was dumbfounded. I had no idea he would be there. But he was.

Later he explained that my mother couldn't get away from her job, but he had a few days coming so decided to drive on down, "just to see the planes come in, you know."

He had driven 600 miles just to "see the planes come in." If that wasn't a magic moment I don't know what is.

I was told early-on in the Navy that the first squadron tour becomes the most memorable. I believe that to be true. No doubt about it, duty in VA-85 was packed with experiences that would live on, probably for a lifetime. But now it was time for a change of pace so, after three years with the fleet, I received orders to shore duty in Washington D.C.

three

Desk Duty

"Well," I asked, "whatdaya think of my T-28?"
"Nice plane," said Dad.
"Nice, son," said Mom, "but it takes two to fly it?"

By the summer of 1963 I was officially on shore duty, but it
wasn't all paperwork. Those of us assigned to desks flew what were
called proficiency flights in T-28s (some also flew the SNB Beech)
at the Naval Air Facility located on one side of Andrews Air Force
Base, just outside the nation's capital in Maryland. These allowed
us to keep our hand in, although the hops consisted mostly of
cross-country flights referred to as "out and ins." I was quite lucky
in having a great job working as an associate editor on the staff of
Naval Aviation News, a monthly magazine distributed to fleet and
shore activities.

I worked for Commander Paul Jayson, the talented editor, and
a lady named Izetta Winter Robb, the managing editor. She was a
most gracious person and a consummate master of the English language. For many years she injected her extraordinary capabilities
into the very lifeblood of the periodical. A congenial atmosphere
prevailed in the office. She and the commander and the other staff
members made it a pleasurable place to spend a working day.

I found an apartment on the thirteenth floor of Southern
Towers in suburban Virginia, a few miles from the city. One
weekend a pair of Marine pilots, friends of a friend, flew a helicopter to nearby Quantico and headquartered with me while they did
a little socializing. Late Sunday afternoon the major and the first
lieutenant thanked me for the hospitality and as they left, one of
them said in an anticipatory tone, "See ya sooner than ya think!"

I was lounging in my apartment a couple of hours later when I
heard the sound of a piston engine accompanied by the unmistak-

able clatter of helicopter blades chopping through the air. Startled, I went to the picture window that looked out over the swimming pool where a crowd of sunbathers had been frolicking. At the moment they were motionless, heads craned skyward toward the noise.

The sound intensified and then, incredibly, there was a horrific change in the light, as if an eclipse of the sun had just taken place. A whirlybird swung into view directly over the pool at cockpit-to-eye-level with me, thirteen stories high. It hung there loudly at perfect attention. Inside the cockpit I could clearly see the square-jawed faces of the major and the first lieutenant. They wore puckish grins as they hovered over the pool, seemingly oblivious to the consequences should the engine quit.

After a moment they saluted in unison and banked the machine sharply away, leaving behind them an awesome silence. I shook my head as they flew into the distance. Those guys have got guts, I thought. I wasn't so sure about their brainpower, however.

"See ya sooner than ya think" was right.

I was sent on assignment to the West Coast and piled into a C-131 at Andrews for the trip. The passenger list was heavy with brass: an admiral, several captains, some commanders, a couple of senior government civilians, and one other lieutenant in addition to me.

We were somewhere over Oklahoma and had entered a storm, a billowing caldron of gray and black clouds. So turbulent was the weather that the plane bucked like a Brahman bull. A commander sitting amidships jabbed nervously with his arm toward the window.

"The wing's oilcanning!" he shouted.

Baggage that was strapped down in the aft section of the plane tore loose and skittered back and forth across the deck, banging into the bulkheads. We rose and fell and swayed in our seats with sickening repetition. One gentleman, a corpulent civilian, had a visit to the bathroom—make a "head" call is the Navy terminology—and careened his way to the john, stumbling several times like a fullback shedding tacklers hell-bent for the end zone.

Except for that single remark that carried above the clamor—"The wing's oilcanning!"—all of us rode along in silent agony. What in heck *is* oilcanning, I wondered. The seconds became minutes. The minutes grew to a half hour. Finally, after nearly a full nervous hour in the heavy weather we broke out and gave a collective sigh of relief.

At a refueling stop, I listened as some of the officers evaluated the flight. We were standing around the airplane.

"I said my prayers," remarked one.

"I thought the old number was up," said another.

"The commander with the jabbing arm said, "Yep, she was oil-canning, all right."

I ran into the pilot, a grizzled lieutenant commander who had come up through the ranks.

"The old bird sure was oilcannin'," I said.

"The C-131 can hack it," he declared.

Later, in an aeronautical dictionary, I discovered the meaning of oilcanning: "a noun; the action of snapping in and out, or the condition of a skin or covering deformed by this action."

I gave thought to that definition and the implications of it, then said to myself, "Thank you, C-131, for keeping your seams together!"

Jim McNally, a comrade from VA-85, was also on Washington duty, and we used to join forces on proficiency flights. We were returning from Jacksonville to Andrews one miserable winter night, and I was in the front seat at the controls. We were about twenty minutes from the airfield when we were jolted by a violent charge of precipitation and turbulence. It was as if a truckload of heavy slush had been unexpectedly cast against the T-28 with great force.

The plane shivered and so did I. The nose pitched up, yawed crazily right and left, then dropped down. I lost spatial orientation and developed an instant case of vertigo. I was dizzy and straining to keep control of the machine. Jim was better composed than I.

"You're doing all right," he said reassuringly.

We flew out of it, motored in and landed, very happy to be on the ground. Some time later we were in operations closing out our flight plan. We joked with the duty officer about the terrible flying conditions and how we had conquered the elements, then left for home. Safe in my living room that night there was a news bulletin on television. A Pan American airliner had gone down very near the same place we encountered the slush. It had apparently been struck by lightning and exploded in the air. All the vacationers and crew who were returning from the Caribbean were killed.

Such gruesome and tragic moments in aviation make all of us pause and grieve and wonder. Ernest Gann put it well when he titled his book about flying: *Fate Is The Hunter*.

In Washington I became acquainted with a "desk driver" who had many hours in his log book, including combat time in Korea. A navy captain, he and I flew together a few times in the T-28 and crossed paths occasionally in the old Main Navy Building on Constitution Avenue where we worked. In our conversations, some of them conducted over the intercom during long, quiet legs on out-and-ins to places like Brunswick, Maine, Cleveland, Ohio, and South Weymouth, Massachusetts, a picture emerged of how much flying meant to him. Although these hops in a tandem seat trainer were better than no flying at all, the captain knew his piloting days were numbered and that he would not return to the fleet as an operational flyer. He also told me how he recaptured the earlier days of his career in the air and how doing so helped him through never-ending sessions of paperwork, reports, and studies—the trappings of desk duty.

"I daydream," he explained, "I settle back in my chair, toss my feet on the desk, and stare at the tower of papers I'm supposed to be working on until they become a blur. I close my eyes and let my mind grow long. It takes a while, but I soon find myself back at the controls, doing what a pilot is supposed to do, and that means flying."

The following is an interpretation of the captain's repetitive daydream:

> I drifted slowly. Like a leaf propelled by the breeze, I floated far away beyond the shore and over a distant sea. Then, as in a zoom-like projection, I was carried from the high skies downward toward the water. Onto a giant ship and into a cockpit.
>
> There was sound. A magnificent roar. I planted my heels on the deck, toes firm on the rudders, left hand at full throttle, fingers extended over the catapult grip (to prevent inadvertent reduction of the power lever when jolted into the sky). I scanned the gauges. All the lights were right. All the needles where they should be. I looked down at the launch officer and his crew. They were eyeballing me, waiting for my salute—the signal that authorized them to unleash the steam-powered piston that would fire my jet down the track and off the end of the boat.
>
> I snuggled back into the seat and pressed my helmet against the headrest, eyes fixed straight ahead. I was ready. The jet vibrated beneath me, straining to burst away. I saluted.
>
> It was a jaunty salute, of course. It was executed with an alacrity equal to that of the catapult shot itself, which was an exercise in swift, blurring power—a glorious explosion of energy. I was in command, in the midst of a million, finely guided yet titanic forces.
>
> My flying machine and I were rifled into the air mass. From zero to 140 knots in a couple of seconds—ecstasy! Quickly, I retracted the wheels and flaps and was in a vigorous ascent, up and away from the carrier.

I leveled off at sixteen thousand feet and stabilized at 300 knots for the rendezvous. In the expanse between me and the flattop, I saw the arrow-like shapes of the wingmen, gems on a necklace laid out straight, rising obediently toward me.

They were soon gliding into position alongside, like filings lured to a magnet. I let them labor there in tight parade position for a time as I guided them toward the practice target ashore. Satisfied with their efforts, I pumped thumbs over my shoulders. They slipped back away from me into a free cruise disposition.

We were a streamlined quartet, undulating smoothly, not unlike a school of fish, as we sped through the sky toward the beach. When we approached the land mass I signaled the formation into a daisy-chain trail. We then began a shallow, accelerating descent so as to arrive over the target range on speed and at the pattern's altitude.

As I studied the scarred earth below and the chalk-white concentric circles around the bull's-eye, I noticed that the aircraft drifted subtly right to left. Twelve, maybe fifteen knots of wind, I figured, were coming from the three o'clock position. I mentally calculated the aim point to compensate for that wind.

"One breakin'," I declared, whipping the aircraft onto its port wing. I drew back on the stick, reversing course, then eased the plane upright to establish an oval tracking route around the target.

As I neared the roll-in point I made a final, split-second examination of switches, altitude, power and speed. Assured they were proper, I keyed the mike and said, "One in."

I flipped inverted and pulled the nose through the horizon. The world was instantly upside down. How many hundreds of times had I seen it this way? I was very comfortable in the cockpit.

I rolled upright, aimed steeply at the earth. My eyes were at one end of an imaginary funnel along the course of which were the amber crosshairs glowing on the gunsight glass. I flew the airplane to align them with the target, which was waiting at the far end of the inverted cone of sight.

With a rapid, corrective wing dip, I adjusted the pipper to a point on the ground two o'clock from the bull, slightly inboard of the 150-foot circle. Airspeed rose toward 420 knots. The bomber's airframe seemed to contract with the intensifying air pressure. The white altimeter needle swept around the black face of the instrument. At the release point I pressed the bomb button on the stick, pickled off a Mark 76 and immediately began a pull-up. I could not see it depart the aircraft, but the simulated weapon escaped from its pylon and began a silent plunge.

Already I was zoom-rising through the horizon, my body compressed by the force of four and one-half Gs. I grunted with exhilaration, filled with the pure joy of this exercise in flying and all the mental and physical dynamics that accompanied it.

"One off," I called. I am young again, I said to myself.

Rate of climb slowed as I banked and glanced over my shoulder. A tiny white cloud wafted across the target's nine o'clock side. The spotter's voice filled the earphones. "Forty feet, two o'clock," he announced. It was a good hit. I smiled.

We repeated the practice assaults with determined concentration, and I scored well on each of them. Afterwards, the ride back to sea was smooth and silent. I tallied my hits on the smudged kneeboard card and knew I would collect a few quarters from those bets we made in the ready room before launch.

The next matter of business was to get aboard the flattop. Weather was CAVU—clear and visibility unlimited; the sea state was moderate. There could be no excuses today.

I brought the flight in close aboard the starboard side of the carrier in echelon. I gazed down the flank. Like the folds in an accordion, the wingmen moved with me in graceful unison. Inside their neatly aligned, Plexiglas bubbles, three helmeted heads were frozen in concentration, eyes looking up the line toward me. As one, our four planes whizzed by the island. We knew that two or three flyers in the air boss's tower would be observing the formation. With pilot-to-pilot critical eye, they would judge the quality of it. They would not be able to fault ours.

We sped beyond the bow and I checked for other traffic in the pattern. There was a single plane dirtied up, downwind. We would guide on him. I glanced at the troops hanging in there, canopy to canopy, wing to wing. Their arms and legs worked the controls with constant, minute movements, invisible to the external eye, but required if they were to remain in perfect position.

I tapped my helmet and pointed decisively at the number two man, then blew him a gloved kiss to signal my departure. I wrapped the plane up with a hard left push and pull of the control column. At the same time I reduced power and clicked the throttle-mounted speed break switch that sent panels from the fuselage out into the airstream to help slow the jet. The plane trembled at the disruption of airflow, then calmed down. The lead was passed. Like a will-o-the-wisp, I was gone from my wingmen.

Speed slowed to 200 knots and with instinctive moves, like a prizefighter's jabs, I slapped down the gear, flap, and hook handles. The silver-stemmed wheels poked out from the plane's body, driven by hidden hydraulic forces. The flaps paid out slowly. The hook dropped precisely into place.

The hook. The exclamation point of naval aviation. The airplane's way of declaring, "I work on the flattops!"

The bomber shook momentarily as wind rushed wildly around the protrusions from its airframe. But it steadied up as the wind adjusted to the contours and the aeronautical design precepts that allowed it to fly in the first place.

I drove on, guiding the machine downwind, stealing a glance here and there at the warship cutting through the sea off to my left. My feet performed a slow-motion tap dance on the rudders while hands and arms managed the throttle and stick.

Turning onto the final approach heading, I was caught up in the familiar glory of carrier aviation's technicolor world. Above was the endless umbrella of pale blue sky; below, the deep dense blue of the ocean; ahead the dull, man-made grey of the ship. At the left corner of the stern the oblong, yellow glow in the center of the glideslope mirror was a beckoning beacon. The datum lights, traffic-lantern green, looked like rigid arms supporting it. There were white stripes outlining the runway, and beyond the fringe of the landing space, the jerseyed blues and browns and reds and greens and purples and yellows of real heroes, the men of the flight deck.

I flew through the unnerving burble—that rough pocket of space created by stack gases and airflow around the island structure—but emerged safely, on a descending invisible string only yards away from touchdown. My eyes danced from cockpit to mirror to deck to cockpit. I dropped a wing and brought it back, correcting lineup. The yellow glow remained centered. On the glare shield in the cockpit, the tiny crimson circle on the angle of attack indicator was lit and proved I was on precise airspeed. Down I flew, the deck expanding. Down, down.

In a mighty cushioned smash my aircraft hit home. It caught its cable, and the machine and I were hauled to a halt. It was a frozen-rope base hit, a soaring sock down the fairway, a slam dunk, an ace. The trap was all of these and then some.

But right after that, all motion stopped. The world grew dim. The ship was no longer beneath me. I was a leaf, floating again.

"How did you do?" a voice said. I could not answer.

"Well, how did you do?" the voice repeated, impatiently.

"OK number three," I said, "and all hits were inside a hundred feet."

"What!" The voice was harsh now and very close to me. I began to come out of the abyss, the land of dreams. Finally, I woke up, partially at least, and focused on the real world of my office. I brought my feet off the desk.

"I mean, how did you do on that report?" asked a man standing behind me, "the one somewhere in that stack in front of you."

I turned wearily in the chair and looked at the inquisitor. "Oh yes, that report," I sighed, "I'll have it in a few minutes."

The man left but before reaching out to the tower of paper, I stopped for a moment and recalled the flight my mind had just logged. I recaptured the image of myself, the wingmen, and all the things we had done. I remembered the dives on target, the glide slope, the cushioned smash. Then the image faded.

I may never go back, I said to myself, but at least I was there. And for now I am content with that.

Griffiss Air Force Base is located in Rome, New York, about an hour's drive from home. I had flown in a couple of times with a Skyraider for short visits with the folks. The first occasion was a month or so after my initial cruise with VA-85. The troops had been very busy and didn't have time to wash the bird that I flew, but that was fine with me. I wanted it to look as if it had been through some tough going.

I knew Mom and Dad would be waiting near the transient line when I got there, so with salty aplomb I wheeled off the runway, slid the canopy back, and waved. As I neared the chocks I rubbed my gloved hand with calculated nonchalance across my name, painted in bold, black letters below the canopy rail. I left my sun visor down for effect even though it was a cloudy day, and took my sweet time after parking before securing the engine. I wanted them to appreciate the throaty grumble of the idling R-3350.

Finally, I shut her down and climbed out, performing the very best emulation of John Wayne disembarking from a P-51 fighter that I could. I nearly stumbled off the wing, which would have demolished my entire exhibition, but recovered. I was heartened to note that an oil slick, common to the Skyraider, was clearly visible abaft the exhaust stacks.

Flight suit rumpled, boots scarred, and helmet bag in hand, I walked over to my parents. We embraced, after which I turned toward the plane and held my arm out to it.

"Well," I asked, "what do you think of my single-seater?"

"Nice plane," said Dad.

"Nice, son," said Mom, "but isn't it awfully dirty?"

Sigh.

Now, on a break from desk duty, I was to arrive with another flyer (who agreed to let me have the front seat to ensure I looked like the pilot in command) in a T-28 which was cleaner, although much less formidable looking, than a hulking, gray A-1. Still, the T-28 in its canary yellow coat of paint had a stylish quality to it, even with the tandem cockpit that accommodated two aviators versus the Skyraider's one.

I waved at the folks as we chugged into the chocks. Certainly they would get a kick out of this brightly colored, single-motored, training plane.

After we turned the engine off, I leaped out wearing an unsmudged flight suit and only partially scuffed boots. I had the same old helmet bag though.

"Well," I asked, "whatdaya think of my T-28?"

"Nice plane," said Dad.

"Nice, son," said Mom, "but it takes two to fly it?"

Sigh.

My mother, incidentally, issued a familiar directive each time prior to my manning up for the return flight to home base following a stopover.

"Now you call us after you get there so we know you made it OK," she would say. And I would mumble a disinterested response. "Make sure you call," she warned.

"Look, Mom," I would plead. "I'm not a kid anymore. I am an officer in the United States Navy. I'm in command of that airplane out there. I really don't think it's necessary for me to—"

"Call us when you get there," she interrupted. Her voice carried that gentle undertone of authority I had known as a youth. It was feminine and endearing on the outside but drill sergeant firm at its core.

I said I would call. And I always did.

I was single and somewhat restless in those days, with a propensity toward searching for different frontiers. In other words I wasn't sure what I wanted to do with my life. I decided to leave the Navy after two years of shore duty even though I was very happy with my job. It was a difficult decision, because if I completed the tour I would more than likely have been assigned to a fleet squadron piloting jets. But I wanted to wander.

The world seemed as stable or unstable as it would ever be. A limited nuclear test ban treaty had been signed in 1963. Martin Luther King gave his "I have a dream" speech in Washington on August of the same year. On the other side of the world, South Vietnam's President, Ngo Dinh Diem, was overthrown and killed. That was in early November, about three weeks before President Kennedy was assassinated in Dallas. In August of 1964, two Navy destroyers, the *Maddox* and the *C. Turner Joy*, were attacked by North Vietnamese torpedo boats in the Gulf of Tonkin. By February 1965, President Johnson had ordered continuous bombing of North Vietnam. Civil rights clashes shook America while fighting in Southeast Asia was heating up. Still, like a lot of people, I thought it would be a short-lived conflict—that business in Vietnam.

So, by late 1965 I was a civilian. I applied for a government position, which I hoped would involve overseas travel, and in the meantime took a short-term job in my home town driving visiting executives back and forth from airports in Syracuse and Utica to the American Management Association seminar headquarters at a nearby lake.

After a month of chauffeur duty I had an administrative position with the government and did get across the Atlantic. I was reading the European edition of *Time* magazine one day and came across the account of a four-plane division of Navy Skyraider pilots who had engaged and shot down a Soviet-built Mig in North Vietnam. Pleased as I was with my civilian job, that story about the A-1s in action set me to thinking about returning to the Navy. In the weeks that followed there were continuing stories in the media about carrier pilots who were right in the thick of battle.

Ultimately, I realized I would rather be there than where I was. In short, I gave notice, came back to the Navy after less than a year out of uniform and by February 1966 was in VA-122, the replacement pilot training squadron at Naval Air Station Lemoore, California. VA-122 was the equivalent to VA-42 from earlier days at Oceana in that it provided refresher training. I had asked for jets, but Skyraider pilots were needed and I was so pleased to be back in a flight suit, I didn't fight it. I was now a TAR—training and administration of reserves—officer, which meant that farther down the line I would be working with Weekend Warriors, civilian reserves who performed Navy duty a couple of days a month and during longer summer training periods. For now, however, I was going back into the cockpit and that's all that mattered.

four

Combat Tour

There were no concentric circles indicating that an aircraft had crashed in the water. There was no fire-filled, blossoming mass of smoke telling me that Pellot had smashed into the ground. Nevertheless, I had the nauseous feeling that I had lost a wingman.

"Pellot, are you up?" I asked one more time, urgency creeping into my voice.

A few more seconds passed, then I heard a mike keyed.

"I'm awright," Pellot reported calmly.

Finally, I spotted his Skyraider, a reassuring profile hugging the wave tops a half-mile distant, pointed *away* from land.

"They're shootin' back there," he said tersely.

"So I noticed," I said, breathing comfortably again, "so I noticed."

Among the major events of 1966, outside of those connected with the war and a growing list of casualties, the first black in 85 years was elected to the Senate, Edward Brooke of Massachusetts. France withdrew all its armed forces from the integrated NATO alliance, and a 25-year-old honor student went berserk atop a tower at the University of Texas in Austin and shot 44 people, killing 14. The killer's actions had nothing to do with what was going on in the jungles of Southeast Asia or the fiery skies above, but in the years to come, with television and a proliferation of media representatives covering the war, the folks back home would experience new and frightening dimensions of the violence, frustration, and heartbreak that is war. And we had to train intensely for it.

While in VA-122 my class of replacement pilots departed Lemoore for a brief spell to sharpen our bombing skills on the practice ranges operated by the Navy base personnel at Fallon, Nevada. This was wide-open, western country, with great desert expanses intermixed with craggy hills and rocky, mountainous terrain. The weather was generally good and featured excellent visibility. The frontier skies were, for the most part, unmolested by the smoke stacks of industry and the exhausts of bumper-to-bumper automobiles. There were numerous targets available, and because the war was heating up, Fallon flourished with squadrons and air wings hurrying to get in shape for the business of combat on the other side of the globe.

Four of us were conducting a close air support exercise one day, attacking targets assigned by a forward air controller (FAC) on the ground. We were operating over what was called the impact range, a generous portion of desert one side of which sloped gently upwards, melding into a chain of barren hills. The FAC was located in a bunker-like command post part way up one of these hills.

In the crevices on the lower flanks of the rolling terrain and on the desert floor itself were old tanks, half-tracks, and the like, basking in the sun. The FAC would give us the coordinates of one of these "targets," which we plotted on small knee-board charts. He would amplify directions in a common-sense manner until we had the particular vehicle he wanted us to strike positively identified. Then we set up a bombing pattern and tried to destroy the rusting hulks.

Commander Al Monger was slated to take over as CAG of an air wing destined for duty in the Western Pacific, WestPac as we called it, and although he would be flying jets most of the time, he wanted some Skyraider flights so he could handle any of his units' missions. He was with us on this particular flight.

We were established in a loose trail formation with what appeared to be decent interval between each other. I was number two man, the CAG was number three. I'm not precisely sure how it happened and neither was the commander. But I rolled in behind the first plane, which was already climbing up, and apparently dove a little steeper than normal. The CAG started in behind me. I dropped a practice bomb and pulled up sharply.

Suddenly, on this bright, cloudless day, I found myself caught in a shadow, and that shadow had to be caused by another flying machine above me. I glanced back and up and saw the looming underside of the commander's A-1. For a terrifying second I thought it was all over, that this was what it was like the instant before a mid-air collision—shadow, and the heart-stopping realization that fate was taking you now.

But we passed each other by inches, literally inches. I was pulsating with fear but all at once joyous at the narrow escape. I felt like a driver who had swung too wide around a mountain curve and skidded perilously along the road's edge before recovering. The grim reaper had swung his scythe, but happily for the commander and me, missed.

CAG Monger was very nice about the matter and did not blame me for almost knocking him out of the sky. He went on to lead some of the most dramatic and successful raids against North Vietnamese targets and was subsequently promoted up the ranks and became an admiral.

(A few years after the close call I ran into him. "Good to see you, sir," I said. "Same here," he said. "Do you recall that time at Fallon when—" I started. "Yes," he said without hesitation. "I remember." We looked at each other in silence. I knew I knew, and I knew he knew—that, but for several precious inches, both of us, in all probability, would not be alive and breathing. We might have been referred to as those two fellows who smacked into each other over the Nevada desert back in '66.)

I received orders to Attack Squadron Twenty-five, which, ironically, was the same outfit that had bagged the Mig the year before in Vietnam. Commander Bill Stoddard was the skipper, a combat veteran who, during the previous deployment, had earned a reputation for aggressiveness under fire. It was gratifying to know that Jim Lynn, Charlie Hartman, and Clint Johnson, three of the four pilots on the Mig flight, were still aboard. (The leader of that historic mission was Ed Greathouse, who was now one of the highly talented instructors in VA-122.) The squadron was part of Carrier Air Wing Fifteen attached to the USS *Coral Sea*.

All hands were busy preparing for the forthcoming return to Yankee Station, a geographic focal point in the Gulf of Tonkin less than a hundred miles from the North Vietnamese coast. I was senior in rank to some of those who had already flown in combat, but attitudes within the command were excellent. My hours in the Skyraider were respected while I sought to learn from those, regardless of rank, who had already faced the crucible of war.

The squadron's slogan, reflected in its insignia, which depicted a hand firmly grasping a bolt of lightning, was "The Fist of the Fleet." And Lieutenant Fred Freckmann was the perfect personification of that slogan. He was a compact, short-necked, square-faced warrior with flair. We nicknamed him "Fearless."

Because we would be launching with heavy loads of ordnance, the Skyraiders almost always were catapulted from the *Coral Sea*

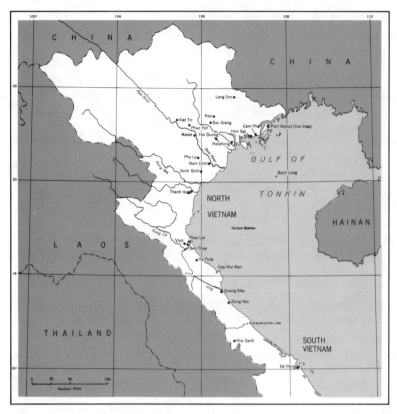

Yankee Station in the Gulf of Tonkin.

rather than sent into the blue yonder by deck runs. We needed the extra muscle, because the bombs and rockets added substantially to gross weight.

On a training cruise aboard the *Coral Sea* off the California coast, Fred was hitched up to the number one catapult on the bow, his canopy slid back, in clear view of people on the captain's bridge. Around his neck he wore a long, white satin scarf. He unfurled one end and flipped it into the windstream just before revving up his engine. It was incredibly long and whipped furiously in the breeze as he roared at full power. He flung an exaggerated salute to the launching officer and, presumably, to the captain behind and above him on the bridge. With a loud whroop! he was tossed into the sky, his white pennant as visible as the star and bars emblem on the wing.

A few of us were in the tower and watched that streaming banner, that symbol of aerial chivalry, and were sent back to an age before we were born. It was World War I and Fred was over the hedgerows of France looking for, and ready to take on, the Red Baron himself.

To my knowledge there were no regulations concerning scarves in the cockpit, but I suspect that allowing one to flap outside it, as did Fred, gave the CO pause. But if the captain was irritated he said nothing. Although the gesture was not to be repeated, we were proud that it took place and that Fearless Fred Freckmann was one of the Fists of the Fleet.

The Spad, as we now called the Skyraider most of the time in antiquated reference to a World War I combat machine, normally functioned in the low-altitude regime, from 10,000 feet down to the deck, but was capable of flying much higher. On cross-country flights, depending on the winds, it was a sound idea to cruise in the mid-altitude airways structure, between 10,000 and 18,000 feet. This required wearing an oxygen mask, which most Spad drivers disdained. We found them cumbersome and restrictive. The jet aircrews who wore masks all the time were simply more used to them than we were.

When we did wear them, however, our radio transmissions were considerably more lucid, our voices nicely modulated à la Edward R. Murrow. Usually we talked through a boom or lip microphone that was held in front of the mouth by a couple of coat-hanger-thick wires mounted on the side of the helmet. The decibel count in the cockpit was notoriously high because of engine noise, and although our own ears were protected by special pads in our helmets, that noise infiltrated the lip mike causing a sort of background buzz when we talked. Our UHF radios weren't exactly brand new either. Quite often we came across like a scratchy, seventy-eight rpm record. When we transmitted through the oxygen masks, though, most interference was prevented, and we sounded just like the jet jockeys.

I was at 16,000 feet, oxygen mask tight against my face (wearing them was mandatory above 10,000 feet), on a gorgeous, sparkling night, flying a round-robin, or cross-country, from Lemoore to the San Francisco area and back. The sky was so clear, the stars so vivid, it was as if the heavens had been scrubbed clean by a legion of angels. For the moment Vietnam was far from the mind, and all was right with the world. The engine was purring, and my own lights—the turtle-back beacon rotating on the fuselage and those on the wing and tail—blended with the evening. The city of San Francisco was aglow. The windows in its buildings were like miniature golden blocks tiered to varying heights. The Bay and Golden Gate Bridges spanned the darkened waters like bejeweled wrist bands.

"Oakland Center," I reported, using the prescribed format for airways flight, to an air traffic controller somewhere on the ground below, "this is November Delta five seven one at Oakland, three five (35 minutes after the hour), one six thousand, over."

There was little airborne traffic in my section of the sky, thus minimum chatter on the radio.

"Roger five seven one," said the controller hesitantly, "Verify you're at one six thousand, over."

"Affirm," I said, short for affirmative, making the *A* long for emphasis, "one six thousand."

"What type aircraft?" he asked.

He should have had that information, but I played along.

"Alpha One," I said, contriving my best baritone.

There followed an awkward silence, and I sensed that the controller was asking his associates what an A-1 was.

"I'm in a Skyraider," I said, "A Navy Skyraider. You know, Able Dog, AD, Workhorse of the Fleet, the Pettigreed Pulverizer, Spad."

"We figured that," said the controller, "but we didn't know you could fly that high. Besides, we thought the AD went out of business after Korea."

My venerable attack bomber had just taken a verbal hit. That fellow sitting in front of a radar screen well beneath me had disrupted the beauty of the night. This flagrant reference to antiquity could not pass unchallenged. I was over the city by the Golden Gate now and turned toward the south. Unprofessional as verbosity on the airwaves was, I keyed the mike to send a long message.

"Ah, Oakland Center," I began, "November Delta five seven one here, listen up, please, and take this down."

Whereupon, aided by the clarity of the oxygen mask transmitter, I delivered a concise history of the A-1 and a summary of its performance characteristics. I told of the Skyraider's conception by engineer Ed Heinemann and his Douglas Aircraft design team; its superlative record battering targets in Korea; its ability to stay aloft for hours on close air support missions to protect friendly troops; the enormous strength that permitted it to carry and deliver extraordinary amounts of ordnance to the enemy; and finally, the nimble maneuverability that allowed pilots from our squadron to actually shoot down a Mig in North Vietnam.

Take that, Oakland Center!

The barrage ended and I cared not whether those on the ground responded. But they did.

"Roger, roger, Navy Alpha One," said the controller hastily, "we have the picture. No more questions. You can contact the center now on frequency———." They were glad to pass me on to somebody else along the route.

I dialed in the new station quite smug about my speech. If my airplane could talk, I think it would have thanked me.

We flew our Spads to Naval Air Station Alameda, across the bay from San Francisco, where they were loaded onto the *Coral Sea* along with aircraft from the rest of the air wing. On a gray morning, with a crowd of family and friends watching, we slipped away from the pier where the carrier had been tied up. We moved out into the bay, and shortly after 0800 I was topside taking a final look at the continental U.S.A. as we passed beneath the Golden Gate Bridge.

Sailors in their blue uniforms and white hats stood at attention shoulder to shoulder along the perimeter of the ship, a traditional ritual when entering or leaving port. Through the years, how many fighting ships and men have sailed under this magnificent bridge on journeys to war, I wondered? How many did not come back?

We paused in Hawaii for a few days of more training, a sort of final examination by Pacific Fleet authorities before continuing on to Vietnam. When we weren't flying, we listened to extensive briefings on the tactical scenario in Southeast Asia. Busy as we were, the ship was tied up at Pearl Harbor long enough for us to have a Mai Tai or two at Waikiki.

Lieutenant (junior grade) Al Nichols, a blond-haired, easygoing native of El Paso, was on his first tour and, like me, new to combat. At an outdoor bar on the beach in Honolulu one night, we listened to Hawaiian music, sipped tall drinks flavored with chunks of delicious pineapple, and watched torches atop tall poles stuck in the sand flicker in the balmy breeze. The ocean waves rushed toward us in huge curls and foamed onto the beach with a whooshing sound that coalesced with the easy lilt of the music.

"It is difficult to believe that in another couple of weeks we will be dropping bombs and maybe getting shot at now and then, isn't it, Al?" I said.

He was staring at the ocean and probably thinking of his wife and two young boys.

"Very hard to believe," he sighed, "very hard indeed."

We steamed on to Cubi Point in the Philippines after leaving Hawaii, and while operating briefly in that area before proceeding to Yankee Station, the ship suffered an engineering casualty. A serious one. Major repair was required on one of the propeller shafts and the *Coral Sea* had to go into dry dock at the Naval Base in Yokosuka, Japan. We flew the planes to Naval Air Station Atsugi, not far from Yokosuka, to operate out of there while the carrier was being mended. The feeling was like that of school kids who learned that the fall semester has been delayed. Delayed but not canceled.

We stayed at the Atsugi BOQ and took turns standing squadron duty officer watches aboard the ship. The air-conditioning system had to be turned off except in a couple of spaces on the *Coral Sea* because of the repair work. As a result, it was incredibly hot in the ready room where we stood the watch and in our staterooms where we retired. It was late summer and without ventilation, duty day was one big Turkish bath. The temperatures had to be in the 100s, and we dripped with perspiration throughout the day and night of still, stale air. I recalled a story about carrier men in the Pacific in World War II who faced similar discomfort on the less-sophisticated warships of their day. They liberally consumed citrus drinks and doused themselves with Ammens powder in the struggle against the heat and consequent itching it engendered.

Our situation was less severe, especially since we were assigned only a single watch apiece during the stay in Yokosuka. Still, Nick Daramus, a lieutenant (junior grade) from Ohio who had a lot of green ink in his log book (combat missions were posted in green compared to blue or black for most flights and red for night time), asked an interesting rhetorical question.

"If we were civilians," he said, "would we go on strike, stage a boycott of the carrier, or ask for better wages?"

The night of my watch I could not sleep. I positioned a fan that was nearly as big as a T-34 propeller next to my bunk. It pushed the stagnant air around but helped little. I took a cold shower every half hour or so and in between them, lay naked on the bed dozing a few minutes at a time.

But if there was exceeding discomfort inside the ship, there were delightful evenings outside, especially on the patio at the Atsugi Officer's Club. There, we consumed beef and chicken teriyaki impaled on long sticks, roasted to delicious perfection over hibachis.

The ship was ready for action in about two weeks, and the night before we left Yokosuka Al Nichols and I went ashore and found a charming restaurant. We removed our shoes and put on wooden sandals given us by a lady wearing a lovely flowered kimono. She led us to a small private room with a lone, glass-less window overlooking a garden. We sat on cushions on the floor, and the fact that the lady in the kimono couldn't understand us—nor we, her—bothered us not. We gestured our way through the ordering process. It was raining and the pattering sound of the drops striking the leaves was very soothing.

Before cooking a wonderful mixture of vegetables and chunks of beef in a huge wok, the waitress set before each of us a slender cup without handles. It was filled with what looked like raw, whipped eggs.

"What do we do with this?" I asked Al.

"I grew up near the Mexican border," he said, "ask me a question about tacos or enchiladas."

"Ah, well," I said, "down the hatch." I drank the mixture. It was uncooked scrambled eggs all right. I shuddered and quickly put the moment out of my mind.

Except for that, the dinner was memorable, and although we didn't talk about the days ahead, we knew there would be uncertain times and that in all likelihood, some of the air wing flyers—maybe even somebody from our squadron—would not see home again.

Finally, the *Coral Sea* moved into the tropical waters of the Gulf of Tonkin and joined many other Seventh Fleet ships dispersed strategically in the Yankee Station area. (Yankee Station was the jump-off point primarily for operations against North Vietnam. Earlier in the war there was a Dixie Station as well. It was the springboard for flights into areas below the seventeenth parallel or demilitarized zone, the DMZ.)

I was scheduled on the first launch of the first day of combat for the ship. I was assigned a rescue combat air patrol, the popularly known acronym for which was RESCAP. I was to fly wing on Lieutenant (junior grade) Charlie Hartman, a cheerful officer with combat credentials that included that successful duel with the Mig. He knew his stuff.

What fascinated me most about that initial sortie was seeing the enemy's land for the first time. We launched just after sunrise and set up a holding pattern in trail with an Air Force HU-16 Albatross a few miles off the central North Vietnamese coast. The Albatross was a twin-engine amphibian that could pick up a downed flyer in the water but was not very useful over land in a rescue situation. We were to stay with it pending further instructions.

VA-25 Skyraider launches on combat mission from USS Coral Sea. *(PH1 R.A. Elder)*

It was a sultry day and I had sweated profusely while preflighting my aircraft, even in early morning. (With rare exception all of us lost weight in Vietnam, probably due to the sweltering heat more than anything else, because we ate very well and usually got sufficient sleep—although seldom eight hours at a time. Oddly, we didn't notice our diminishing physiques because the loss was happening collectively, and we all seemed to be changing at the same time. Despite the discomfort caused by the humidity, we found refuge in the ship's clean, cool rooms. We often wondered how miserable it must be for the gound troops living and fighting in the steaming jungle without similar relief.)

As if suspended from an endless train of low clouds, a curtain of haze hung over the verdant stretch of land known in military terms as Package III, North Vietnam having been divided into seven segments from the demilitarized zone north. An attractive beach ran along the coast, and behind it was a forest of green trees and underbrush. Farther beyond were huge squares of rice paddies. The terrain was mostly flat, although at some points hilly peninsulas jutted out into the Gulf and accentuated the raw beauty of the countryside. From my position, high and away, the enemy's land looked as tranquil as the green pastures in David's psalm. And that is what fascinated me, the serene look of a country afire with war.

The first two hours of that mission nearly lulled me to sleep with boredom. Occasionally, Charlie and I, like performing seals, would whip into an aileron roll or two, as much to stimulate ourselves as to entertain members of the Albatross's crew who gathered at an open hatch aft on the plane's starboard side to take pictures of us. But mostly we droned on in a ten-mile-long elliptical pattern waiting for something to happen.

About five minutes before a section of Spads from our squadron was to relieve us, something did happen. It had been perfectly quiet without any radio chatter for some time when a strong voice, devoid of panic, shattered the calm like a bullet breaking glass.

"You're hit—you're hit—bail out now!"

The voice was so clear it seemed as if it came from a few feet away. Despite the economy of words, I could picture the troubled pilot rocketing straight up out of his cockpit, fired into the sky by the automatic ejection system. His seat would tumble away from him and the parachute would stream out, instantly fill with air, and slow him down with a strenuous jolt. Below, his jet fighter-bomber, aflame and disintegrating, would plunge toward earth.

"He's got a good chute," said the same voice, "Diamond Two has a good chute!"

There followed a rapid sequence of transmissions, during which an elaborate exchange of information took place and the network of search-and-rescue (SAR) units sprang into action. I was reminded of a scene from a western. The wagon train had been rolling along uneventfully when all of a sudden Indians appeared atop the surrounding hills, converging toward the pioneers at the gallop. A sort of chaos ensued before cooler heads took over and put things in order. Such was the case here. Another voice, distinctively authoritative, announced, "This is Crown One. I am the on-scene commander. Knock off the chatter and proceed as follows."

The pilot was down a hundred miles west of us near the Laotian border. Crown one was an Air Force pilot in that vicinity and would coordinate the rescue attempt. Charlie and I were ordered to detach from our Albatross, rendezvous with a Seasprite helicopter—call sign Green Dragon—just off one of those jutting peninsulas, and escort him to the scene. A Jolly Green (Air Force rescue 'copter) would approach the flyer from the west. It was a two-pronged effort.

We dove down and away from the HU-16, increased speed, and hurried toward the waiting helicopter several minutes south.

En route, I heard some cackling in my earphones. Charlie was trying to tell me something. I pulled up close aboard his aircraft. His radio sputtered as he transmitted, and I couldn't understand him. To my profound dismay I had the sickly feeling that my flight leader was in trouble himself. He tapped his lip mike, made an exaggerated thumbs down motion with his right hand, then slapped the side of his helmet several times with his left, following that with an exaggerated thumbs up. Next he patted the top of his hard-hat and threw me an Uncle Sam Wants You!, arm extended, index finger pointed directly at my face. Translated, this pantomime meant: "I have lost my transmitter, my receiver is OK, and you've got the lead. I will continue as wingman."

"Expect the unexpected," is a revered adage in aviation. Say it isn't so, Charlie, I thought forlornly. Please say it isn't so.

My stomach was doing flip-flops, but I patted my helmet and looked away from Charlie signaling I was in control. I tried to sound undisturbed when I said, "Roger, I've got the lead," but my heart wasn't in it.

In addition to attack missions, search-and-rescue duty could send us virtually anywhere in the entire theater of combat. So we had to prepare and carry many detailed charts. Before coming on the line in Vietnam we spent hours building maps under the tutelage of our air intelligence officer, Jay Stone, an illustrious lieutenant (junior grade) from Baton Rouge. Jay's ambition was to one day become the governor of Louisiana, but this aspiration did not detract from his duties.

Each map when spread out was bigger than a card table top. We folded them accordion style for stowage and easy access. I say *easy* with reluctance. For me, trying to fly the plane smoothly and manipulate a chart, not to mention plot a course on one, was a test of dexterity that I most often failed. I was a keystone cop in the cockpit when it came to such matters.

Jay checked our charts very carefully to ensure that we had accurately marked the known AAA—antiaircraft artillery—sites. We used blackened circles for these, which made the maps look as if they had been spattered with ink, lots of ink.

Therefore, racing toward the Green Dragon, I fumbled through the stack of maps, selected the one for Vinh and the neighboring area, nearly tore it up laying it open, and somehow worked out a route to the downed pilot. My aircraft bobbed like a cork on rough water as I inadvertently hit the controls while playing with the chart. The course I chose looked like a reverse check mark. That is, we would go feet dry, head southwest for a time, then northwest, navigating clear of a nasty concentration of ink spots.

The Seasprite was circling impatiently near Cap Mui Ron, like a dark green, mechanical moth buzzing around a light bulb. When the pilot saw Charlie and me approaching, he said, "OK, Canastas, let's go!"

His enthusiasm was stupefying. He sounded like our coach in college trying to ignite us from the doldrums so that we would explode out of the locker room and crush the opposition. The circumstances were far more serious, of course, and the tone of his voice was less "sis boom bah" than "a man is in trouble and it is our job to help him, now!"

"Roger, Green Dragon," I said, "head two one zero degrees."

Immediately, almost pivoting in space, the helo swung around to a southwest course. Charlie and I set up a weave pattern over him and we were soon crossing the beach. Frankly, in those initial moments over the green pastures, I was too busy to feel fear. I'm sure it was there to some degree but suppressed to a lower level of consciousness. There simply was too much to do to dwell on that negative emotion.

At the same time, in the early going, it occurred to me that the slowest thing in the world is a rescue helicopter over North Vietnam. The Green Dragon's best speed was about one hundred and fifteen knots, fast for him, perilously slow for us. He was at 5,000 feet and we flew above that, jinking continuously. The idea was for us to be able to pounce instantly on any source of ground fire. Guiding and protecting the helicopter was our principal obligation while the helo's goal was to retrieve the flyer from the jungle. The jinking was critical. It meant constantly changing altitude and heading to confuse enemy gunners. So, all the way, Charlie and I dove and climbed and banked, eyeballing the Green Dragon and the terrain below.

"Come right to three two zero degrees," I directed the Green Dragon after we had traveled inland about twenty miles. I was surprised at the authority in my voice.

"Roger, Canasta," said Green Dragon turning northward.

Now we were over the jungle, characteristic of North Vietnam's western flank. It was an endless rolling carpet, lush, green, forbidding. Here and there, rising up through the green, were sharp formations of limestone, brownish-black in color, called karsts. A dirt road or two looked like script wandering across the landscape.

The homing needle of my direction finder began to quiver on

the twelve o'clock position of its dial after about fifteen minutes on the northwestern course we were taking. It responded to Crown One's transmissions, which were frequent and reflected an SAR effort in full progress.

Something caught my eye off to the east as I was banking over the Seasprite and I turned my head in time to see an Air Force jet diving steeply. It was close to the ground and, like a ricocheting bullet, angled sharply upward. Shortly, an enormous cloud of radiant orange, fringed in black, erupted from the floor of the jungle. There was another silvery glint. It was the number-two plane, and he too, ricocheted above a blossoming technicolor explosion. So that's how real bombs look hitting a real life target, I thought, wondering what the target was in what appeared to be a no-man's land. Probably a hidden truck park. The North Vietnamese were experts at concealing their rolling stock during the day. Welcome to the conflict in Southeast Asia, I said to myself.

A few miles ahead I saw several columns of white smoke rising from the carpet. Signal flares probably. There was a covey of airplanes circling the smoke, and below them—hovering close to, and almost touching, the canopy formed by the abundant trees—was a helicopter. It had to be the Jolly Green. He was in there already.

We checked in with Crown One who ordered us to keep our distance and stand by. The Jolly Green, he said, was in the process of making a pick-up. I pictured the survivor on the ground listening to the sound of the helicopter, its rotor blades spanking the wind in a distinctive staccato. How reassuring that sound must be to someone in the alien wilderness. At the same time, as Charlie and I wove over the Seasprite, I worried that we had come all this way for nothing and that we would not partake in the rescue.

"Diamond Two is on the hoist," reported Crown One, a hint of jubilance in his voice, "they're bringing him up now."

Thankfully, before ejecting, the pilot managed to get some distance away from the guns that hit him. Neither enemy troops nor the guns themselves were an immediate threat. So the helo crew and the covering aircraft were able to do their work without serious distraction.

"He's coming up," said Crown One.

Like a fish on a hook, the man who was Diamond Two clung to the harness on the end of Jolly Green's steel cable as it was reeled up into the machine. This took what seemed an interminable amount of time, and the moment the survivor was finally pulled into the hatch by waiting crewmen, the helicopter wheeled away like a horse abruptly changing direction and sped off to the west.

"Canasta and Green Dragon, this is Crown One, you're cleared to return to home plate. Thanks for coming anyway."

Just like that it was over. All that way and nothing to show for it except the experience. But the pilot was safe. That was the important thing.

On the return trip to the Gulf I saw the Seasprite and her crew in a new perspective. Here they were lumbering along deep into enemy territory nearly as vulnerable as a turkey at a "shoot." Yet they did not hesitate, did not falter, did not look back. They charged ahead in what I thought was a quintessential exhibition of courage. And courage, according to Webster, is "the attitude or response of facing and dealing with anything recognized as dangerous, difficult or painful, instead of withdrawing from it."

In the Korean War the rescue helicopters came to be known as hovering angels. On this day I believe that I saw the halo on the angel. I am not referring to the perfect circle formed by the blurring blades that powered the Green Dragon through the sky, although that image has metaphysical qualities about it that could apply. Rather, it was the palpable spirit that emanated from the Seasprite and those inside it—the persuasive force that motivated those men to undertake such dreadful labor.

I also wondered if I could have led us on a more direct route to the scene, cut corners, and beat the Jolly Green. Had I been too cautious? I felt like apologizing to the Green Dragon, but didn't.

When we reached the sea the Seasprite detached to return to its destroyer.

"See you later, Green Dragon," I said weakly.

"We'll get 'em next time, Canasta," the pilot answered confidently.

Later in the ready room someone asked Hartman if we had encountered ground fire.

"They winked at us a couple of times," he said, removing his Mae West. "But we were too high for that small arms stuff to bother us."

"Winked?" I said. I tried to make it not sound like a question.

"Sure," Charlie chuckled. "You saw what looked like flashing lights on the ground just south of Cape Mui Ron, didn't ya."

"Oh *that* small arms stuff," I lied, contemplating whether I would have noticed even if Charlie had had a good transmitter and told me about it.

"Certainly." Winking, I thought. A new word for my combat vocabulary.

Commander Stoddard was killed on the second day of operations. He had just led a bombing attack on a storage facility near the coast and was descending with his flight from 5,000 to 1,000 feet over the water abeam the city of Vinh. A series of three surface-to-air missiles (SAMs) burst from their launching pads somewhere near Vinh and raced toward his Skyraider with fierce precision. The first and second exploded fairly close to him and some shrapnel probably slammed into his plane. The third, a monstrous silver bullet, blew up directly in front of him creating a lethal, red-orange cloud. His Skyraider pitched up helplessly then fell off on a wing and nosed down into the sea. Commander Stoddard and his aircraft were gone into the deep six.

If we had not been aware of it before, the loss of the skipper, a vigorous, popular man, made all of us solemnly aware of our own mortality. I was with Lieutenant Commander Robin Bacon and other wing flyers in the air intelligence spaces briefing for a flight when word came through that the CO had gone down. There were no histrionics, no outbursts of rage, no slamming of knee-boards to the deck in abject frustration. In their stead, glum expressions came over us, accompanied by momentary silence as each person in that room let his own mind absorb the doleful news. We had lost a respected shipmate, a leader of men, and his death diminished us all. The pause did not seem long enough. But in the tradition of warships, the briefing and flight operations went on.

Topside a couple of days later, wearing white uniforms, we swayed as one, trousers flapping in the gentle wind, while the chaplain helped us say goodbye to our commanding officer. A Skyraider, the one with the skipper's name on the fuselage, was parked adjacent to the pulpit, and all was quiet as the carrier rose and fell on the slowly heaving sea. The minister was reading from Scripture when a startling disruption took place.

A latching device that "froze" the stick in place to prevent damage to the controls from high winds, somehow became disconnected. Perhaps the bolt in the lock had not been fully inserted and for one reason or another freed the stick. Whatever the cause, the ailerons, elevators, and rudder flapped briskly for two or three eternal seconds, then became perfectly still. Did a sudden breeze cause this? No one seemed to feel it. Was it our imagination? Maybe. Who knows.

"My God," whispered Jay Stone next to me in ranks, "you'd think the skipper was saying goodbye to *us!*"

I said nothing then nor later but privately gave the incident considerable thought.

Commander Jim Burden, an affable, serious-minded naval officer, moved up from his XO spot to fill the breach as commanding officer. It is the nature of military life that even though a key individual has gone, there is no major change of pace, no drastic alteration to the way of doing things. Commander Burden was the new boss and we went about our business accordingly. In addition to the rescue patrols and attack missions, we flew armed reconnaissance flights, going after targets of opportunity like truck parks, petroleum-oil-lubricant (POL) facilities, and the like. In the squadron's previous cruise, pilots sometimes flew recces (wreck' eeze) as they were called, for incredible durations, eight hours or more in length. Now, flight times were less grueling but still seldom, if ever, less than three hours. And for two-thirds of that period, except when orbiting offshore on RESCAP duty, flyers were exposed to the threat of ground fire.

In the first few days a number of our Spads were hit by both small arms and larger weapons, like thirty-seven-millimeter shells. The North Vietnamese were also building up their surface-to-air missile inventory, and missile sites began to proliferate not only around Hanoi and Haiphong but farther south as well. When the skipper was shot down, the powers above were forced to reconsider the Skyraider's role in the war. After some time it was ultimately, and I suppose inevitably, determined that the Spads lacked sufficient maneuverability to operate in areas where SAMs were likely to be positioned. As a result, our missions were restricted to armed reconnaissance along the coasts, rescue patrols, and the more satisfying close air support and bombing hops below the DMZ and in Laos. The decision was a blow to us because we began to feel a bit like second-stringers.

At the same time, in the days that followed, we engaged in some successful rescue efforts, which were gratifying, and we also found occasional worthwhile targets along the coast, not to mention in South Vietnam and Laos.

One afternoon, Lieutenant (junior grade) Holt Livesay and I were flying low over the muddy shallows off the northern coast when my oil sump warning light came on. You never get used to

The author taxies on flight deck for combat mission in Vietnam.

those red beacons. Their sudden illumination provokes instant unrest in the gut. Because we have been trained so well, however, the tempests are usually short-lived, reason prevails, and calculated decision-making follows.

Statistically, engine failure seldom follows a sump light, but procedures demand that we *expect* the power plant to fail. I keyed the mike.

"Five seven four," I transmitted to Holt, "I have a sump light, turning east." Livesay, a cool veteran from the last deployment who wanted to become a lawyer when his tour was over, rogered and came up quickly on my wing. I started to climb.

"Watch your altitude," warned Livesay firmly. I was about to make a rookie mistake. Holt realized that even though we were over the water, we were within range of SAMs. Close to the surface we were relatively safe but higher, the eyes of radar could more easily search us out. I pushed the nose down quickly, embarrassed at my poor headwork and thinking that yes, sir, with a rapid analytical mind like that, Holt would make a good attorney some day.

We sped toward the *Coral Sea* and although the engine ran perfectly, the light stayed on. Unfortunately, the carrier's crew was re-spotting the aircraft for launch so I was ordered to land on the *Constellation*, which was a few miles away and had an available clear deck.

Trouble was, "*Connie*" had just begun a stand-down day, her first in more than three weeks of day in, day out operations. They weren't exactly glad to see me coming down the glide path. Anyway, Holt stayed aloft and later recovered normally, and I trapped aboard the *Constellation*. The mechanics went to work right away on the plane, pulled the sumps, and discovered a couple of minuscule metal fragments that had caused the warning light. They removed these and ran up the R-3350 for a good half hour without any problems. The aircraft was cleared for flight, but the ship decided not to launch me till the next day. Because the *Constellation* was completely loaded with people, I was ushered below to the dispensary where I stayed the night on a bunk they had there. While I slumbered amongst the forceps and tongue depressors, troops from the host ship were busy with paint brushes. In the morning, when I saw my aircraft in the hangar bay, my jaw dropped. It wore a patchwork pattern of rainbow colors the length of the fuselage and on the tail and wings.

Funny?

Not funny. The VA-25 troops would have to spend many a man-hour cleaning the bird. They were busy enough without make-work like this. I complained to various officers on the *Constellation*, who listened politely but, understandably, could not get caught up in what was to them a low-priority issue.

"Look," I pleaded, "tradition allows such pranks when one lands on the wrong carrier by mistake. I came here intentionally. There's a difference!" I sensed I wasn't going to get any action from the hosts. Tired heads nodded in agreement, so I let it go at that.

I was catapulted off in late morning and flew back to the *Coral Sea* feeling uneasy about the reception I would get from our troops, whom I was dearly fond of, and specifically, one wise old sailor named Waller, the maintenance chief.

The crew was very dismayed when they saw the paint job and realized the labor involved to scrub down the machine. Chief Waller flung a few verbal accusations at his counterparts across the way on the *Connie*, then ordered the paint removed. Waller was a superb and respected leader. He had silver, crew-cut hair, and a wise twinkle in his eyes that could convey a full range of emotions from supreme contempt to kind accommodation. I received a look somewhere in between and withdrew to the security of my stateroom, thinking about sump lights.

During the Vietnam War a medical study was made to determine the stress load on pilots operating from carriers at night and flying in combat. To the surprise of some, it was discovered that pilots experienced more pressure and anxiety trying to land on the flattop in the dark than when they were engaged in combat. Interesting.

In any event, whether over enemy territory or trying to get aboard, a key factor after the sun went down was instrument proficiency—flying those gauges—and having a keen sense of where your wingmen were at all times. We turned our lights off during attacks to make it as difficult as possible for those on the ground to draw a bead on us. It was essential, therefore, to coordinate movements with whoever else was in the sky with you. It also followed that we went out in two-plane sections, although occasionally we traveled in larger numbers. One big difference between day and night operations was that we were encouraged to use the radios in the latter, especially during the critical phases of an attack. It was bad enough to be hit by groundfire, but running into a wingman was nothing less than tragic. Talking to each other helped.

One night Al Nichols and I dropped flares over a well-traveled highway a few miles inland in central North Vietnam hoping to illuminate some trucks. The flares, which descended under miniature parachutes, lit the ground brightly for a minute or so. I saw what I thought was the road and possibly some vehicles on it and rolled in to drop a bomb. I got steeper than I wanted, thus faster than desired, pickled off a 250 pounder and pulled up. As I transitioned from the bottoming-out point to climbing flight I came so close to the flare that I saw the shroud lines connecting the canopy to the flare cannister itself. The apparatus had a weird, nightmarish glow to it caused by the blinding light and streaming smoke from its burning chemicals. I was also desperately worried because I had committed a tactical sin. I had actually dived *below* the flare, exposing myself to the enemy. It was like being center stage in a darkened theater with a spotlight on you.

Gunfire rose up toward me, its tracers like neon probes. They reminded me of searchlights prowling the sky during a London blitz. It was as if I were frozen in the deathly embrace of the guns while the shells exploded all around. Actually, I was all the time climbing and instinctively jinking toward the east and the sanctuary of the sea.

The probes stopped as I retreated farther into the dark, getting as far away as quickly as I could from that flare.

"You OK, five seven nine?" called Al.

"Affirm," I said, concealing a sigh.

"They were really hosin' you down in there," said Al.

"Roger that," I said.

"Don't worry," Al said, "I'm right behind you."

There was something strange about the event, but I didn't realize it until moments later when it occurred to me the guns made no sound; that is, I didn't hear them. Heretofore, I'd only seen antiaircraft artillery in movies, where there was always the noise of flak exploding—thud, thud, thud, or crack, crack, crack! But in the air the ack-ack appeared and went away like a motion picture without a sound track. Anyway, a thought by Winston Churchill suited the occasion: "Nothing in life is so exhilarating as to be shot at without result."

On a rescue patrol one placid afternoon, Lieutenant (junior grade) Bruce Marcus and I sneaked our way across the glossy stillness of Haiphong Harbor. We stayed low, under 200 feet, far enough from the shore to be relatively safe from North Vietnamese guns but close enough for a good view of the land and a scattering of islets east of the harbor. These islets, some hardly big enough to support a single building, poked up through the water like knuckles in a partly submerged hand. There was stark beauty to them. On the mainland, villages near the buff-colored beaches, along with a few magnificent-looking homes perhaps symbolic of a colonial past, overlooked the sea in pastoral calm.

Not far from this panorama, which in other times might have graced the pages of *National Geographic* magazine, a growing roll call of American men, shot down from the perilous skies of war, languished in prison camps. It was a startling paradox.

Lieutenant Dean Woods from VA-25 was on a recce flight when he was shot down about twenty miles south of Thanh Hoa in hilly, thickly forested jungle. For several days Dean evaded the enemy while rescue efforts, impaired by weather and other problems, were made to get him out. All failed and Dean was captured. (He survived his ordeal and was released with other prisoners more than six years later in 1973.)

Others, meanwhile, were paying the ultimate price. In the air intelligence spaces there was a clipboard hanging from a bulkhead; it held a sheaf of daily dispatches that in dispassionate terms summarized air combat reports. We devoured these like stockbrokers reading a ticker tape—not only to absorb the strategic knowledge contained therein, but to check for names of friends and acquaintances who might have been shot down.

Too many good people were captured. Too many lost their lives. One day I saw the name of my Abraham Lincoln friend from primary flight training days at Saufley Field. I hadn't seen him since we flew together in the T-34. He was killed on a raid over North Vietnam.

And the losses weren't confined to the battlefield. As the days rolled on, there were accidents on the flight deck. A petty officer from our squadron, a young ordnanceman, was crushed to death when a fully loaded rocket pod, nearly the size of a trash can, came loose from its pylon and fell on his chest. On a night launch, a sailor inadvertently moved into a spinning propeller and died instantly.

While we did our thing in the Spads, the jet pilots of the *Coral Sea* and other carriers pressed on as well. As they did so, I developed a new level of respect, if not veneration, for them. The reason can be expressed in two words: Alpha Strikes.

These were types of missions the very mention of which sent shivers up the spine. Our Spads didn't directly participate in them, but they did maintain SAR orbits nearby. To me, the Alpha Strikes had to be the most dangerous attack operations in the history of aerial warfare.

Thirty or so planes, heavily loaded with bombs, rockets, missiles, and guns, flew en masse against the most heavily defended targets ever known. The fighter-bombers of the fleet (the Air Force flew similar strikes also), and the unarmed reconnaissance planes that followed them in to film the damage, literally plunged into the valley of the shadow of death. From the floor of the valley, rising up to thwart them, were fusillades of antiaircraft artillery of every size, accompanied by swarms of surface-to-air missiles.

The men who led these flights were a breed apart. Usually they were air wing and squadron commanders or XOs, but other highly experienced, less-senior officers also spearheaded the onslaughts.

"What a responsibility those flight leaders have," Jay Stone remarked one day after briefing a group for a major strike into the

Hanoi area. "Brains, guts, physical skill. They have 'em all. The stakes are different, but they're like pro football quarterbacks with the pressure to win directly on their shoulders."

As tough as it was on the leaders, I didn't envy any of those who had to fly the Alpha Strikes. Needless to say, it was on such raids that a major portion of the casualties took place.

After more than a month on station we retired to Cubi Point in the Philippines for a few days rest. Actually, Cubi Point was part of the sprawling Subic bay naval complex. It consisted of a beautiful harbor with mountainous fingers of land forming a natural barrier around it, an airfield, and numerous other facilities. At the Cubi officer's club, one side of which was all glass permitting a scenic overlook of the harbor, we were talking one night with a lieutenant (junior grade) from one of the air wing Skyhawk squadrons. He was a veteran of half-a dozen Alpha Strikes. Young as he was, there was a gaunt look about him, especially in the eyes, that gave him age beyond his years. I figured that expression derived from a combination of factors, among which were prolonged anxiety and lack of sound sleep. I trust the condition was temporary in nature. He was describing one of the Alpha Strikes to us, from his vantage point as a wingman somewhere in the middle of the pack.

"The target was a railroad yard outside of Hanoi," he began. "We crossed the beach at high altitude and after going feet dry north of Haiphong, the leader started us down, accelerating gradually.

"Keep in mind, when you're as heavy as we were with all those bombs aboard, it's like trying to run with a sack of cement on your back. You just can't maneuver very well. We heard the warblers (electronic signals indicating active enemy radar) right off and knew the SAMs were angled up from their pads toward the sky—and us."

He paused to collect his thoughts.

"What comes to mind," he said, "is a scene from one of those movies about the Middle Ages where one horde of warriors is storming the castle walls against another horde. The guys on the ground are shooting arrows and slinging spears and catapulting boulders from those giant sling shots. The troops in the castle are doing the same, plus pushing the ladders away and pouring buckets of hot oil all over.

"Well, if you're in the middle of a fight like that, a sort of chaos is going on. Viewed from a seat in the theater, however, there's a simplicity to it all. There's the castle and its defenders on the one hand, the attackers on the other. No holds barred and may the best man win.

"Same thing on a strike. We go in with one force against another. Give it all you got and good luck. Anyway, a few miles from the roll-in point the SAMs and triple A started coming up at us. Trying to dodge them and stay in the same section of sky as the other planes—formation integrity, they call it—is where the chaos comes in.

"There's none of this every man for himself stuff, of course. Radios were busy and everybody was helping everybody else, calling out those telephone poles (SAMs) and the flak.

"The leader found the target and signaled rolling in. Someday I'd like to see a film of thirty jets diving all at once on a pinpoint target. Being in the middle, all I could do was to hold on for dear life, try not to hit the planes next to me, and pickle the bombs when the leader and the rest did.

"Well, we did pretty well on the railroad yard so they told me later. I wasn't about to look back at the time. Once the bombs were gone, once the sack of cement was off the back, it was like the difference between running in the mud with clodhoppers and sprinting around a board track wearing spikes.

"We hauled out of there at full power, weaving and jinking and tracking out to sea. Going home from there was the easy part. Everybody made it that day. Three birds took hits, which wasn't bad, considering. I'll take that score anytime.

"It's a lot more complicated than I've described it," he said in closing. "Let me just say that I wouldn't want to make a living flying Alpha Strikes."

By early 1967 I was a lieutenant commander, and time was flowing right along. We stayed at sea for long periods, a month or more at a spell, which promoted the swift passage of days and nights. We were seldom bored. Frustrated maybe, but not bored. For instance:

As an air intelligence officer, Jay Stone stayed aboard ship, but he always wished he could go on missions. The fact that he loved to listen to our tales of combat when we got back made him better at his job, I think. Deep down, however, he would have preferred to be out there where the shooting was. AIs, unfortunately for Jay, were duty-bound to the ship, out of the line of fire.

He was at his podium one morning explaining the code words of the day, issuing radio frequencies to be used, and pointing out the latest SAM and AAA hot spots. Lieutenant Commander Ralph Smith from our outfit, a pipe-smoking, easy-going veteran with a log book full of flight hours in the Spad, was sitting near the podium listening attentively. He was wearing his thirty-eight caliber pistol and ammunition belt, a common practice.

Somehow one of the bullets became dislodged from the belt. It struck the tile floor in a way that caused it to fire, producing a deafening report. The bullet slammed against a bulkhead at Jay's end of the room, which prompted him to hit the deck with amazing speed, and ricocheted crazily for a second or two motivating everyone else to seek cover. Then having run its course, the bullet dribbled to a stop.

Happily, although heartbeats had accelerated from normal to triphammer speed and back again, there were no injuries. Calm was restored, Jay manned his podium once more, and a pilot in the back of the room stood up.

"Stone," he said, "you now have the distinction of being the only air intelligence officer in WestPac to be shot at."

Jay hesitated for a moment, remembered part of that Churchillian phrase, and said, laughing, "without result!"

The Cubi Point officer's club in war time was the Pacific equivalent to the one called Breezy Point on the air station at Norfolk, Virginia. It has been said that if you were patient enough, you would meet every flyer you ever knew in naval aviation at Breezy Point. Cubi was a crossroads through which many carriers passed on the way to the combat zone. If you had the time, you might just see all your old friends coming through there, too.

One evening, I recognized a tall figure from desk duty days in Washington. I was surprised to see him, because he'd gotten married a couple of years back and was thinking seriously of leaving the Navy to fly with an airline. He had been a Skyraider pilot, and I remember him wanting to get into jets after his shore-duty tour— if he changed his mind and elected to stay in.

"Great to see you," I said, "but what are you doing here? I thought you were going to drive 707s."

"The detailer promised me jets, I took him up on the offer, and here I am, flying A-4s."

We chatted for a while, then went our separate ways. Small world. A month later I was reading the dispatches. My tall friend was lost on a night bombing hop.

Another evening, in the game room at the Cubi club, I noticed a Marine ground officer who was on a break from some very tough jungle-fighting duty in South Vietnam. He looked extremely weary, as if he had been in and out of far more than his fair share of scrapes. He was unwearying himself with a glass of spirits and systematically pulling the lever on a one-armed bandit. He would slip a coin into the machine, pull the arm, study the cycling lemons and oranges and cherries, then start all over.

He wore a unit insignia on the sleeve of his jacket. I don't remember the graphic inside the circle of the emblem, but written on the pennant that rimmed the lower half of it was his outfit's numerical designation followed by five words. The words spoke rather scornfully of his unit's fate and helped explain his weary look: "One Good Deal After Another."

We returned to California in February, took some time off, made the expected turnover of personnel, and began preparations for going back to Vietnam again in a few months. I experienced a changeover in personnel myself. I had kept in touch with a young lady whom I met when stationed in Washington, and an intensification of the relationship between us culminated in our wedding. We set up housekeeping in Lemoore.

A war in the Middle East had thundered for six, intense days in June, during which one of our information-gathering ships, the USS *Liberty*, was attacked at a terrible loss of life. Race riots erupted in New Jersey about a week after the nation celebrated its 192nd birthday. A doctor in South Africa, Christiaan Barnard, performed the first successful heart transplant operation. Action in Southeast Asia, however, was the day-in, day-out central theme in American life.

Part way through the home stay, the air wing went to Fallon for extensive weapons training. Like a football team getting ready for the forthcoming season, we needed the practice.

Aside from flying, which occupied most of our time at Fallon, there were two activities that flavored the busy semester in the clear-aired Nevada desert. One of these was gambling. Ma's Roadhouse Inn was a landmark where Ma herself dispersed wooden coins to us as soon as we entered. We exchanged these for free drinks and were thus softened up for the blackjack and roulette tables that she often manned in person. Ma was a gray-haired, honest, and kindly lady, but she was also very shrewd with a deck of cards. If we lost, however, we blamed the cards, the wheel, or the one-armed bandits, never Ma. For reasons as patriotic as they were financial, naval aviation was very big with her and most of the other Fallon establishments where games of chance flourished. We were welcome visitors.

The pinball machines in the BOQ lounge on the base were the focus of a second pastime. They represented a form of gambling with consequences far less severe than those involving felt-covered tables and tall stacks of chips. We competed for beers and maybe a quarter now and then. No one got terribly hurt in the wallet.

One of the delightfully noisy, colorful devices had a special appeal. It featured a single set of flippers at the playing end which, if actuated (by buttons on the side of the machine) in a timely manner, kept the silver ball alive, swatting it up the slightly sloped face of the apparatus toward a battalion of plastic-covered lights. When struck, the electronically keyed targets increased the score, which was recorded in a little window on the face of the upright portion of the machine.

In the center of the sloped board, amidst the battalion of lights and framed by rubber pedestals, was a narrow opening through which, one at a time, passed a series of metal placards of varying numerical value. They marched by like ducks at a shooting gallery. More points could be tallied here, so smart players concentrated on them rather than targets in the periphery. The idea was to keep each of five balls (one at a time) careening geometrically as long as possible, avoiding to the last their disappearing plummet through an opening behind the flippers. A crescendo of bells and chimes combined with the rapid clacking of the scoring mechanism was a sure sign that a player was having a good run.

In the back of my father's tobacco and magazine shop in Hamilton, New York, we had, over the years, a progression of pinball machines. Frankly, I cut my teeth on them. So it was with sly confidence that I pursued the Air Wing Pinball Championship along with my partner, Lieutenant (junior grade) Bruce Marcus. Bruce had been a college halfback, which fortified his competitive spirit, and had trained for pinball work in various pool rooms, bowling alleys, and recreational centers in his home state of Texas. Although the championship matches were informally conceived, many fellows were inspired to participate in them.

Throughout the first week we were unstoppable. By a process of elimination we fended off a string of worthy contestants and were riding high. Action peaked in the evenings, and we reveled in the cheers and jibes from flyers in flight suits wrinkled from sweat who formed around us in horseshoe-shaped crowds, sometimes three deep.

Marcus and I were jaunty as roosters entering the second and last week of the training evolution. We handily dispatched three sets of challengers Monday night. Tuesday afternoon he and I flew a combined rocket and gunnery hop and completed a night bombing mission before convening in the lounge at the BOQ. Each of us had pulled a lot of Gs and were pleasantly fatigued after a day and night in the cockpit. But we were not too tired for a little flipper action and accepted a match with two gentlemen from one of the Skyhawk squadrons. Each partner would play a game each and the best team score dictated the victor.

I recognized the lieutenant but the commander was new, having just checked into his outfit as executive officer. He had a lean, dark look about him. His complexion was smooth and swarthy, his eyes black. A neatly-trimmed mustache enhanced his Latin good looks. He projected a self-assurance that presumably bode him well at the controls of an attack bomber. Here in the lounge, it gave him the demeanor of a night club owner straight out of a George Raft movie.

He approached the pinball machine tentatively, flipped the flippers several times, and examined it as if it were a patient on whom he was about to commence surgery. Bruce and I exchanged wary glances. We felt like a couple of prospectors whose gold nuggets were all of a sudden in jeopardy because of a new gunfighter in town.

The games began. The commander quickly had the machine humming and obeying every flip like an obedient robot. Pings and chimes and clacks filled the air. The lights flickered brightly, the balls blurred toward targets with startling accuracy. The score rose at an unprecedented rate. We had come up against a pinball pro.

"Where ya from, commander?" I asked during a break in the action.

"Bayonne, New Jersey," he said. "I cut my teeth on machines like these."

It was a statement of fact rather than a boast. He and his partner went on to destroy us. It was a bitter defeat, the only good thing about it being that the commander and his colleague were not obnoxious in victory. Unseated from our pinnacle, Marcus and I retreated quietly from the lounge as the horseshoe of observers closed around and cheered the new champions.

"The trouble with naval air," I said dejectedly to Bruce as we walked down the darkened corridor to our rooms, "is that sooner or later, no matter where you go, you always run into somebody who is better than you are."

The *Coral Sea* scheduled a Family Day Cruise out of Alameda, a great opportunity to show the wives and kids what we did for a living. Unfortunately, the weatherman didn't cooperate and fog rolled in from the sea, shrouding the coast and the area where the air wing had planned full-scale operations to give the families a genuine look at naval aviation, *Coral Sea* style. So, instead of going beyond the Golden Gate, arrangements were made for the ship to slip away from the pier at Alameda and anchor in the middle of San Francisco Bay. At least the folks would experience the abbreviated sensation of a huge warship under way.

Al Nichols and I had pounced on the schedules officer some time earlier when we learned that VA-25 was to provide a couple of pilots to make takeoffs and landings during the cruise. We got the hops and Bruce Marcus was assigned as back-up.

Because there was little wind and the ship, while at anchor, couldn't generate its own, the proposed aerial demonstration had to be modified. The jets come in fast for their landings and could not safely recover without plenty of wind on the nose to slow them down. In the best traditions of the theater, however, the show did go on. A couple of Phantoms took off from the runway at Alameda and made flybys. These were dramatic enough but really were only soup and salad when a main course was in order. It was left to the Spads to carry the day.

We *could* operate from the flattop, wind or not. Because of our comparatively slower speeds, we didn't need anything on the nose to slow us up. The propeller-powered attack bombers would show the folks how it's done.

Vulture's row was packed, and like stars at center stage, Al and I went about preflighting our machines, which were poised on the bow catapults. We were wearing combat fatigues, bright green baseball caps with Fist of the Fleet emblems in the center and our bright orange Mae Wests.

"Be cool and casual," I cautioned Al, "make it look like another day at the office."

"Roger that," he said, slinging me a thumbs up.

I sneaked a glance toward the island structure, knowing my wife was up there. It would have been un-cool to wave, so I didn't. Since we were the only two planes involved, it was like having the entire waiters' corps at the Top of the Mark serving us dinner. The plane captains and catapult crew quickly had us ready. In no time at all we were running up the engines and ready for the shot.

In full view of the families on board, observers who had flocked to the edge of the air station, and an impromptu crowd that had gathered across the way along San Francisco's waterfront, we bolted into the sky, one after the other. Clouds of steam rushed up through the catapult track in our wake as we bellowed up and into the carrier landing pattern.

There was a touch of surrealism about this episode, I thought. Here we were, a pair of fighter-bombers more at home over the high seas or an enemy target, winging low over peaceful waters surrounded by the earmarks of civilization. Our intent was to plunk down on a portable runway held in place by an anchor while thousands upon thousands of eyes focused on us from vantage points on shorelines, bridges, and buildings that rose sharply from the land.

Nearly sixty years ago on a chilly January day, a twenty-four-year-old ex-farm boy from Iowa named Eugene Ely had motored over these very same waters in a fragile flying machine. It was 1911 and his Curtiss biplane, which was hardly more than a crude T-shaped framework of wires and tubes and kite-like wings and tail, vibrated along at a brisk sixty miles per hour. His destination was, like ours, a ship at anchor in San Francisco Bay with a landing runway on part of its deck. On that day, Ely did what no one had ever done before. He landed his aircraft on the wooden platform that had been constructed over the after section of the armored cruiser *Pennsylvania*. Crude hooks mounted on the underside of his plane snared manila lines that were stretched across the makeshift platform and weighted down by bags of sand.

Following his historic "trap," people on the ship cheered, horns from tugboats and other vessels blasted away, and fire sirens wailed in jubilation. Even though he was a civilian, Ely had given naval aviation a huge boost, proving that planes could land on ships.

We did not expect sirens or horns, of course. It was thrilling enough just to be part of the episode. And, no matter how routine daytime carrier landings might have become, like Ely we could not let ourselves get careless, especially coming down the glide slope. Without the wind, our approach speed was considerably faster than normal, which meant less time for corrections.

But we did all right. We made a couple of landings each and were quite smooth throughout, as a matter of fact. There were no wave-offs, no stultifying off-center engagements of the arresting wires, no hook skips. As a bonus, because of the ebullient mood that pervaded the ship, the air boss let Bruce Marcus into the act. I turned my plane over to him during a brief pause in operations so that Bruce could go aloft and massage his ego.

It was a grand day, and after the show was over guests were allowed on the flight deck. I lingered near our planes on the bow with Al and Bruce. My wife found her way through the crowd and came up to me, smiling proudly. I put on that old haughty-tilt-of-the-chin look and smiled back.

"Nothing to it," I told her, "nothing to it at all."

Too soon the interlude at home was over. We returned to Yankee Station where it didn't take long to get back in the groove. One afternoon, with the sky an unusually clear and radiant blue, I flew a coastal reconnaissance mission with Lieutenant (junior grade) Dale Pellot. A serious-minded, easy-going type, Dale was hard-working and flew very well. He was an excellent wingman. He didn't mind a bit when we called him Pellot the Pilot, either.

Visibility was perfect, and the dark green underbrush along the north central coast contrasted vividly with the narrow strip of buff-colored beach. Jay Stone had briefed us that groundfire had erupted briefly out of that underbrush a day earlier, so Dale and I figured it was worth a rocket run or two. The area was beyond known surface-to-air missile danger zones.

I double-checked the coordinates Jay had given us, figured a roll-in point over the sea and maneuvered the flight into position for an attack to the west.

"Fire in pairs (two at a time)," I told Dale, referring to the Zuni rockets we were carrying in pods on either wing, "and recover seaward."

I set my switches, called rolling in, and wrapped the plane up nearly inverted before snapping back, nose down, with the gun sight reticle aimed nicely at the forest below. I loved to fire the Zunis. These were larger rockets than the 2.75-inch, folding-fin types that we carried most of the time. The Skyraider could carry Zunis and the smaller rockets simultaneously (see R. G. Smith's jacket illustration of two VA-25 Spads at night) not to mention a combination of bombs and 20-millimeter ammunition. About as thick as the forearm on a weight lifter, they were about four feet long with a dangerous-looking, tapered steel warhead. When fired, they rushed from the pods with a force hefty enough to shake the airplane.

At release altitude I pressed the trigger on the stick and the rockets whooshed powerfully away. I pulled up, bending the Spad sharply around over the water.

"Rollin' in," called Pellot, a few seconds later.

"Roger," I said, looking over my shoulder but not seeing him.

Suddenly, where there had been blue sky I saw a barrage pattern of white puffs saturating the airspace where Dale had been. It was as if a batch of kernels had been tossed in the air and instantly burst into popcorn. Under other circumstances the sight of the miniature clouds blossoming against the azure background might have induced poetic thoughts. On this day they set my heart to pounding. I feared Dale had been hit.

"Check in, two," I said.

There was no answer.

"Two, ah, check in," I repeated.

Still no answer.

I dove toward the surface and turned back to the beach searching for him.

"You OK, two?" I asked, hopefully.

There were no concentric circles indicating that an aircraft had crashed into the water. There was no fire-filled mass of smoke telling me that Pellot had smashed into the ground. Nevertheless, I had the nauseous feeling that I had just lost a wingman.

"Pellot, are you up?" I asked one more time, urgency creeping into my voice.

A few more seconds passed and then I heard a mike keyed.

"I'm awright," Pellot reported calmly.

Finally, I spotted his Skyraider, a reassuring profile hugging the wave tops a half-mile distant, pointed *away* from land.

"They're shootin' back there," he said tersely.

"So I noticed," I said, breathing comfortably again, "so I noticed."

VA-25 Spad releases bombs on combat mission in Vietnam.

It was a clear but moonless night, and we had been over Laos working with forward air controllers who lit targets for us with flares. Safety, or should I say, survival, depended on a mastery of instrument flying and an acute sense of where your fellow flyers were in the sky, especially during strenuous, high-G pull-outs from diving runs. When the sessions over land were done, it was relaxing to sit back and drone home to the carrier.

We were about ten miles offshore when I looked toward the land. My field of view encompassed a span from just below the de-militarized zone, north to the central coast of North Vietnam. Perhaps it was a weird coincidence or just an unusual perception on my part, but for the moment, that section of the world wore a striking pattern of lights, startling silver-white on pure black.

At varying altitudes parachute-retarded flares were moving like slowly descending stars toward the earth. Rising from the ground in sporadic bursts, presumably aimed at the stars and the airplanes that had dropped them, were slim fingers of groundfire—some in solid lines, some like a sequence of hyphens. Cauliflower-shaped flashes signaled bomb impacts.

In a short time the lights went out and the horizon was dark again. It would ignite once more soon enough. But as we flew on, I wondered if it was a paradox that violence and all the ramifications of it could accompany such wondrous beauty.

Motion pictures, which were shown every night in wardrooms, mess-deck areas, ready rooms, and many other spaces, were one of the pressure-relief valves that characterized life at sea. The Navy did its best to get current films to us, and with rare exception, we looked forward to the two or so hours of escape that viewing the movies provided.

A ship's company officer, one of the dentists on board, loved westerns and, for that matter, any story that served up violence in heavy dosage. Oddly, whenever he attended a movie, he carried in his hand a small, counting device with which he clicked the evening away.

"Commander," I said to him one night after a show in the wardroom, "curiosity has gotten the best of me. I have to know. Just what are you adding up with that thing?"

"Why, casualties, of course," he admitted without hesitation.

"Casualties?" I said.

"Sure," he said. "I keep a running tally of the fatalities the folks in Hollywood manage to put before us on the silver screen."

"What's the total now?" I inquired, more convinced than ever that naval aviation is a world of numbers.

"Three hundred and seventy-five," he declared, "counting from the day we left San Francisco. Last Sunday's double feature really boosted the total. Clint Eastwood gave me thirty-six in *A Fist Full of Dollars* and fourteen more in *For A Few Dollars More*."

Among the Spad's unheralded virtues was a low-frequency (LF) radio. It served in a direction-finding capacity mostly, while primary communications were handled with the ultra-high frequency, or UHF, radio. I particularly liked the LF, because on dull RESCAP patrols (we flew these without the Albatross on the second deployment) or on point-to-point flights out of the combat zone we could tune in broadcasts on the Armed Forces Network.

Once, when I was overhead the ship about seventy miles from land, I picked up a sports broadcast. The Houston Cougars with their great All-American, Elvin Hayes, were playing the UCLA Bruins with their tremendous star, Lew Alcindor (Kareem Abdul-Jabbar). It was the biggest basketball game of the year. I was in the delta—or holding—pattern, enjoying the near-perfect reception afforded by the LF radio and asked the troops in approach control, whose frequency I was monitoring on the UHF, if they were interested in my relaying progress reports of the game. They surely were.

So, with the help of the Spad and its LF radio, a touch of athletic excitement taking place in Texas, U.S.A. was passed on to some fans in the USS *Coral Sea* on the other side of the world in the Tonkin Gulf. I was a regular Curt Gowdy for a while.

Just as the first half ended I received a Charlie, which meant I had to land and terminate my sportscasting duties. But half was better than nothing, and eventually I learned the final score. Houston won.

During breaks from combat we had shore leave and liberty in the same watering spots of the Far East we knew the year before. Although we seemed to spend more time at Cubi Point than anywhere else, we did get into Hong Kong to enjoy the bustling activity and enchantment of that marvelous place. And even at sea there were moments of relaxation that allowed us to forget the fighting. Bob Hope gave the *Coral Sea* and her crew one of those moments.

He had brought Raquel Welch, Barbara McNair, and his customary retinue to Yankee Station. For reasons never made clear to us, his itinerary included the USS *Constellation* and excluded us. We were incensed. We had been in combat for months and the *Connie* had just arrived from the States. It wasn't fair! We needed Raquel and Barbara far more than those other fellows. Protests boomeranged off bulkheads in every level of the ship, from the machinery spaces and below all the way up to the far reaches of the superstructure.

Alas, despite our complaints, we were stuck with show business on celluloid, that is, movies in ready rooms and other places. Oh, how we yearned for the three-dimensional presence of the man and his ladies.

But wait! An announcement rippled through the ship, and mouths, which had resembled the inverted cursive letter U, flip-flopped. Bob Hope was coming to see us after all. When he learned how long we'd been on duty in Vietnam, he arranged for a small contingent from his troupe, led by himself, to fly from the *Connie* by COD (carrier on-board delivery aircraft) to the *Coral Sea*.

Subsequently, the hangar bays were jammed to the rafters, and on a makeshift stage, the mini-band played, Raquel wiggled, and Barbara sang. The beauty of the women projected dramatically to the crowd, but it was the gentleman with the ski-shoot nose who stole the show. He wore a yellow flight deck jersey with blue baseball cap and, lazily swinging a golf club, chatted and joked with us. It was like a visit from an uncle that everyone in the family revered and enjoyed.

The peripatetic demands of Hope's schedule exceeded those of most prominent individuals, even the likes of a Secretary of State. Yet he came to our ship when he didn't have to. He climbed into a COD, was catapulted from one flattop to another, made the trap, and with that brand of humor known all over the world, made us laugh at the perils of landing on an aircraft carrier. His devotion to the men and women in uniform was graphically demonstrated by the simple fact that he came to see us. But even that gesture was exceeded by a few words he spoke toward the end of the evening. The throng in the hangar bay grew still as several thousand Navy and Marine Corps men listened to him talk about the folks back home.

"I want you to know," Bob Hope said earnestly, "that we're behind you and what you're doing out here." He went on and mentioned the dissenters, the skeptics, those who insisted that the U.S. was poisoning the world by fighting in Vietnam. "They are there," he admitted, "but so are the others, the majority of Americans. They support you. Remember that."

I suppose the veracity of his remarks could be debated until the sun sets in the east. But for me, and for a lot of others that night on the high seas far from home, the man with the famous smile and the enormous heart made us feel pretty good.

Not long after that we had a rest and recreation period in Japan. I returned early from shore leave one night and saw a cluster of officers and sailors sitting in folding chairs in hangar bay one. They were listening to a soft and elegant-looking lady who stood at a microphone singing a soft and elegant-sounding song, an old favorite. A man played the upright piano beside her. The lady and the voice were vaguely familar. I was sure I had heard her before. I joined the cluster.

Good lord, it dawned on me. The woman was Frances Langford. Like Bob Hope she had traveled the globe to entertain the troops since World War II. There was something very warming about the scene and the perpetuity it reflected. The warmth was heightened by the knowledge that there were people like Ms. Langford to sing the same songs with the same voice, soothing another generation of servicemen.

Marcus and I were returning from a bombing mission one overcast afternoon, cruising over the water northbound toward the ship alongside a wall of rain clouds that towered to nearly 10,000 feet. A movement caught my eye from three o'clock high, and I was astonished to see a pair of Spads, one behind the other, three or so thousand feet above, diving out of the gray-white wall toward us. I knew the other airborne A-1s from VA-25 were well north of the ship. Our visitors had to be from a sister Skyraider squadron based aboard another carrier. Well now, I thought, as the competitive juices began to flow, what have we here? There was an enticing spontaneity to this encounter. I chose my words carefully and keyed my mike.

"Four Oh Seven," I said to Bruce (our aircraft side numbers had been changed to the 400 series for this cruise), "combat spread [meaning move away slightly for maneuvering room]. Bogeys at three o'clock high, diving. I'm adding power now. Stand by to break right."

"Roger," Bruce said without delay, banking over to my left side and slipping back a couple of hundred feet from me.

Had I used the word bandit rather than bogey, it would have implied that the approaching planes were authentic enemies. Marcus understood this the instant he saw the Skyraider silhouettes speeding toward us. Neither the North Vietnamese nor the Viet Cong had A-1s.

Without having to say a word, each pilot in the four cockpits reacted instinctively to what was to become a swirling, whirling, gut-stretching dogfight. We were four knights of the realm, two against two. The first pair had thrown down the gauntlet, the second had taken it up. This would be an exercise in aerial skill without malice. It was a pick-up basketball scrimmage sans spectators. The impromptu nature of it, however, did not diminish the desire for victory, although the main goal, since the opponents were friends, was to give a good accounting of ourselves.

"Break right, now!" I ordered. I stood the Spad on its wing and yanked the stick back mightily into my lap. I squeezed my stomach muscles and grunted against the force of Gs imposed by the pulling turn. The attackers whipped over us and seeing us turn, banked toward us.

"Reverse!" I cried to Bruce, swinging steeply to the left to try and get behind the bogeys.

My body, and I'm sure those of the three others, was tensed up from head to toe. All mental and physical faculties were prickling. I felt sweat building on my forehead. The bogeys were sweeping sharply around, well to the left of my nose, inside a sort of makeshift lufbery circle. (The lufbery circle is a maneuver named after World War I flyer, Raoul G. Lufbery, in which two or more aircraft follow one another in a spiral or approximately horizontal

Division of VA-25 A-1s.

circle.) Bruce and I couldn't quite get them (the bogeys) on our nose for a decent shooting angle.

The bogeys, probably intentionally, ran into a tall, bulbous-shaped cloud that stood apart from the wall, disappeared momentarily, and emerged from it in a climbing turn toward the partition of weather to the east. When the bogeys penetrated the wall I had to make an instantaneous decision. Do we follow or break it off.

We pursued.

"Maintain this altitude," I said to Bruce. "Take up one one zero degrees. I'll stay on zero nine zero."

I was gambling, perhaps unwisely, that the wall was not excessively thick and that we could poke through on the other side in a short time. Since we would lose sight of each other and have to fly on the gauges individually while in the soup, the heading differential would prevent us from ramming into each other.

Flying inside the opaque mass straight and level gave us a sort of reprieve from the action, although later, Bruce likened the color of the clouds to a grayish, dismal-looking medicine he once had to drink for an upset stomach. Happily, we pierced the wall in less than a minute. It was like emerging from thick jungle into an open savannah. Our prey, meanwhile, had cleverly maneuvered into a perch position above the wall. As we emerged into the savannah, they pounced on us.

There followed another swift, twisting, and spiraling tussle. At one point Bruce and I slapped down the wheel, flap, and speed-brake handles, bringing our machines to a near halt in mid-air. The attackers were only partially fooled, but the maneuver allowed us to neutralize the bogies.

And so it went for a solid, invigorating ten minutes. Finally, spent, sated with the intense, unadulterated excitement of it all, the dogfight ended by mutual, unspoken consent. The parties withdrew from each other to proceed on separate ways.

Marcus and I joined up and as we cruised over the gray waters toward our carrier, I looked at my wingman. His face was lit with a broad, up-from-deep-down smile. So was mine, I suppose. Neither of us said anything, because there was really nothing to say. The scrimmage was over. It would be fair to call it a draw. The knights were going back to the castle, and it mattered not whether we won or lost, but how we played the game.

Technology and a quirk of Mother Nature combined one day in the war to bring a moment of delight to an Air Force fighter pilot and his wife. The pilot was returning from a mission and switched radio frequencies to obtain landing clearance at his South Vietnamese home base. He was amazed when he heard what sounded like a tower control operator at Travis Air Force base— Travis being located thousands of miles away in California.

"Travis tower," he asked, "This is Red Rock Two Oh Seven, how do you read me?"

"Loud and clear," was the reply.

This was stupefying, the pilot thought. He had been stationed at Travis, and in fact, his wife lived on the base. The transmission was so clear it was as if he was approaching the runways at Travis rather than an airfield in the war zone.

He reduced power to a maximum endurance setting in order to remain aloft as long as possible, then explained the circumstances to Travis and enquired if they might arrange for his wife to get to the radio so he could say hello. The Travis people swung into action, and a few minutes later a very surprised and elated Air Force wife in the United States was chatting with her husband flying a jet in the skies over Vietnam.

Somehow, the atmospheric conditions had allowed the radio waves of similar frequencies to travel an incredible distance from one side of the earth to the other. My guess is that that was one conversation neither the pilot nor his wife would ever forget.

Airman Apprentice Langdon was a happy-go-lucky sailor just out of his teens who got into trouble often. Although he was not one of VA-25's shining lights of military decorum and efficiency, he was good-humored and functioned well enough in nonchallenging tasks to be of value. He was not destined to become a petty officer and really didn't care about that anyway. His usually tousled, thick black hair flopped over an innocent, Tom Sawyer-like face. He was placed on report with some regularity but usually for minor infractions, despite that facade of innocence.

The city of Olongapo was immediately outside the gate of the Subic Bay complex in the Philippines. It had a rather notorious reputation and was not very high on the list of preferred liberty sites. Still, it was a place to go if for no other reason than to get off the base. It had plenty of bars and plenty of girls.

Langdon found himself in double jeopardy one evening. He had been written up for missing a muster earlier in the week but was not restricted to the ship, pending a captain's mast—a captain's mast being a proceeding wherein an alleged offender faced the CO of the ship directly and depending on the outcome, was subject to disciplinary action. Langdon was advised to stay out of further trouble, at least until the mast.

He went ashore, ventured through the gate, and entered into the alluring, but sometimes troublesome, world of Olongapo. Not long thereafter he was taken into custody by the Shore Patrol and returned to the ship. Seems he was discovered in a saloon clearly marked "Off Limits," a definite no-no.

I had the squadron duty next day, and he was assigned to clean up the ready room.

"Langdon," I asked him, "what's the story? You already have one offense hanging over your head. You knew that place was off limits. Yet you went out there and jumped from the frying pan into the fire."

"Sir," he said, "I am innocent. No one will believe me, including you, but here's what happened."

I sat back in my chair very interested.

"I was walking down the street past this certain recreational establishment," he began, "when all of a sudden, the door of the place burst open. A bunch of people roared outa there and onto the sidewalk fightin' like alley cats. Just like one of those brawls in a western movie. Somehow I got caught up in the scuffle; you know, like being pushed along in a crowd at a rally or somethin'. I was trapped in the midst of those alley cats. It was brutal. I was sort of swung around, like on a carrousel, and flung *inside* the door of the place!"

"Please go on," I said suspiciously.

"Well." he said, "I bet it was no more than thirty seconds later when the guys from the Shore Patrol, wearing their black arm bands and carrying night sticks, arrived on the scene. Right away they spotted me. Two of 'em came up to me, one on either side, and took me by the shoulders. I was hauled out of there real fast-like. Now how is that for bad luck?"

Langdon paused and noticed my expression of doubt.

"See," he sighed, shaking his head, "I knew you wouldn't believe me."

I stared into his puppy-like eyes.

"You're right, Langdon," I admitted. "I *don't* believe you. You tell a good story but I just don't buy it."

At which point the sailor tried but failed to suppress a smile which built up from the corner of his mouth, grew rapidly, and blossomed into a laugh.

"It was worth a try though, wasn't it, sir?" the guilty party said.

I failed to suppress a laugh of my own and said, "I suppose so."

Airman Apprentice Langdon added spice to the stew.

What a great hop! Larry Ramsey, a first-tour lieutenant (junior grade), and I received an urgent summons from a forward air controller southwest of DaNang.

"I've got a patrol trapped by the Viet Cong and they have wounded," said the FAC. "A helo is standing by to haul 'em out, but there's too much groundfire. Can you sanitize?"

"Affirmative," I said, sanitize being a civilized term for suppressing the enemy with a fusillade of ordnance from the air.

The chopper was circling slowly a mile or two to the east. Except for the huge white cross on its fuselage, it was olive-colored and barely discernible against the deep green of the jungle and the thick carpet of trees and underbrush along the slopes of the rolling hills.

"Watch for automatic weapons," cautioned the FAC.

As I examined the terrain below, one of the trapped soldiers dashed out from an outcropping of trees adjacent to a small clearing. To my surprise, he flung a bright orange marker, about as big as a cardtable top, onto the ground, then scampered back to cover. With the marker as a reference point, we were instructed to fire into an area thirty meters northwest of it. This was just like a programmed training exercise, except that a miss here could harm our own troops. We had to be very careful.

We set up a pattern, swooped in, and had at it. With rockets, bombs, and the twenty-millimeter cannons we worked around the marker, guided by the FAC. Combat is no athletic contest, but for a few moments I felt like a basketball player with a hot hand. I remembered a long ago game in high school when I couldn't miss a shot. The ball left my fingers and sailed toward the hoop and through the net whether I was close in or well away, off balance or on. It was as if my movements were influenced by an external force that willed me to score. The ball gravitated almost supernaturally to its target.

This day in South Vietnam was a little like that. Whatever altitude or airspeed I had at the roll-in point, I was able to rapidly adjust aim point with dive angle and score near-perfect hits. Rockets spurted from the pods, bombs plunged from the pylons, and the twenty mike-mike spat from the guns—all striking enemy emplacements within a meter or two of where the FAC and the soldiers wanted them.

We were Winchester—all ammo gone—in thirty minutes. We had been shot at by small arms fire and some automatic weapons but weren't hit. Because we were able to keep the Viet Cong ducking, it probably prevented them from taking effective aim on us. Importantly, the helo was eventually cleared in and the patrol, with its wounded, was plucked from the jungle and carried to safety.

Wish all the missions were like that.

Toward the end of our Yankee Station duties, the USS *Pueblo* was captured by North Koreans and waves of apprehension rolled through high places. Commander Cliff Church, who had relieved Commander Jim Burden as our squadron skipper, told us about it. He explained that we would be extended for a few more days on Yankee Station and eventually sent to Sasebo in Japan for a time before deploying on a short tour in the Sea of Japan as part of a strategic show-of-force. Then we would go home.

There wasn't an overwhelming groundswell of hate and discontent over this unexpected alteration to plans. There was certainly no exultation either. We took it with a "what's a few more days here and there" attitude, right? Wrong. We took it because there was not a single thing we could do about it.

My last combat hop was a nighttime affair with Pellot the Pilot. After delivering some ordnance near the DMZ, we were called in on a RESCAP that had just gotten under way. Dacron Two, an Air Force Phantom fighter-bomber, had been shot down. The pilot and his radar officer parachuted into a narrow valley between sharply rising hills. From the charts, which I studied by penlight with my customary maladroit technique, theirs was not a promising situation. The terrain was rough, and because of the surrounding peaks, a helo wouldn't have an easy time finding them. Plus, a weather front clouded over the area. On the other hand, their location was remote enough to be of limited strategic importance and that meant that enemy ground forces weren't an imminent threat.

Dacron Two Alpha, the pilot, had a good emergency radio and was talking to his still-airborne lead plane. The status of the radar officer, Dacron Two Bravo, was unknown. He hadn't answered any calls and his beeper, or distress signal, worked for a brief time but stopped for one reason or another.

In deference to tactical efficiency and procedures that had been set down since aviation's earlier days, the names of two human beings had been converted to numbers, letters, and in this case, a type of fabric. Under the circumstances I would have preferred talking to those fellows on the ground using their real names. I think they would have liked that better, too. Anyway, we moved in and began an orbit as the Dacron lead plane, running low on fuel, was leaving.

"We'll rendezvous with you two in the club tomorrow," he transmitted to his colleagues in the jungle below. Even though Bravo gave no indication he was OK, the leader wisely included both men in his message. Maybe Bravo's transmitter was inoperative, but his receiver was functioning. Dacron Alpha, in response, clicked his emergency radio microphone twice. I am positive that he would like nothing better than a stiff drink at the club bar the next day.

I wasn't so sure about that rendezvous. We were high and clear over the clouds but the SAR network reported that a band of weather hugged the valley floor. The night and the shroud of rain-filled fog precluded a rescue helo from even trying to go after them. Hopefully, conditions would improve in the morning. The Dacrons were so near to us, I thought, and yet so far away.

"Dacron Two Alpha, radio check," I transmitted routinely every five minutes or so. It was important to let the survivors know we were standing by, even though they might have been able to hear the sound of our engines.

"Two Alpha, loud and clear," he answered each time in a surprisingly firm voice.

"Dacron Two Bravo, this is Canasta, do you read, over?"

There was only silence from Dacron Bravo. I wondered how far away he might be from his pilot. A few yards? A few miles? It was a perplexing question that might never be answered.

The search-and-rescue coordinator was monitoring the situation at command headquarters, probably at Da Nang, and decided that no rescue try would be made till daylight. Disheartening as it must have been, I relayed this information to the survivors. I also verified with Dacron Alpha that there were no signs of enemy troops in the vicinity.

Unusual, I thought. Here were Pellot and I, clean and comfortable, winging freely through the clear night sky over two fellow American military men, trapped in the dark, wet jungle. The four of us were, for the moment, caught in a weird and isolated capsule of space on planet Earth. Yet there were two distinctive environments within that capsule: Pellot's and mine, one of hope and optimism because this was our last combat mission; and the Dacrons', one of severe apprehension if not downright fear.

We orbited for more than an hour and were relieved on station by Air Force Skyraiders, the Sandys.

"Good luck," I transmitted lamely to the Dacrons.

"Thanks, Canasta," said Dacron Alpha, his voice still strong.

I could not rid myself of the picture of the man huddled against the chill in the black of night, flight suit torn, bruised, hungry, and thirsty. He was in a kind of purgatory preserved especially for fighting men without regard to sin or innocence.

Over the sea, on the way to our sanctuary, Pellot and I flew along in silence. The elation we might have felt about having the war behind us was subdued. It was well after midnight when we landed and shuffled into the ready room, which was vacant but for a couple of stragglers and Marcus, the duty officer. Bruce lunged toward me, grasped the waist-level CO_2 toggles on my flotation gear and yanked them down. Compressed air, accompanied by a loud hissing sound, rushed into the pockets, ballooning them to nearly inner tube dimensions.

"You're home free!" Marcus cried.

I could only shrug my shoulders.

Not long after leaving Yankee Station for the last time we were in Sasebo, and after several days there, entered the Sea of Japan for limited operations. The flight schedules were hardly hectic. Every other day each pilot flew (would you believe it?) a practice bombing mission using targets located on the Japanese mainland. The air was so icy, the temperatures so savagely cold that even thermal underwear and the cumbersome exposure suits that sealed our bodies from neck to feet couldn't completely ward off the elements.

Frustratingly, the extra clothing caused us to perspire while inside the ship before manning up. There was a provision for specialized air-conditioning in the ready room whereby we plugged hoses from the exposure suits into receptacles in the floor next to our seats, allowing air under pressure to be pumped inside the suits for cooling. Even so, by the time we unhooked and made our way to the flight deck, we were sweating. For me, stepping onto the roof in the Japanese winter was like walking into a meat cooler room, naked. Once in the cockpit, however, with the canopy closed, engine running, and heater on, we were OK.

When we flew from the ship those two weeks in March 1968, I was very pleased that our eighteen-cylinder R-3350s held up so well. The water temperature ranged from forty to fifty degrees, the air temperature well below that. So, should the engine decide to stop and one had to ditch, say a hundred miles from the ship, chances are one would become an ice cube in a matter of minutes, even with the protective gear. A rescue helicopter would really have to hustle to reach you in time.

Most flyers have pondered at one time or another whether they would, in the event of an aerial mishap, elect scorchingly hot or deadeningly frigid conditions to endure, assuming only those two extremes exist. I would choose the steaming jungle and its reptilian population, no matter how much they terrify, over the Arctic. Happily, the options usually were between the two.

As it turned out, no one had to go into the water. There were no aerial mishaps. Another ship relieved us to continue the show-of-force, and those that made it through Yankee Station made it to the friendly shores of the U.S. of A.

I pray the Dacrons made it, too.

We returned to Yokosuka, and those of us lucky enough to fly home rather than ride the ship boarded a stretch DC-8 at an air base outside of Tokyo for the journey. We arrived at Travis Field in California from Japan by way of Anchorage, Alaska, about twenty hours after leaving the land of the rising sun. We piled into a C-131 for the final run to Lemoore and a reunion with wives and families. I was most anxious to see my wife again for the first time in eight months, not to mention our daughter who had arrived on Christmas Eve while I was in the Far East.

It was a bright, cloudless California day and for obvious reasons there was an electric air of excitement among us in the transport. We landed and the C-131 rumbled briskly toward the ramp adjacent to the operations building where everyone was waiting. I had a growth of beard and my blue uniform was badly rumpled, but I didn't think my wife would mind. For no particular reason, I was in the back of the plane and would be the last man out. Jay Stone was filing out ahead of me, and since he was planning his reunion in Louisiana and had no one waiting, I tossed him my movie camera.

"How about recording this event for posterity?" I asked. He agreed and disembarked while I lingered a moment near the hatch. Finally, I stepped out and hurried down the ladder, seeing my wife and that little bundle immediately. It was easy because by the time I emerged, everybody else was tangled up in embraces.

Stone filmed away as I gathered up the loved ones in my arms. After a while my wife asked, in a voice tinged with anger, "How come you were the last one out of the plane? For a minute I thought you weren't aboard. Not anxious to see us, maybe?"

I made some quick and decisive reassurances to the contrary

then said, "Well, I saw Cary Grant do it in a movie once and—"

"Listen, pal," she interrupted, "a Cary Grant you're not. Next time you come out with the others or I'll bop you over the head!"

"Wilco," I said, explaining that that was an aviation term meaning "understand and will comply."

The movies came out very well.

It would be five years before the prisoners of war would come home. A close friend from VA-85 days, Jack Fellowes, who had been shot down and captured early on in the conflict, was one of them. So, too, was Dean Woods from VA-25, who was taken on our first cruise, and Al Nichols. Al had two combat tours as a Spad pilot with us, returned to Vietnam flying A-7 Corsair jets, and fell into the hands of the enemy about a year before the war ended.

At this point I ask the reader's indulgence while I jump ahead to 1973 when I was assigned to a reserve squadron based at Naval Air Station Alameda. One morning word filtered down that a plane-load of POWs was being diverted to Alameda due to bad weather at its original destination, Travis Air Force Base. A number of us hustled down to the receiving area to see the men come in.

Necks craned and eyes searched the mist-shrouded horizon as the C-141 carrying them, a jet-powered behemoth, settled onto the runway. Even though the POWs aboard could not hear it, cheering erupted from the bystanders. I thought for a moment of Commander Stoddard and another VA-25 pilot, Lieutenant (junior grade) Joe Dunn, who was shot down and declared missing, and all the others who wouldn't be coming back. How many people in this country of ours really appreciated the sacrifices they, and the men approaching us in the Starlifter, made. I wondered.

The huge aircraft taxied slowly toward the impatient audience, which was formed into a huge V by restraining ropes. News media personnel stood behind a battery of cameras perched atop tripods on a raised platform at the apex of the V. The transport drew to a halt, its engines sighing into silence. It was as if the curtain had been raised in a theater. A red carpet ran from the exit door of the gleaming C-141 toward the edge of the crowd. Just beyond the door was a podium with a spray of silver microphones mounted atop it. The disembarking ladder was swung downward by a crewman, and a nervous quiet fell over the onlookers. A voice from somewhere in the background broke the stillness.

"The senior member of this group of returning Prisoners of War—Captain Harry Jenkins, United States Navy!"

A burst of clapping greeted the tall, gaunt Navy flyer who walked directly to the podium and spoke briefly. Though his remarks were similar to those of other repatriated Americans in their gratitude to the President and the people of America, the speech carried its full measure of drama. To me, Captain Jenkins and those that followed him out of that aircraft after he talked, were larger than life itself. They filed from the plane, beaming. One man, an Air Force B-52 aircrewman, was carried on a stretcher, swathed in white sheets and blankets. He raised his arm proudly, fingers forming a victory sign, à la Winston Churchill.

A Navy lieutenant commander waved jauntily. Several women and children near a bus that was waiting for the POWs held aloft a banner bearing the lieutenant commander's name in brightly colored letters. When he saw this, the officer charged toward them and scooped nearly all of them up in his arms.

As one Air Force colonel strode by toward the bus, an apparent friend of his in the crowd shouted his name. The colonel slowed his pace and looked into the sea of faces, smiling but failing to recognize anyone. For those close enough to see, the expression on his face embodied both the heart-lifting spirit and the doom-like travail that had characterized the POWs' horrible ordeal. The man's face was lit with joy but his dark eyes were sunken and tired, surrounded by concentric circles firmly etched into his flesh. There was also a trace of bewilderment in those eyes, caused, I believed, by the resounding welcome.

One of the squadron flyers standing next to me that day later confided, "It was a bit difficult to keep a dry eye out there. I had the feeling that 'There, but for the grace of God, go I.'"

Jack Fellowes told me after he got back, "I really wouldn't welcome the opportunity, but if I had to, I'd go through it again. I feel that strongly about this country of ours." He had been a captive for more than seven years!

That sort of remark reminded me of an incident that occurred not long after Captain Jenkins's group returned. There's a tradition in Navy officers' clubs that stipulates that "He who enters covered here, shall buy for all a round of cheer." Many a man has unexpectedly lost a pocketful of money by forgetting that rule and wearing his hat into the bar.

One night at the Alameda club much of the conversation centered on the returning prisoners. People were three deep at the bar. Tables were packed. The music was loud.

A lieutenant commander, who had been incarcerated for about seven years, was enjoying one of his first evenings on the town in the continental U.S. in a long, long time. He wore dress khakis, and as he approached the entrance to the bar he placed his bridge cap on his head and patted it down firmly.

A young officer went up to him, touched his elbow and said, "Sir, better remove that hat. It'll cost you."

It's intentional," the lieutenant commander said, smiling. He charged forward and shouted, "Hey, everybody, look at me!"

The message spread like flames on oil. All heads swung toward him. He deliberately pulled the hat down tighter on his head. Someone recognized him as a POW and passed the word around.

"Bartender," ordered the lieutenant commander, "set 'em up for the house!" The applause lasted for minutes.

I consider that a classic example of the spirit of naval aviation.

So was the case of Dieter Dengler. He was the Navy lieutenant shot down early in the war. Captured, he escaped, was recaptured, and escaped again.

Wretchedly emaciated, he walked and crawled for days through the jungle. He was on the threshold of death, clinging to life by the threads of hope and true grit. He was ultimately saved by a helicopter crew literally minutes from eternity. He later described those final moments in the wet heat and cruel underbrush of a war-torn land.

"I knew I was going to die," he said. "But my goal was to make it to the next ridge so that I could die seeing the ocean. That's what I wanted to do."

"Why the ocean?" he was asked.

"Because I'm in the Navy. I've seen much of the sea, and that's where the carriers are. I said to myself, 'If I can't make it home, at least I can make it to the top of that ridge so I can see freedom. Freedom is the ocean and that's our territory.'"

Which calls to mind a rhetorical question voiced by a character from James Michener's *The Bridges at Toko Ri*, the book that helped spark my early interest in naval aviation.

A carrier pilot had been shot down over North Korea and was ultimately killed by ground troops despite gallant efforts to rescue him. Alone on the flag bridge, the admiral said some words that are, on occasion nowadays, recalled with innocuous cynicism by newer generations of flyers:

"Why is America lucky enough to have such men? They leave this tiny ship and fly against the enemy. Then they must seek the ship, lost somewhere at sea. And when they find it, they have to land upon its pitching deck. Where did we get such men?"

It is one of the glorious truths and inspiring mysteries of our time that somehow, somewhere, when needed, we have been able to come up with them.

five

Jets

"A.J.," I said, "I'm impressed. That's really thoughtful of your troops, letting us taxi into the hangar out of the rain so we don't get wet."

"Hell," A.J. scowled, "we don't care about you jet jockeys gettin' your pretty flight suits drenched."

My jaw dropped at his strident tone.

"It's the cockpits I'm worried about," he said. "If we park you on the line, some of you dodos leave the canopies open so long climbing out that the seat packs and parachutes get soaked. And that costs my people extra work!"

Finally, the jets.

During desk duty days I had ridden a couple of times in the rear seat of a T-33 with Stan Cobb (the man who got married with HELP written on the soles of his shoes). He was at the test pilot school in Patuxent River, Maryland, and I drove down from Washington to log a few hours in the jet trainer he flew, which might facilitate my own transition later on. Because I was a passenger and only had my hands on the stick for a tame aileron roll or two, they were forgettable flights. They did let me experience the different sounds of turbine-powered machines and the innate sensitivity of the controls, especially at altitude, but that's about all.

In the spring of 1968 I was assigned to Attack Squadron Forty-Five based at Naval Air Station Cecil Field, Florida, where I would learn to fly the jets and become an instrument flight instructor. I would never forget the Spad, of course, but I looked forward to the change. Someone asked me how a pilot would describe his relationship with a plane he had flown for many years.

"It's not quite like loving a woman," I said, "but it is far more than being fond of a durable, old sweater."

VA-45 operated the TA-4 Skyhawk. Skipper Hinman's aircraft is shown here.

The new sweater in my life was the tandem-seat TA-4 Sky-hawk. Like the Skyraider it had a string of nicknames: Tinker Toy, Scooter, Bantam Bomber, Mighty Midget, and perhaps most popular, Heinemann's Hot Rod. Ed Heinemann and his design team at Douglas Aircraft's El Segundo Division in California had struck pay dirt with their Skyhawk, as they had with the SBD Dauntless, the Skyraider, the F4D Skyray, the A-3 Skywarrior, and many others.

The TA-4 was a derivative of the single-seated Skyhawk that first flew in 1954 and was a simple, low-cost, lightweight attack bomber. About forty feet long, its wing, technically defined as a modified delta planform, had a span of less than thirty feet. This allowed it to maneuver on carrier decks without the need for a wing folding mechanism. It and its successors were subsonic, cruised easily at about 400 knots at altitude, and could carry heavy loads of bombs and other ordnance. It was one of the most durable and effective aerial weapons of the Vietnam fighting. The A-4 was very shifty in air-to-air combat, although its primary mission was air-to-ground attack. It embodied the Heinemann trademark of fundamental simplicity throughout its design. It was a nifty, responsive machine and in all the time I flew it, I never heard anyone decry it.

On my first flight in the TA-4 with an instructor in the rear seat, I rolled down the Cecil Field runway and rose into the sky with so few manipulations of arms and legs compared to those needed to fly the Skyraider, I wondered, somewhat nervously, what procedural steps I had omitted. We reached a hundred knots on the takeoff roll in no time at all and the machine seemed to leave the strip of its own accord without any help from me save for keeping the throttle full forward.

The sound of the engine, which like most jets when I heard them as a spectator was like the sustained prelude to a thunderclap, was a bit more subtle than the deep roar of an R-3350. But it exuded a sort of smooth and graceful strength that was absent in the Spad. If the R-3350 called to mind an elephant thumping across the jungle, the Pratt and Whitney J-52 in the Skyhawk suggested a racing jaguar.

It was quite a change not having a propeller whirling in front of me. In fact, one of the most noticeable differences between the Skyhawk and the Skyraider was that in the former I felt as if I was well out front at the point of attack, whereas in the latter there was a lot of machine between me and the nose.

"An airplane is an airplane is an airplane," said one of the pilots undergoing transition with me. "One flies like the other."

I didn't totally agree. But no matter. I was happy as a bird just to be in the cockpit of a jet.

As the story goes, VA-45 was formed with two dozen individuals as a nucleus, and during my tour we had two great skippers, Commanders Don Reh and Al Hinman. Its insignia depicted a swaggering, cigar-chomping blackbird (from the poetic excerpt "four and twenty blackbirds baked in a pie" in reference to the twenty-four who started the squadron) who wore a derby and struck a challenging pose with boxing gloves. The unit had a reputation as a class outfit, a "Gentleman's Squadron" it was called, in deference to the fact that most of the flying was conducted during normal daytime hours (two hops a day per instructor, usually, with administrative duties in between), albeit in all weather conditions. Also, pilots needed to fly only four night hours per month, a comfortable commitment.

The idea was to be outbound from the parking lot, heading for the comforts of home by four-thirty P.M. each day. Folks seldom worked weekends, except for duty days and occasional cross-countries. It was a nice change of pace from combat duty.

After an extensive series of transition hops capped by a group of this-is-how-you-teach-instrument-flying flights with seasoned instructors, I began flying with students. Actually, those we trained were already designated naval aviators en route to squadrons from the training command, or fleet-experienced flyers satisfying annual instrument requirements. Normally, instructors rode in the front seat while the trainee occupied the rear where he flew under the dreaded hood, a canvas cover that came up over him like the top of a baby carriage. This forced him to operate the aircraft with reference only to the gauges.

On one of my first instructional sessions, my student and I landed in a downpour, one of those typical afternoon thundershowers, Florida style, that swept through the area. As we were taxiing toward the flight line I called the duty officer on the radio to check us in.

"Bring her into the barn," he said, meaning that I should bypass the parking line and guide the Skyhawk directly into the hangar. The rain pelted down, but we were snug and dry inside our glass cocoon. Still, I was confused. Did the duty officer really mean taxi into the hangar? We never did that in Spads.

A plane captain wearing rain gear, looking much like a Gloucester fisherman, waved us past the row of jets and pointed at the huge building that housed the maintenance department on the ground floor, and the squadron's administrative spaces along the outer sections above. Terrace-like walkways ran the length of the second story on both sides of the hangar.

I aimed the jet at the gigantic sliding doors which, as if by secret signal, began to slide open with biblical drama. A waiting plane captain guided us in out of the downpour, and the engine reverberated in the cavernous space. I noticed a number of people along the terrace looking down at us. Their attention, coupled with the powerful whining sound of the J-52, filled me with a momentary sense of omnipotence.

"Pretty neat, letting us in out of the rain like this," said my student over the intercom. "They don't want us to get wet."

"That's affirmative," I replied, figuring gentlemen squadrons did this sort of thing as a matter of course. "VA-45 is a class outfit."

Boy, I thought, I'm really up there with the tailpipe set now. No wonder jet pilots always looked clean and tidy compared to us Spad drivers. We shut down, climbed out, and went about our business.

A little later I ran into Commander A. J. Smith, the maintenance officer. A tyrannical sort by reputation, I was to learn that he knew airplanes and how to take care of them probably better than any person around. He actually wrote new procedures in maintenance management that were being used throughout the Navy. At the same time he was an earthy type with a temper. He had been an enlisted aircrewman in World War II, earned aviator wings later, and worked his way up the ranks flying fighters and an assortment of aircraft along the way. He flew regularly as an instructor in the TA-4 as well. A. J. had abundant brown hair clipped in a crew cut, which gave him youth, and a weathered sun-tanned face, which when the occasion necessitated, could convey the wrath of Moses coming down from the mountain. And like VA-45's blackbird, he also favored cigars.

"A. J.," I said, "I'm impressed. That's really thoughtful of your troops, letting us taxi into the hangar out of the rain so we don't get wet."

"Hell," A. J. scowled, "we don't care about you jet jockeys gettin' your pretty flight suits drenched."

My jaw dropped at his strident tone.

"It's the cockpits I'm worried about," he said. "If we park you on the line, some of you dodos leave the canopies open so long climbing out that the seat packs and parachutes get soaked. And that costs my people extra work!"

Burst that balloon.

On the day in July 1969, when astronauts Neil Armstrong, Edwin Aldrin, and Michael Collins were scheduled to rocket to the moon from Cape Kennedy, I was airborne with a student. We had planned our route to be near, but not too near, the launch site at liftoff. We headed south out of Jacksonville and climbed through a quilt-like blanket of clouds that ran unbroken to the horizon. At a safe standoff distance, clear of the airways, we set up an orbit.

"Should have ignition right about now," I said to my companion after checking the time. Then, precisely as scheduled, we watched as the Saturn rocket pierced the blanket trailing a ball of fire and smoke, powering straight up. Up, up it went, relentlessly, an enormous projectile in what seemed like slow motion. Higher it climbed until, like a Fourth of July sparkler at burnout, it disappeared from view.

"I believe," I said, "that we have just witnessed an historic event."

The pilot behind me clicked his mike twice in agreement.

Fearless Fred Freckmann, a former Fist of Fleet from VA-25, had preceded me at the Blackbird squadron. Aside from our Spad backgrounds and an eagerness to enjoy the merits of shore duty, we shared a propensity for punctuality, at least when it came to the flight schedule. We usually flew twice a day, and counting briefings and administrative duties, it was important to adhere to launch and landing times. Most fellows were content to motor into the fuel pits within fifteen minutes, give or take a few. (The fuel pits were actually a refueling station complete with pumps and below-ground tanks, located in the throat that led from the taxiway paralleling the runway to the parking ramp. We disembarked there and the crew gassed up the aircraft for the next flight.) Spurred by competitive fervor, Fred and I decided to compete to prove who was the most punctual. Using the honor system we agreed to record arrival times for a week, at the end of which we would compare scores and elect a winner. The award was a mythical gold star signifying pride in work. Importantly, there could be no excuses because of weather or mechanical difficulties.

Although we trusted one another, Fred or I would go out to the pits, schedule permitting, when the opponent was due in. Such gestures had psychological impact and put pressure on the other guy.

I was on hand one day when Fearless braked his Skyhawk to a halt precisely on time. He shut down, raised his canopy and held one arm up, pointing to his wrist watch with his other hand. (We synchronized our watches daily. Olympic Games timekeepers had nothing on us.) Fred had a broad, dominant jaw, and when he grinned his smile took on Cheshire cat proportions.

"Precision!" he shouted, "is the name of the game!"

I retreated back to the hangar realizing I was up against a real pro.

For a while it was nip and tuck and we were both doing nicely. The secret to the timing was in the way we managed the final twenty minutes aloft. On the majority of training hops the last portion was devoted to making a series of instrument approaches, usually at Cecil Field or Naval Air Station Jacksonville, a few miles to the east. Since the students needed a certain aggregate of approaches over the course of the syllabus, we tried to give them several per flight. Depending on the type of approach, an instructor could predict with some certainty how long a complete circuit would require and base his arrival time on that.

As in any endeavor worth undertaking, concentration and practice led to triumph. Fearless bested me in both categories and at week's end won the gold star.

"All right," I said during my concession speech. "You win. But I hereby offer a new challenge."

"Sure," Fred cackled with harmless condescension, "name it."

"Brown bags," I said.

"Brown bags?" Fred said, arching his eyebrows.

"The guy that brings in the best brown bag lunches in the next week wins."

Fearless puffed up his chest, which was already as muscular as a stevedore's, and said in a loud voice, "Accepted!"

Flying, especially instructional flying, was physically and mentally taxing. The body needed substantial midday nourishment to carry on. Many of the fellows relied on snack bars, others brought lunches from home in paper sacks—brown bags. Since Fred and I were brown baggers of long standing, it would be a fair contest.

On the first day I revealed a carton of milk, black olives, a mound of potato chips, and an appealing sandwich made with thick slices of fresh bread that my lovely wife had bought for me. Inside the slices was a layer of lettuce and generous cuts of imported Genoa salami plus a slab of provolone cheese that extended beyond the boundaries of the bread. For dessert there was a plump, fuzzy Georgia peach.

"Try and top that, Fearless," I said.

We were sitting at a table in the back of the ready room, and several officers hovered around us. With great care Fred opened up his brown bag and slowly extracted from it a thermos bottle and numerous items of different size wrapped neatly in wax paper. He arranged each item before him like a kid playing with toy soldiers. There was a collection of plump, shiny olives, half of them black, the other half green; a row of intermingled celery and carrot sticks fresh from the garden; a perfectly formed red apple which had been buffed to advertising page perfection; and a plastic container of fluffy, golden-white tapioca pudding. The crowning glory was a sandwich of Dagwood Bumstead dimensions featuring rich red stripes of pastrami, Swiss cheese, lettuce, tomatoes and rich-looking, delicatessen-style rye bread.

"I'm not done yet," said Fred, unscrewing the cup of his thermos. "Watch carefully." He poured lemonade from the container and said, "Notice the pulp and a lemon seed here and there. Undeniable proof that this drink has been made from scratch with fresh lemons."

The accolades began to flow and I tried to slide my repast off to the side so that the comparison of the two would be less drastic.

"I'm still not finished," announced Fred. Whereupon he unfolded the last waxed paper item, a large square of white cake capped with thick green frosting. It was not just any thick green frosting either.

"Observe," said Fred, raising the cake and holding it abeam of his right shoulder, next to the VA-45 patch he wore. (I did not mention it earlier but the blackbird in our insignia was posed against a light green background.)

"You will note," said Fearless, "that the color of this frosting exactly matches the green in our squadron patch. My wife worked very hard to achieve that color." He returned the cake to the table and I slumped to my elbows in defeat.

"It's no use, Fred," I said dejectedly. "This is only Monday. I don't think I can take anymore. You are the winner. I will challenge you no more."

Fred, a true champion, flashed a Cheshire cat grin, the bystanders went about their business, and I moved to a corner of the ready room and ate my lunch in silence.

Shore duty had its diversions.

After a year in VA-45 I was well settled into the routine and considered myself a fair instructor. I had never given any one a "down," or unsatisfactory, grade on a hop, preferring instead, in those rare cases where it was needed, to give a flyer a few more minutes to smooth out a particular deficiency. I was inclined to give a second, and sometimes a third, chance, so to speak. If a student was consistently unsafe in handling the aircraft on instruments, it was to his own benefit that he not continue as an aviator. But there were few, if any, who came to us with that problem. I suppose I had become what was called a "Santa Claus," an easy grader, a soft touch. Perhaps I was influenced by my own training command days when I received more than a fair share of "downs" and lived in an almost continuous state of apprehension. I had empathy for those who, like me, had to struggle through. I also believed that a lot of pilots, myself included, undergo a sort of metamorphosis when operating under the penetrating eye of an instructor. They fly much better alone than with a teacher scrutinizing every move.

Anyway, a lieutenant (junior grade) named Smith, who was headed for an A-7 Corsair (attack bomber) squadron and was undergoing replacement pilot training at VA-174, also based on Cecil Field, had some trouble getting through his final instrument check ride. He had already been given one "down" and another might lead to the long green table, or pilot evaluation board. That could spell an end to flying days. I was assigned to take him up on the re-fly.

We got airborne and Smitty went through the first half of the flight in an acceptable manner. When we went into the approach phase he became, to put it gently, disorganized. He wavered back and forth across the proscribed course clumsily, letting the airplane fly him rather than the other way around. His altitude control, in close to the field where it is most critical, was erratic. The nose of our Skyhawk rose and fell like a rowboat in a storm. I couldn't pass him based on that demonstration.

"OK," I said, taking the controls, "I've got it. Pop the hood and take a breather."

We climbed to altitude and after a few minutes I said, "Look, Smitty, I know you can do better than that."

"Roger," he said, almost inaudibly.

"You can hack it," I said.

Next time around Smitty was better, far from perfect, but smoother and safer. Buoyed by that success he made a couple of excellent precision approaches, and I had no reservations whatsoever in giving him an "up."

A month later VA-45 was playing arch-rival VA-174 in a base league flag football game. I was the quarterback for VA-45. Smitty, who was compact and well-proportioned, was a receiver and defensive cornerback for the opposition. It was a late autumn afternoon, and a small crowd—just a few people really—gathered along the sidelines to watch. Pride was at stake. The Skyhawk versus the Corsair.

It was no contest. We were destroyed. From opening kick-off to final whistle we were humbled. Lieutenant (junior grade) Smith was as quick as a cat, with the leaping ability of an antelope. He intercepted the first pass I threw, another one in the second half, and caught two of his own quarterback's throws for touchdowns.

Afterwards as I was trudging off the field, head down, Smitty sprinted by.

"Good game, sir!" he yelled jubilantly.

I stared at my feet. "Gratitude, Smitty," I muttered. "You've got no gratitude."

A sharp-looking commander with prematurely white hair took the instrument course at VA-45. Skipper of an A-7 squadron based at Cecil Field, he looked well-groomed and authoritative even in a flight suit. He was the young pilot on the recruiting poster, fifteen years later.

He listened carefully to my briefing, asked a minimum of questions, and later, under the hood on the climb-out, took the controls with a concise, "I've got it."

From the very beginning I knew he was different from all the others I had flown with. Had he been a nugget, I would have felt like a baseball scout watching a Willie Mays play for the first time. With the commander at the controls the airspeed needle adhered precisely to designated speed, not a centimeter off the mark. The same was true for the heading indicator. He executed a complicated maneuver called the Charlie pattern perfectly. It required him to make timed turns, reversing after 180 degrees of travel, all the while descending or climbing at 1,000 feet per minute. He was faultless.

"Beautiful control, sir," I heard myself saying, so impressed was I by his technique.

He was, I imagine, something most flyers are not—a natural in the cockpit. I'd never seen anyone, including a couple of VA-45 instructors who had flown virtually nothing but instrument-type flights for two years and who were absolutely first-rate in ability, do better. It occurred to me that his equivalent in the arts, or medicine, or athletics—any profession that demanded uncommon dexterity, intelligence, and concentration—would have stood apart from his contemporaries, like a Willie Mays.

During a break with the hood back I took over for a while.

"Teach instruments before, sir?" I asked, as we flew high over the Florida landscape.

"No," he said.

"If you don't mind my saying so," I went on, "maybe our positions should be reversed. You teach, I learn."

"Well, I don't know about that," he said. "But I admit I never have had much trouble making an airplane do what I want it to do."

I liked his modesty but envied his skill. After the flight I consulted the operations officer and suggested a reduced syllabus for the commander, which was agreed upon. Naturals are a rare breed and need to be appreciated.

In late 1969 I was ordered to Naval Air Facility Detroit, which occupied one half of Selfridge Air Force Base, on the shore of Lake St. Clair in Mount Clemens, Michigan. So I packed up the family—there were two children now—and we left sunny Florida for the state that, on a map, is shaped like a mitten. I was to help set up a jet attack program for the Naval Air Reserves who drilled on weekends and for longer periods in the summer. Commander Bob Graham, a veteran A-4 pilot, was my boss. We flew singleseat A-4Bs, which were functional although somewhat antiquated compared to the newer TA-4s I had been flying. We also had a T-33, a two-seat trainer built by the Lockheed company. Called the Shoot-

Skyhawk.

ing Star, it was an aging machine with straight wings and fuel tanks on their tips. It was slower than the Skyhawk, cruised at about 300 knots, but made up for its undramatic performance with reliability. The old T-bird would get you where you wanted to go.

One bright and cold winter day with the Midwestern skies crystal blue and the sun shining like a gold piece, I took off in the T-33 destined for Naval Air Station Glenview, just outside of Chicago. In the back seat was Lieutenant Bob Springer, a reserve pilot in the A-4 program. We were dressed arctic-style with exposure suit inner-liners and thermal underwear beneath our flight suits. Below us, the earth was wrapped in white, and beyond, Lake Michigan looked like a sheet of blue steel. As we neared Glenview, the skyscrapers of Chicago poked up from the land at the edge of the lake like dark monoliths.

We landed uneventfully on a runway patched with snow and taxied to the operations building where I was to deliver a package from the maintenance department people at Detroit to their coun-

terparts at Glenview. I shut the engine down, and when I opened
the canopy, a ferocious, numbing wind whipped against my face. I
felt as if I had been slapped with a curtain of ice. It reminded me
of those days in the Sea of Japan a couple of years back.

"Good Lord," I said to the plane captain as I climbed out,
"how cold *is* it here?"

"Chill factor is forty below, sir," he said, clouds of moisture
puffing from his mouth. "The wind makes the difference. I swear
it comes straight from the North Pole!"

"You're probably right," I said. I unbuttoned one side of the
T-33's nose compartment, where we could store a few items, held it
up with one hand, and pulled out the package. I let the door down
and with Bob trotted into operations, chased by the vicious breeze.

The package delivered, we had a cup of coffee while the aircraft was refueled. A little later I told Bob to climb in, that there
was no sense in both of us freezing while preflighting the aircraft.
Flowing with self-sacrifice, I told the plane captain to stay inside.
I'd handle his duties and call when ready to wind up the engines.

"One of us turning blue is enough," I said. "I'll signal you to
come out and man the starter."

A few moments later both Bob and I were strapped in, canopy
locked, and taxiing out to the duty runway. Snow was heaped in
orderly masses along our path, and like the runway, the taxi route
itself had some patches of ice and snow scattered about.

Everything was in order and we began the takeoff roll. In the
dense cold air we reached takeoff speed quickly and left the
ground climbing easily. As we passed through 500 feet aimed toward Lake Michigan a curious, subtle movement caught my eye.
What I saw brought my heart to the proverbial stop. I had failed to
secure the fasteners on the starboard nose compartment door and
it was cracked slightly open. Had I let the plane captain do his job
we probably wouldn't be in what was now one serious predicament.
The open door was only a couple of arm lengths from me but
there was nothing I could do from within the cockpit to correct it.

We were at 150 knots and to my despair, the door suddenly
flipped full out, fell back, and opened again, like a window shutter
in the wind. Although I felt no adverse effect on the aircraft I
knew that we had to get back on the ground quickly.

"We've got a problem, "I said to Bob, trying to sound calm.

"I see it," he said, also trying to sound unruffled. "What are we
going to do?"

"Turn back and land. Advise the tower that we have an
emergency and are returning."

I turned left gently, in a shallow angle of bank, as if being extra cautious might placate the errant door. It didn't. It continued to wave perilously, almost rhythmically, like the wings of a soaring sea gull. I flew downwind for an interminable length of time as Bob talked to the tower. We were the only plane in the area so traffic wasn't a problem. I made some intense, private solicitations to the man upstairs as we turned onto the final approach leg. The door was still flapping gracefully, ominously.

"Are you OK?" asked Bob. Which was his way of asking what the chances were of the door tearing off and banging into us with unknown consequences. Or worse, would the wind effect over the nose section be disruptive enough to spin us out of control? I surely didn't know.

"We'll be all right," I said.

And we were. We touched down safely, a blessedly beautiful feeling under the circumstances, even though the door fluttered through most of the roll-out. We taxied back to the line and got

Charles Cooney, Naval Aviation News art director, created this view of the nose compartment door opening on wintry day at NAS Glenview, 1970.

properly buttoned up. In a few minutes we were airborne for home base again, and Chicago was behind us.

Several days later I was reading through a sheaf of messages that were routinely passed down the line to our office. They covered a variety of naval topics, including aircraft accidents. One concerned a recent mishap in a T-33 with two pilots on board. They had launched from a Navy installation in New England. Investigators weren't positive as to what had happened, but all indications were that both the port and starboard nose compartment doors of the Shooting Star had come open after takeoff. Both men were killed. I imagined the grotesque picture of the plane plummeting from the sky like a felled mallard. Then I thought of Bob and me and our flapping door. Scary.

In the name of the Father and the Son and the Holy Spirit. Amen.

Late in the afternoon of another winter day the executive officer of NAF Detroit, Commander Dick Egelund, passed the word that he needed to see some officials at the naval base in Minneapolis. Could we get him there? Why certainly we could.

The T-bird was prepped and we were soon airborne, westward bound chasing the setting sun. Metropolitan Airport, serving the Minneapolis-St. Paul areas of Minnesota, was no stranger to winter white. It lay in the heart of a snow belt. One of our reserves, an airline pilot who flew out of the field, had cautioned me.

"It can be hazardous if you're not careful," he said. "That's one big skating rink under hard-packed snow once you get off the runway. Taxi gently."

We arrived at twilight and an accommodating tower controller guided us by radio across the sprawling complex to the Navy side. The runway had been mostly clear, but the taxiways and parking ramp were encrusted with snow and ice. I drove the T-33 oh-so-slowly over the treacherous ground, creeping really. I tapped the brake pedals a bit too much at one point and the Shooting Star swung rapidly around as if the right wing wanted to get in front of the nose.

"Slippery, isn't it?" said the XO, who was a transport pilot and had plenty of cold-weather flying experience behind him. He wasn't worried at all. Meanwhile, I longed for the sultry climate of Cecil Field and other points south. We reached the parking apron in near darkness, and when I climbed out I felt the brisk wind that swept snow in flurries from one bank to another. They must be a hardy lot up in this neck of the woods, I thought. This was no

Christmas card scene. This was the Yukon with brick buildings, lumbering snow removal equipment, and enormous airplanes that grumbled lethargically to and from the runways, anxious to get up and get away from it all.

If familiarity breeds contempt, unfamiliarity breeds insecurity. As the cloak of night fell over the land of lakes, the XO's meeting droned on. I paced the floor in operations like an expectant father wanting the thing done and over. "Come on, XO," I kept muttering, "let's get back to Detroit." I reviewed the field diagram chart on the wall for the umpteenth time. I never have been good at puzzles, and the schematic display of the field's taxi routes surely resembled one. That, coupled with the tundra-like conditions, made me long for the simplicity of the flight deck where you slammed into the wires and were practically escorted to a parking place.

Finally, his meeting was over. We manned up in the bitter cold, doing the best we could with stiff fingers and fumbling flashlights to secure ourselves in the cockpit with all the harnesses and clamps and straps. I thought of the Navy's aircrews from Antarctic Development Squadron Six, the guys who supported Operation Deep Freeze, a long-running research project on the globe's southernmost continent. They operated in conditions far worse than those in Minnesota. They had to be awfully good at their job, or part crazy—perhaps both. They had to land in "white-outs," when wind and snow totally obscured their view, and live for half a year at a time in a world of bulky parkas, frozen beards, wild winds, and rugged work. They would laugh at me for being concerned about the comparatively modest challenge imposed by a little snow, darkness, and unfamiliarity with an airfield's geography. (Sid Wegert from VA-85 days became a C-130 pilot with the development squadron and absolutely loved the duty, saying it offered some of the best and most challenging flying he had ever experienced. He was one of the finest pilots I knew and wasn't crazy at all.)

Ah well, it turned out that the tower controllers handled me like a baby, as if they knew the apprehensions of a T-33 pilot trying to weave his way over icy ground around Boeing 707s, McDonnell Douglas DC-8s, and snow banks shaped like miniature mountains. Nearing the approach end of the duty runway I noticed, off to my left side, a flashing pattern of lights, like a celestial constellation, outlining a gigantic passenger plane. It dwarfed us like a grandfather gazing down upon a grandchild, or a monster about to consume its prey—depending on one's perspective.

"Little jet T-bird," a voice said over the radio, sounding as if it came from deep within a cavern, "one step farther and I'm gonna gobble you up!"

Was it my imagination? Did that voice come from the celestial constellation? Was that a chuckling noise I heard immediately after?

"Continue straight ahead," directed a formal voice from the tower, "the runway is on your nose."

We got into position, were cleared for launch and churned down the strip gathering power quickly in the frigid air. We seemed to leap skyward after only about 2,000 feet of travel. If I didn't know better it was as if the Shooting Star was as much in a hurry to get out of Minnesota as I was.

"Navy Four Five One," said the tower, "turn left to one zero zero degrees and have a good trip." Simple as that we were on our way, and my fears dissipated in direct proportion to the increase in slant-range distance from the airport.

A couple of hours later we descended into Detroit where a light wind was blowing straight down the runway. It's always nice to get back home, and the smooth, steady wind made it nicer. It allowed me to place the T-33 on the glide slope for a text book, ground-controlled, precision approach. I felt as though I was sus-pended from a clothesline, angled slightly downward, as the T-33 descended. We touched down on centerline, smack between the twin rows of white beacons outlining the runway.

"Nice approach," said the XO as we rolled toward the end of the strip.

"Thank you, sir," I said.

It was nearly midnight as we taxied in to the flight line, and two distinctive thoughts went through my mind: this journey to Minnesota was an enriching experience, but I could never imagine myself volunteering for duty in Operation Deep Freeze.

The rains of spring came, washed away the snow, and were a prelude to the green Michigan summer. The Skyhawk program at Detroit was flourishing with both A-4s and the Shooting Stars, a second T-33 having been received to augment operations.

A much heralded air show for general aviation aircraft, mostly small, private airplanes, was scheduled one summer Saturday at a small field outside of Detroit. It was billed as a fly-in, which meant that anyone could come, park their aircraft, and enjoy the festivi-ties. Officials for the affair asked, "Would one of your Skyhawks make a fly-by? The folks would really appreciate seeing the Navy in action."

"Not only will we fly by," we said, "but the pilot will perform a special maneuver for you—a one-half cuban eight. How would you like that?" They would love it, they replied.

There's nothing quite like a high-speed pass, low over the ground, especially when it climaxes in a sensational zoom-arc through the sky. It thrills the crowd and satisfies any theatrical urge the pilot might have. I volunteered for the mission and as a precaution checked with various officials to ensure that the maneuver was legal and that all safety measures were adhered to.

"The stage will be clear," I was promised by the air show's sponsors. "All aircraft will be shut down and parked well before your overhead time, absolutely."

I took off from Selfridge and flew south toward the strip, which was west of the city. The old nerve ends were in a nice state of stimulation, and I looked forward to buzzing by the civilians and hauling the Skyhawk through a three-quarter loop followed by a diving, aileron roll recovery, escaping in the same direction from which I had come.

Nearing the site I was chagrined, however, to see a multitude of private aircraft flying in omnidirectional disarray, ascending from, and descending to, the field. Planes banked and swooped and rose blissfully, like birds that had discovered a freshly seeded lawn. I was coordinating my time on target with radar controllers at the metropolitan airport, but they could only report "many, many 'targets' in the area." They were unable, therefore, to call traffic for me and left it up to my discretion whether I wanted to penetrate the flock of birds and make an appearance.

My time overhead arrived. I circled and waited, hoping the air would be clear. But it stayed cluttered. If anything, the population of small flying machines increased. So finally I told the controllers I was going home and broke out of my orbit headed north. I swallowed my anticipatory joy and accepted the fact that there would be no show business today. I must admit I was saddened by this lost opportunity to dazzle the crowd.

"How did it go?" asked my plane captain on the flight line after I had shut down the Skyhawk and climbed out.

"I'm dumb," I said with melancholy in my voice, "but not dumb enough to mix it up with happy birds." I gazed skyward for a moment, a distant look in my eye. "I'll get my curtain call some other time," I muttered.

The plane captain looked at me as if I were crazy. Puzzled, he shook his head. He was still shaking it as I slung my helmet bag over my shoulder and began to walk slowly back to the hangar.

One cloudless and balmy summer afternoon I was flying a routine hop with one of the reserve pilots who was in the back seat of the T-33. It was a perfectly gorgeous day, and I was counting daisies in the sky as we swooped low toward the runway on our final landing approach. I eased the nose up into the landing attitude as we neared the touch-down point. I didn't sense anything wrong right away. We were aligned nicely with the strip, there were no other planes in the vicinity, and airspeed was all right, if a knot or two fast. We droned down closer to the dark grey concrete, which passed below us in a blur.

Instinct told me something was amiss, however, and I glanced at the landing wheel indicators, three little windows on the lower left face of the instrument panel, one each for the main mounts, a third for the nose gear.

The wheels were up! Something was amiss all right.

I rammed the throttle forward, kept the nose where it was, had a microsecond to realize that my career in naval aviation was about to reach a black conclusion, and held on for dear life. I also entreated the ultimate power above to reach down and keep that T-33 aloft until it generated enough speed to climb safely away. We plowed forward, dangerously close to the runway, skimming along nearly its full length before I was able to ease the nose up and coax the machine into a climb. Whew! We made it.

We came around again and with the wheels triple-checked down along with the flaps, which had been set properly the first time, landed. Neither the tower operators nor the pilot behind me caught my bonehead error. This fortified the axiom that one should look out for himself, especially one who operates flying machines.

The truth is, since the inception of retractable landing wheels in aircraft, pilots, albeit infrequently, have made unintentional gear-up landings. Seniors constantly warn flyers to use the checklist provided to prevent such negligence. Obviously, I had been counting daisies rather than reading and complying with the checklist and narrowly missed paying the price for it.

Somebody told me once that making such a landing is like trying to sit down in a chair that a prankster suddenly pulls away. The sitter has a fraction of time to recognize his predicament but, in most cases, is powerless to do anything about it. An ungainly collision with the floor is inevitable. Boy, was I relieved to avoid an ungainly collision with you know what.

After the postflight debriefing, I jogged over to the athletic field where our flag football team, of which I was a member, was already practicing. Chief Petty Officer Dale Maners (pronounced May-ners), a technician in the maintenance department, who was a fine athlete with a sense of humor that could sometimes bite, saw me coming.

"Hey, sir," he said, "we watched your bird come over without those legs down. Thought sure you'd pancake that baby in."

"Right, Chief," I said, "I was lucky this time."

"Yes, sir," he said, "we figured you'd miss practice. When a pilot makes a gear-up landing, the brass tends to jump on 'im with hobnail boots!"

"I know, Chief," I said, anxious to get the episode out of my mind. "But do you mind if we practice now?"

"Sure, sure," Maners said. "Now let's see, do we have a *check-list* for that pass-option play—" There was both a needle and a little bite in that word check-list.

While at Detroit I had the opportunity to fly an A-4 to Griffiss Air Force Base near my home town in New York State. My parents had seen the T-28 and the Skyraider. Now they would get a look at a slim and speedy-looking jet. Neither the T-28 nor the Skyraider evoked from Mom and Dad the sort of glowing admiration and awe I felt was my due. On the first two occasions I was like an actor auditioning for a coveted role in a play, only to be told, "That's fine, but don't call us, we'll call you."

Surely the Skyhawk—the Mighty Midget, Heinemann's Hot Rod, the Bantam Bomber—would change that and draw a full measure of oohs and aahs.

I landed at Griffiss and taxied in. Canopy up, my arm over the side, I caressed the fuselage with a sort of nonchalant authority. I had tightened my oxygen mask an extra hitch for the final half-hour of flight so that the stress lines temporarily formed by the contours of the mask would stay imprinted on my face a bit longer than normal. I approached the parking ramp, the engine hissing nicely, and saw my mother and father standing side by side near the door of the transient line building.

I unhitched one side of the mask and let it hang loosely. With my shiny white hard hat, the mask dangling, and my crooked arm draped over the fuselage like a taxicab driver, I had to look like a veteran warrior of the skies.

I waved, drawing the machine to a halt, and sat there a moment letting the engine produce its special noise, like steam under pressure escaping from a pipe, then closed the throttle. I unstrapped and disembarked slowly, ensuring that my ejection seat harness, which resembled a turn-of-the-century bathing suit and was worn over my forest green flight suit, was fully zipped and that its silver connecting clamps were clearly exposed. I removed my helmet, pulled a fore-and-aft cap from the shin pocket of my suit, fitted it onto my head, and descended the ladder that was attached to the fuselage below the cockpit.

It was an overcast day, unfortunately, which prevented my highly polished, steel-toed flight boots from glistening in the sun. But otherwise I was satisfied that my parents would be quite taken by this show of style.

We embraced, after which I stepped back and, like a car salesman revealing the newest model, gestured toward my Skyhawk.

"Whatdaya think of my jet?" I asked.

"Nice plane," said Dad with an unconvincing bob of his chin.

"Nice, son," said Mom. Sensing that that endorsement fell short of the mark she added, "It's very cute."

I sighed the deep sigh of frustration. First the T-28, then the AD, and now the A-4. I simply could not turn them on. Even more distressing was the fact that in the course of our visit, which occupied several hours, neither my mother or my father asked me how those oxygen mask lines got etched on my face.

After a year at Detroit the Navy ordered me to Naval Air Station Alameda in California as officer in charge of a reserve force unit, Attack Squadron Three Zero Four, the Firebirds. I would be boss of the outfit in the absence of a selected air reserve commanding officer who would come in weekends and other times when his civilian schedule permitted. I packed up the family (three children on the rolls now) for a tour of duty out West.

VA-304 flew A-4Cs, an updated version of the A-4B Skyhawk, and was headed by an American Airlines pilot, Commander John Thompson. He was an energetic, talented officer and a great pilot. In the two-and-a-half years I spent with the Firebirds, I was fortunate in having people like Thompson and his successors—Commander Pete Hammes, who flew for Pan American, and Commander Jerry Kirk, a brilliant aeronautical engineer who worked for the Ames Research Center (a field laboratory for NASA that was located adjacent to Naval Air Station Moffet Field at the southern end of San Francisco Bay)—showing the way. We functioned with an active-duty nucleus of officers and enlisted men running the show most of the time, augmented by citizen sailors and officers on weekends and for active-duty training periods, especially during the summer. It was rewarding to see the outfit, part of an entire reserve carrier air wing, become almost, if not more, proficient than its counterparts in the fleet. We were loaded with experience, especially at the pilot level, the flyers having been naval aviators, many with Vietnam experience, before leaving the active rolls of the service to become airline pilots, lawyers, teachers, businessmen, what have you.

We even had a classy insignia. On a field of black, a firebird, outlined in red, grasped a bone-white human skull, raising it, according to the legend, from the ashes. Our tactical call sign had an affinity with that emblem. It was *Graveyard*, and I loved the undiluted force of it when transmitting on the radio: "This is Graveyard Four Zero One, checking in, over."

During one phase of readiness training we flew to Pensacola for carrier qualifications and staging out of Sherman Field, taking turns flying the Skyhawks out to the USS *Lexington*, the training command's flattop, for our landings. One afternoon six of us were over the Gulf of Mexico with an A-3 Skywarrior tanker aircraft in company when we ran into a billowing squall line of mean-looking thunderstorms. We were curtained off from the *Lex*, which was on the other, or southern, side of the squalls. The band of weather meanwhile forced us northward toward land.

What was unnerving, however, was the meteorology report that crackled through our earphones. Gusty winds and rainstorms had built with such unanticipated speed and ferocity that even forecasters at Pensacola were stunned.

"Sherman Field has been temporarily closed due to extremely high winds and heavy rain," came one report. We had launched from there less than an hour before. Furthermore, all fields within a 200-mile radius were shut down. Those of us aloft in our small jet planes had less than one hour's fuel remaining.

Now, I had practiced aerial refueling before. It was one of the prerequisites for getting checked out in the Skyhawk at Cecil Field. But I never had to do it for real. To veteran jet pilots it was a routine procedure. For me, either I plugged into the tanker and took on precious gas or I might well be in very deep trouble. I was apprehensive about this real-life need to take on a huge drink from that service station in the sky.

We took turns lining up behind the large, twin-engine tanker and its refueling apparatus, a lengthy hose streaming in the wind at the end of which was a conical receptacle called the drogue, or basket. The first three Skyhawk pilots slid neatly into place and each guided his probe, a spear-like projection that ran alongside the right-hand fuselage and extended beyond the nose, precisely into the drogue. Once connected, fuel flowed under pressure from one aircraft to the other directly into storage cells.

The Skywarrior pilot flew smoothly despite the roiling build-ups that seemed to surround us, and when my turn came, I moved in directly behind and below it, concentrating on the airplane rather than the drogue itself. Eyeballing the drogue alone could be futile because it had a life of its own and flew lazy circles, swaying gently like a submerged tree branch in a swift-moving stream. If you picked up visual keys on the more stable Skywarrior and homed on them, however, the Skyhawk almost naturally was in position for final closing on the drogue.

My initial groping jabs at it were embarrassing. I felt the eyes of my squadron mates on me and believed I was a regular Dilbert demonstrating how *not* to aerial refuel. Had the circumstances been less critical, I'm sure my colleagues would have issued some clever references to my airmanship. But this was, under the circumstances, a serious situation and no one was laughing.

Anyway, as luck and determination would have it, I managed to jam the probe into the drogue and hold it there. I scanned my fuel gauge and experienced one of the most reassuring sensations ever as the white needle on the fuel quantity dial gradually arced away from the "empty" end of the gauge.

The reprieve provided by extra fuel, coupled with a semiclear pocket of weather, allowed us to break out into the surprisingly uncluttered, but still blustery, southern side of the squall line. We found the *Lexington* amidst the white caps, descended eagerly and landed aboard. Ironically, it was my first jet carrier landing and seemed anticlimactic compared to the unsettling experience earlier.

We stayed aboard the ship waiting for better weather, especially for reduced winds, before continuing our qualifications. While chatting in a ready room set aside for our temporary use, one of the pilots in the flight said, "That's a nice feeling—getting a drink of fuel when you need it badly, isn't it?"

"Yes," I said, "a very nice feeling."

I wish I could have found better words to express with proper dramatic impact just how nice that feeling was.

By 1971, despite periodic bombing halts, reduction in U.S. forces, and various peace initiatives, the conflict in Southeast Asia continued. Economic troubles stateside led President Nixon to freeze wages and prices. Communist China, in a move that could hardly have been envisioned a few years before, was granted United Nations membership, and publication of classified documents referred to as the "Pentagon Papers" stirred even more controversy about America's conduct in Southeast Asia. Also, the Watergate crisis, which would lead to the downfall of President Nixon, began when a group of men broke into the Democratic National Committee offices in Washington D.C.

Meanwhile, at Alameda we got a new bird to fly, the A-7 Corsair II. Built by the Vought company, it had been combat-tested in Vietnam. It was specifically developed for precision air support of front-line troops and tactical zone bombing and had demonstrated it could handle those missions most effectively. It was considerably bigger than the Skyhawk, with a thick fuselage and roomy cockpit. It was nearly fifty feet long with a wing span of just under forty feet, the wings being mounted on the upper fuselage. It had a single Pratt and Whitney turbofan engine that emitted a sort of hollow but potent metallic whine and produced about 11,000 pounds of thrust. (Our Corsairs were the A-7As. Later versions had more powerful engines and more sophisticated weapons systems. These were in use by the regular Navy squadrons.)

Like the Spad, the Corsair had long legs and could stay aloft, depending on the mission, for several hours. In the tradition of attack planes, it was subsonic but had mobility. It bore a close resemblance to another Vought product, the F-8 Crusader, which had a slimmer, longer fuselage than the A-7 and served primarily as a fighter. Our new plane also had a distinctive, huge air intake—large enough to allow a man of almost any size to climb through—beneath a rounded nose.

Some enterprising and apparently well-read plane captains in VA-304 nicknamed each of the airplanes and painted the imaginative titles in bold letters on the landing wheel doors of the aircraft. There was Zeus, Pegasus, and many others—including my favorite, Beowulf. Beowulf was the hero of an Anglo-Saxon folk epic I remember studying in my Middlebury College days. According to the eighth century story, Beowulf was a mighty warrior and once fought a dragon that was ravaging his kingdom. To me, Beowulf

VA-304 A-7 *with San Francisco in background.*

represented a thunderous, Viking-like presence, all strength and agility. So it wasn't a bad handle for a heavy-hitting flying machine like the Corsair.

Naval Air Station Alameda is situated across the bay from San Francisco, and one night I was waiting for takeoff clearance at the approach end of the north runway. It was a cool, clear evening, and I sat there in the spacious cockpit with the engine idling beneath me, enjoying the panorama.

The stars above harmonized with the man-made lights of earth—lights that gleamed from buildings on San Francisco's magnificent skyline and those that sparkled from the sprawling landscapes of Oakland, on my side of the bay, and all the other communities that rimmed the body of water, north to south. The flashing lights of my A-7 blended in as well. They counted a visual cadence on the pavement below as I waited for instructions from the tower.

Finally, a voice sounded in my earphones. "Graveyard Four Zero Four, Alameda radar control needs to calibrate some of its equipment this evening. Would you make a series of GCAs (ground controlled, precision approaches) for us?"

This was like asking a kid if he would enjoy free access to the cookie jar. In the first place, because Alameda lay in a high-density air traffic zone—the Oakland airport was a hop, skip, and jump to the south of the air station, San Francisco International was a few miles to the west, and at the southern end of the bay was Naval Air Station Moffett Field—it was virtually impossible to get multiple practice approaches. We usually had to fly elsewhere for them and be content with a single, final approach and landing at Alameda. I was only going out on a round-robin anyway and agreed without hesitation to help out.

"I'm all yours," I said.

Nothing adventuresome or of earthshaking significance took place in the next sixty minutes of my life. When I look back at the log book for that particular sortie, the entry contains only the bureau number of the plane, the flight code, the time aloft, and the numbers indicating a half-dozen precision approaches with touch and gos at the end of each. The digits and letters are written in red, signifying night work. What the log book could never show was that those sixty or so minutes were totally absorbing, if not poetic, in nature.

"A thing of beauty is a joy forever," wrote John Keats nearly 200 years ago, and San Francisco and its surroundings that night were a thing of splendid beauty. I was like a sole owner and occupant of a chunk of airspace that extended from the ground up to 3,000 feet and encompassed a five-by-one-mile rectangle horizontally. In that imaginary box I felt as if the Corsair and I had been miniaturized and let loose in a display case at Tiffany's. We were surrounded by diamonds all aglitter against the black velvet of night.

The controllers issued terse, simple commands: "Turn left to three two zero degrees"—"commence descent"—"cleared to land." I obeyed with easy assurance, calling on my experience as an instrument instructor, and guided the A-7 around the pattern with as much grace and precision as I could muster. It was just me up there, on the receiving end of personalized handling, roaring through the night skies of one of America's most dazzling and eye-pleasing places.

Afterwards, when I reached the maintenance desk in the hangar, I made some small talk with a few of the troops. I signed off the aircraft and turned to head for my office, which was on the other side of the hangar. I turned back and faced the men, wanting to tell them about my last sixty minutes in the air.

"Forget something, sir?" one of the men asked.

It occurred to me that there was no suitable way I could convey to them what I had experienced. I stood there dumbly and finally said, "No, I guess not."

How can you explain what it's like to be in a Tiffany display case that would have inspired even John Keats to take up quill and parchment?

Tom Scully was a spirited young lieutenant in VA-304, who loved flag football as much as I did. Tom was an aggressive pilot, a highly regarded and trophy-winning bomber, knew the A-7 inside and out, and applied the same brand of fire and dedication to athletics as he did to flying. He was compactly built, ran fast, and was the in-house purveyor of pep talks. He slapped us on the back and told us to go out there and fight, fight, fight, win, win, win!

In the days preceding the annual confrontation with Alameda's Marine unit, we practiced with special fervor. Beating the leathernecks would bolster our egos and elevate Firebird pride. During working hours we stole moments here and there for impromptu skull sessions, during which we diagrammed plays and talked strategy. While Scully provided vivacity, Personnelman First Class Jackie Pierson, our best all-around athlete, contributed his brainy football sense to the cause. I lent philosophy.

"What we've got to do," I urged repeatedly in the days before the game, "is hit 'em hard right from the start. I mean crush 'em physically. Put 'em on notice we came to play."

"It's war!" cried Scully.

Pierson agreed, but was the type who believed that action was more powerful than words and that success would be measured on the patch of green between the goal posts.

Game time arrived. We were not overwhelmed by the Marines in their scarlet jerseys and genuine football trousers, even though our tattered orange T-shirts and "miscellaneous" pants paled next to them. In a pre-kickoff huddle along the sidelines, I reiterated my "crush 'em" thoughts. All hands grunted in agreement as we shuffled our feet nervously. Then Scully let out an unintelligible, blood-curdling call-to-arms that converted us to Apaches on the warpath. We burst from the huddle and sped to our positions on the field.

We kicked off to them, and Pierson broke through the wedge formed by the Marines in front of the ball carrier to pull one of the runner's flags from his hip. (Each of us wore two bright strips of cloth on either hip attached to a belt by velcro material. When one of the strips was yanked away, the ball carrier was considered tagged and play stopped.) On the very next play their quarterback stepped back briskly to set up for a pass. We had studied their patterns and had a good idea of what to expect. The quarterback reared and heaved the ball down field. It arced toward Scully's defensive zone around the forty-yard line.

The intended receiver, who was at least half a foot taller than Scully, leaped for the ball. So did Tom. With the sort of determination that propels men beyond their limits, our man towered into the air with his opponent and swatted the ball away. In the process, however, there was a god-awful collision accompanied by a sound that a bare fist would make slamming into a side of beef. That sickening noise shot through the sky like a bullet, causing a fearful silence to fall over the field. The Marine and the lieutenant tumbled grotesquely to the ground, one heaped on top of the other.

After a few seconds the Marine, who was groggy but otherwise unhurt, got up from the grass. Scully, our prime source of spirit, lay there like a sack of grain, eyes open but clearly stunned. I rushed to his side. There was no sign of fracture, no blood, and he could move his limbs.

"Are you OK, Tom?" I asked, which was a rather stupid question under the circumstances.

"Yea," he muttered, "I'll be all right in a minute."

His head had apparently struck the Marine's shoulder. With a grimace, massaging his head, he repeated, "I'm all right. I'm all right." And he was. A true warrior, he insisted on staying in the game.

Well, I thought, my psychology backfired. The Marines got in the first, body-busting lick instead of the other way around. The leathernecks had gained momentum and the game was hardly under way. As it turned out, it was a close contest throughout, but we had the lower score when the man in the striped shirt blew his silver whistle ending the affair.

"You know," I said afterward to Scully as we walked back to squadron headquarters, "those Marines are tough. When the shootin' starts I'm glad we'll have them around."

"Yea," sighed Scully rubbing an enormous goose egg on his head, "and the next time we play football, it wouldn't be a bad idea to have a few on our side either."

I had occasion to fly an A-7 back East, and put Griffiss Air Force Base on the itinerary. I simply had to give the folks a look at the Corsair and try one more time to shake them up with one of naval aviation's finest pieces of hardware.

I wheeled into the parking area, slowly, positively, the glorious roar of the engine producing a decibel count measurably greater than the T-28, the AD, and the A-4 I had presented to them in sequence over the years. I shut down the engine and climbed out, putting on a sort of firm-chinned, steely-eyed, captain-on-the-bridge look—as if I had just personally berthed the USS *Forrestal* at Pier Twelve in Norfolk.

"Well," I said to my parents who, marvelously, had hardly aged and looked the same as they did the first time I showed up years before in that T-28, "tell me what you think about that attack bomber out there."

I pointed to the handsome, freshly washed jet with the bright orange paint scheme on the tail, the thick fuselage, and the snub nose with its menacing look. "Some piece of hardware, wouldn't you say?"

"Nice plane," said my father.

"Nice, son," said my mother, "but isn't it sort of fat around the middle?"

Sigh. My shoulders sagged along with the rest of my body. It was no use. Maybe if I had a rocket ship?

I was promoted to commander while in VA-304, and although the events are unrelated, my wife and I had child number four. The squadron's blend of active-duty and reserve personnel was achieving a productive state of readiness, and we traveled to Naval Air Station Fallon's "proving grounds" in Nevada to demonstrate it.

A-7A Corsair II carrying a full load of bombs and rockets on its wing and fuselage pylons.

Most of us had a lot of time behind the gun-sight reticle, whether in Southeast Asia or other places, and we established a closely monitored competition to see just who really was "top gun" among the Firebirds. During an intense week of bombing, strafing, and rocket firing, scores were carefully tallied, and some fierce rivalries developed. When the final tabulations were posted on a chart that resembled a tote board at Churchill Downs, the scoring was so close that a mere point or two separated individuals.

I was crushed to find myself at the end of the list. It did not lessen the impact to realize my hits weren't substantially different from those in the upper brackets. I was Tail-end Charlie and it was very embarrassing. Here I was, a so-called full-time flyer, bested by part-timers, the reserves.

There was no self-effacing way to get through the customary, end-of-deployment wing-ding. All hands gathered at a small club on the base for a relaxing, if not boisterous, celebration. The preceding days had been exhausting, and a few spirits and lively conversation were in order. But I knew that somehow the truth of the final ordnance scores would come out and I had no place to hide.

Inevitably, Commander Jerry Kirk, the skipper, himself winner of the Golden Bomb—representative of unsurpassed scoring in a bombing derby held among all West Coast light attack squadrons—tapped a spoon to a glass and ordered quiet throughout the club.

He issued various awards for strafing and dive-bombing and rocket-firing winners, then called me forward to the improvised stage in a corner of the room.

"And now," he said seriously, "it gives me great pleasure to present to the Firebird officer in charge the following award."

Whereupon he unfurled a square-shaped flag in squadron colors about the size of a street sign. Sewn into the cloth was a revolver, its barrel curved lazily downward, a plume of smoke emanating from the tip. In large letters beneath that were the words, *Bottom Gun,* followed by an exclamation mark.

The crowd broke into loud cheers and I forced myself to laugh, despite the pain of shattered pride.

"Speech! Speech!" people began to shout.

I held up my hands and the room grew quiet.

"I've worked very hard for this award," I said with the best stage baritone I could muster. "And no one deserves it more than I."

There was a clapping and a wall-shaking round of unforced laughter. I retreated into the crowd thinking of all those great troops in VA-304 and the expert attack pilots who could put the ordnance on target as well as any flyers I had ever been associated with.

I'm glad those shooters are on our side.

six

Final Approach

But what can replace those marvelous moments in the air when, far across the waters, the profile of your own flattop comes into view, and you key the mike to make your homecoming report: "See You."

After Alameda I was ordered to desk duty in Washington, where I would spend my next years in the Navy as editor of *Naval Aviation News*. Peace pacts theoretically ending the war in Southeast Asia were signed in late January 1973, with our POWs coming home in groups shortly after that. The total number of dead was some two million people, more than 46,000 of them Americans. The draft also ended in 1973 and the inevitable cut-back in military forces loomed on the horizon. I still managed to get proficiency flying for a while; after a time that was stopped. Ultimately, I managed only an infrequent hop here and there as time passed. Meanwhile, a fifth child rounded out the family lineup, quite a household full.

Whenever I could, I jumped at the chance to get back in the cockpit. On one occasion, while visiting some units at Lemoore in California, I rode in the back seat of a TA-4 Skyhawk with a young lieutenant. We went up over the Sierras, and after some air-to-air combat practice with a flight of A-7 Corsairs, we drove on over the mountains, enjoying the colorful autumn morning from 25,000 feet.

"Would you like to fly it?" the pilot asked.

"Of course," I said.

"You've got it !"

I jiggled the stick confirming I had the controls, and he threw up his arms to show he was off them. It's like riding a bicycle. You don't forget how. It comes back quickly. Of course, there's not that much to do at altitude; just keep a light grip on the stick, hold the nose level with the horizon, enjoy the feel of the machine and all its mechanical wizardry laboring easily.

Another flight on another day some time ago on the other side of the country came out of the memory bank and paraded through my mind. I was in VA-45 at the time and flying a senior officer from Cecil Field in Florida north to Andrews Air Force Base near Washington, D.C., where he had to attend a meeting. His active flying days were behind him, and when I asked if he'd like to fly for a while he enthusiastically took over and didn't surrender the Skyhawk to me until a couple of hours later on the final approach to landing.

"These days," he said after we had shut down and were walking toward operations, "I appreciate every moment of stick time I can manage. Thanks. It was a tonic."

Over the Sierras, too few years later, the coin had flipped. Now it was me grabbing at minutes, which passed too quickly. We were soon on the ground, trekking to the hangar.

"Thanks," I said to the lieutenant. "It was a tonic. Served in a shot glass," I added, "but better than no tonic at all."

So, the flying days were over. In their place came other duties, administrative or managerial in nature, and I had to content myself with pictures from the memory book, recalled in dull or quiet moments to keep up the spirits. A sampling from the album:

—Leading a flight of four aircraft into the break ("up the slot" was the terminology we sometimes used in earlier days) over the runway with all canopies aligned as if our planes were impaled by an invisible skewer; then peeling away from each other in cosmetic interval for landing.

—Slipping into a trail position behind the lead Skyraider and adjusting the rpm control so that I could look through my propeller arc to number one's and match the speed of his. This produced a perfect picture of synchronized rotation, as if our props were one and the same, and created identical shadow patterns.

—Flying at low level over a sparsely populated group of cream-white, sunlit Dodecanese islands; awestruck by the emerald beauty of the Aegean and the way its waves rushed onto the craggy shores, only to retreat leaving beards of foam where sea and land met.

—Being somewhere in the pack along with eleven other Skyraiders on a fly-off from the carrier, headed for home shores after half a year deployed to the Mediterranean.

—Moving along at 300 knots and tightening up so close to the lead jet that I could theoretically reach out and touch its wing; and at that proximity listening to the hollow roar of its engine in addition to my own.

—Standing on the flight deck late at night amidst the parked airplanes after a heavy day of operations and listening to the carrier creak as it heaved slowly on the tranquil sea.

—Being cinched down on the catapult, like a bronco straining at the rodeo gate, the engine howling, heels planted on the deck, helmet snug against the head rest, left hand at full throttle with fingers grasping the catapult grip, right hand steadying the control column between my knees; vibrating as one with the aircraft, saluting crisply, waiting the limbo-like one or two seconds before a steam-driven piston below deck slams forward and slings me and my machine into the sky with a thunderous thuuuwack!

—Recalling some of the great terms and call signs of naval and military aviation, the salt and pepper of tactical language: Really Ready, Atom Buster, Mustang, Honeybee, Cannon, Handbook, Graveyard, War Ace, Sandblower, Magic Carpet, Warbonnet, Buckeye, Canasta, Inferno, Corktip, Stallion, Misty, Sandy, Jolly Green, Holly Green, Railsplitter, Idaho Spud, Climax, Able Dog, Feet Wet, Feet Dry, Scooter, Winchester, Short Skirt—try saying that last one five times fast.

Then there are the culinary pleasures that in all likelihood I would not have known if I hadn't joined the Navy "to see the world."

For example:

—Steaming paella and cold sangria, which we consumed on the terrace of a seaside restaurant in Valencia, Spain, where Ernest Hemingway himself used to dine.

—French fries, real ones, crisp and gold and served hot in large oval dishes in a cafe on the beach in Cannes, in the South of France.

—That first slug of beer after more than a month on Yankee Station following a four-hour flight from ship to shore at Cubi Point in the Philippines. Thoughtful sailors in the support detachment had iced down the cans in galvanized trash containers and handed them to us after we emerged from the cockpit, exhausted and wrinkled with sweat.

—Lamb roasted in a stone oven on New Year's Eve in a tiny restaurant on the hill, up from the sea, also in Cannes. It was served with chilled white wine in long-stemmed glasses. There were yellow roses on the table.

—More French food, especially escargot, enjoyed in, of all places, Hong Kong, at an establishment called the Normandy.

There were blue and white checkered table cloths and embellishments that gave the surroundings a Renoir touch.

—Unsurpassed fettucini found at a sophisticated place not far from the Fountain of Trevi in Rome. For the next course, diners pointed to the fish of their choice as it swam about in a large tank, unquestionable proof of its freshness.

—And believe it or not, some of the best meals ever, on board the good old *Coral Sea*; like those special Thursday nights with prime ribs or steak, followed by heaping servings of Baked Alaska.

Sooner or later a pilot has to face closing the throttle and listening to his engine sigh into silence for the last time. It is inevitable. What is that moment like? For me it was delicious pain. I said to myself: happily, you have survived. Unhappily, the joys of flying the Navy way are no more. You won't miss the rainswept landings aboard the carrier on dark and worrisome nights. But you will miss the silent exhilaration of breaking into the clear blue from a cloud-shrouded climb-out.

You won't miss the endless weeks at sea away from home. But what can replace those marvelous moments in the air when, far across the waters, the profile of your own flattop comes into view and you key the mike to make your homecoming report: "See You."

Life is a compromise. For every beginning there is an ending. Still, the knowledge of having been a part of naval air soothes. Although all the memories must be shelved in the archives of the mind, they can be retrieved and replayed with a certain relish.

So, there are no regrets for the delicious pain. You have been there on the wing of the high and the mighty and the journey has been a worthy one.

Originally, I thought that I would conclude with the above reflection. An incident took place before the end of my naval career, however, that changed my mind.

I was staying for a time in the BOQ at the Anacostia Naval Station in Washington, D.C., just across the river from the historic Navy Yard, the old gun factory. One spring morning in the late 1970s I saw a young officer gazing out of the glass doors of the BOQ's entrance, which faced a helicopter launch-and-recovery area used by the Marine Corps' special presidential transport unit. It was warm and sunny, a beautiful day for flying, and a highly polished green and white Sea King was practicing touch and gos. The officer, an ensign as I later discovered (he was in civilian clothes), was watching the helo intently, wistfully.

We exchanged hellos and I asked, "Passing through?"

"No, sir," he answered. "I've just been reassigned from Pensacola to a job at the Navy Yard."

"Pensacola?" I said.

"Yes. I was in flight training but washed out. I was flying helicopters, as a matter of fact," he said, nodding toward the Sea King, which was lifting off across the way.

"I'm sorry," I said softly.

"Only two weeks to go," he went on, giving voice to words that must have run through his mind a thousand times. "Had trouble with instrument stage. Just couldn't hack it under the hood."

Both of us were now looking at the helicopter as it clattered up and banked away. Standing there, sensing the hurt in the young man, a long forgotten moment came to mind. It happened that day in 1957 at the air station in Niagara Falls, New York. We were taking our pre-induction flight physicals, and the candidate ahead of me emerged from the examining room wearing a vacant, depressed expression. A few minutes before he was the picture of confidence and strength, the All-American boy ready to take on the world. Now he seemed deflated, beaten down.

He was found to have an astigmatism, an imperfection in one of his eyes, and consequently failed the flight physical. He did not get the chance to even begin the pursuit of golden wings even though, like me, he wanted desperately to become a Navy pilot. It was not to be for him and it was not to be for this ensign.

Surely that man in Niagara Falls adjusted to his disappointment and went on to other things, and this pensive young officer watching a helicopter flying over Anacostia on a spring day would also find his niche.

Measured against the short-lived aspirations of these two, I feel very lucky and grateful to have lived the life of a naval aviator. It has been brimful of challenge, value, and meaning. Indeed, my cup runneth over.